The CNC
Workbook

The CNC Workbook

An Introduction to Computer Numerical Control

Frank Nanfara

Tony Uccello

Derek Murphy

ADDISON-WESLEY PUBLISHING COMPANY

Reading, Massachusetts · Menlo Park, California · New York · Don Mills, Ontario
Wokingham, England · Amsterdam · Bonn · Sydney · Singapore · Tokyo
Madrid · San Juan · Milan · Paris

Library of Congress Cataloging-in-Publication Data

The CNC workbook : an introduction to computer numerical control : includes
   interactive graphic simulation software for CNC milling and turning
   / by TOR Computerized Systems Inc.
        p.   cm.+ 1 computer disk (3 1/2in.)
    System requirements for computer disk: 8086, 80286, or higher;
  640K; MS-DOS 3.0 or higher; EGA or VGA graphics; 2 or 3 button
  mouse.
    Includes index.
    ISBN 0-201-65600-0
    1. Machine-tools--Numerical control--Programming. I. TOR
Computerized Systems Inc.
TJ1189.C654 1994
621.9'023--dc20   94-4362
                                        CIP

IBM, MS-DOS, AutoCAD, Mastercam and any other trade name are trademarks of their
respective owners.

The programs and applications presented in this book have been included for their
instructional value. They have been tested with care but are not guaranteed for any
particular purpose. Neither the publisher nor TOR Computerized Systems, Inc. offer
any warranties or representations, nor do they accept any liabilities with respect to the
programs or applications.

TOR Computerized Systems, Inc. reserves the right to make changes to the software or
the book from time to time.

Reprinted with corrections November, 1995

9 10-CRS-98

Contents

Preface

Computer numerical control programming skills are important to any engineering student. *The CNC Workbook: An Introduction to Computer Numerical Control* is an affordable text and software combination designed to introduce students to CNC and provide them with an opportunity to learn and practice at their own pace. The workbook teaches students about CNC programming, and the software, *TORCAM CNCez*, allows students to create CNC programs and test them in a simulated manufacturing environment.

The CNC Workbook may be used as a complete text for a course in computer numerical control, or as an instructional supplement if CNC is a component of another course. Students can even use this package to learn about CNC on their own, outside of the classroom environment. The software will run on high and low end computers, and is ideal for learning, teaching, and testing CNC programming.

FEATURES OF THE WORKBOOK

The text introduces students to CNC programming and the use of the *TORCAM CNCez* simulation software, providing the student with the basics needed to build confidence in CNC programming.

- Chapters 1 through 3 discuss the basic concepts of computer numerical control, including the theoretical and applied aspects.

- Chapter 4 introduces the student to the interface of the *TORCAM CNCez* simulation software program.

- Chapters 5 and 6 begin teaching the student to program and run simulations. Chapter 5 describes milling, and Chapter 6 covers turning, the two most important and most common uses for CNC programming. Each chapter concludes with five step-by-step tutorials to help the student develop programming skills.

- Chapter 7 describes the basics of Computer Aided Design and Computer Aided Manufacturing.

- Chapter 8 provides extra exercises for the student, including questions to answer and new simulations to program.

FEATURES OF THE SOFTWARE

One of the biggest problems in learning CNC technology and specifically CNC programming is finding time for the hands-on training required on a

CNC machine tool. *The CNC Workbook* lessens the student's dependence on traditional classroom-style learning and maximizes the amount of hands-on CNC programming time available to each student or trainee. Using the software allows the student to perform dry runs of all CNC programs in a simulated manufacturing environment. By using *TORCAM CNCez* to test a program, the student needs to use a CNC machine tool only for final confirmation of a design.

Two other key features of this learning system are safety and comfort. Since this software will emulate a CNC milling machine or CNC lathe, the student can do all the necessary CNC programming training and later write, edit, and test new CNC programs on the computer. Since a CNC machine is not actually being used, both the student and the instructor can learn in a safer and more comfortable environment.

One special feature of *TORCAM CNCez* is that the on-screen simulator and the programming editor are interactive. As the user creates and edits CNC programs, the screen graphics immediately show the result of each new step, providing instant feedback. Students will know immediately which part of their program generated which result.

For users with prior knowledge and experience with CNC programming, the *TORCAM CNCez* simulation software can be used to test existing CNC programs which follow the EIA/ISO standards, and to write and edit new ones. The workbook may be used as a reference guide, or the user may select the HELP menu option on the screen for assistance.

A WARNING TO THE READER

The objective of this workbook and software combination is to teach CNC programming. It is NOT to instruct the user on machining terms or procedures, nor does skill in the use of the simulation software mean that actual hands-on experience with manufacturing equipment can be eliminated. All speeds and feeds used in this manual have been tested on machinable wax only, and are not recommended for any harder materials or metals.

All programs in this manual have been tested for reliability. Some changes may be required to adopt these programs to non-TORCAM CNC machines. Please consult your CNC machine operations manual.

ACKNOWLEDGMENTS

We would like to thank Daniel Schmidt, Michael Malfara, and Mario DeCarolis for their contributions to both the workbook and the software. We would also like to thank the people who reviewed the manuscript for their comments and suggestions.

Frank Nanfara   Tony Uccello   Derek Murphy

Chapter 1

Introduction to CNC

CHAPTER OBJECTIVES

After studying this chapter, the student should have knowledge of the following:

The evolution of CNC

The process of CNC

The flow of CNC processing

The objectives of CNC

INTRODUCTION

Computer numerical control (CNC) is the process of manufacturing machined parts in a production environment, as controlled and allocated by a computerized controller that uses motors to drive each axis. The controller actually controls the direction, speed, and length of time each motor rotates. A programmed path is loaded into the machine's computer by the operator and then executed. Numerical control (NC) is the original term given to this technology and today is still used by many interchangeably with CNC.

NC technology has been one of manufacturing's major developments in the past fifty years. It has not only resulted in the development of new techniques and the achievement of higher production levels but also has helped to increase product quality and stabilize manufacturing costs.

THE EVOLUTION OF NC

The principal of NC manufacturing has been evolving since the Industrial Revolution, although the actual procedures involved have developed with technology. Early attempts were made at automating production through the use of belts, pulleys, and cams, but manual labor was by far more cost effective than were the development and operation of big, new machines.

It wasn't until World War II was under way that industrialists realized an inability to fill both quantity and quality requirements. Machinists of the day could produce superior quality, but not at high volumes. As the quantity of a certain product increased, the quality decreased due to the human factors involved.

The United States Air Force sought to combat this problem, and to ensure that all U.S. planes were manufactured identically, by inviting several companies to develop and manufacture numerical control systems. Thus the goal behind the development of numerical control was to realize the following objectives:

1. To increase production

2. To improve the quality and accuracy of manufactured parts

3. To stabilize manufacturing costs

4. To manufacture complex or otherwise impossible jobs

NC, along with programmable automation, was also designed to readily accommodate changes in product design and was designed for small-to-medium sized production runs.

Numerical control was also designed to help produce parts that had the following characteristics:

- Similar in terms of raw material

- Various sizes and geometry

- Small- to medium-sized batches

- A sequence of similar steps was used to complete each workpiece.

The first contract was awarded to the Parsons Corporation of Michigan, which had developed a control system that directed a spindle to many points in succession. Although the contract date was June 15, 1949, the demand for these systems was a direct result of the war effort.

In 1951, the Servomechanism Laboratory of the Massachusetts Institute of Technology (MIT) was given a subcontract by Parsons to develop a servo system for the machine tool. At that time, MIT was also working on the development of a computer called the Whirlwind. Consequently, the total NC development project was conducted at MIT.

In 1952, the first three-axis, numerically controlled, tape-fed machine tool was created. A Cincinnati Milicron Hydro-Tel Vertical Spindle milling machine was retrofitted and controlled by a very large vacuum-tube computer. The controller used a straight binary perforated tape as the feeding mechanism. In 1954, Numerical control was announced to the public, and three years later, the first production NC machines were delivered and installed.

By 1960, NC was widely accepted and readily available. Although the controllers used alphanumeric characters in their controlling code, it was still called numerical control.

The majority of these machine tools required coded paper tape to run. The engineers would generate NC code on their computers, then encode long strips of paper tape by punching them with holes. These reels of tape would then be taken to the shop floor, where the operator would insert them into the controller and run them. The tapes contained all the data required for machine operation. The machine tool would then perform the same operation exactly, as many times as required.

Further research and development brought about new generations of NC machines and the subsequent introduction of computer numerical control, whereby a computer is used to control the machine tool, thereby eliminating the bulky and fragile paper tape.

Direct numerical control and distributed numerical control (DNC) describe communications to a machine tool from a remote computer. In direct numerical control, part program instruction blocks are communicated to a machine tool as required and as fast as the machine can accept them. This method of communication was very popular, since it eliminated the paper tape system and increased the maximum length of a program. In distributed numerical control, whole programs or multiple programs are communicated to a CNC machine tool or several CNC machine tools. This process was made possible by the increased memory capacity of CNC controllers. In the early days, controllers could not store programs, thus programs were stored on paper tape. Later controllers were able to store limited-sized programs, but today's can store hundreds of programs on their built-in hard drive memory systems.

From 1955 to 1960, MIT also developed a computer-assisted programming system called APT (automatically programmed tools). The programming language was developed to ease the task of complicated three-axis programming, mainly in the aerospace industry. APT uses Englishlike words to describe the geometry and the tool motions on a part program.

The great advantage of CNC was the ability of the code-generating computer to move from the engineering department back onto the shop floor, where it was directed by the machinist. The computer and machine control unit (MCU) were now one unit, capable of creating the program, then storing it in memory. This also eliminated much of the need for paper tape. With the exception of extremely large programs, most NC programs are stored on the machine tools built in a computerized controller.

Machining centers, which take the place of half a dozen machines, are now capable of many operations—including milling, boring, drilling, facing, spotting, counterboring, threading, and tapping—all on one setup.

CNC is now a well-established technology. CNC machines have become far more commonplace. The number of manufacturing systems has blossomed, and there are greater levels of computerization in most engineering companies.

Computer integrations can be implemented at almost any level—from a simple machine shop with a computer-aided manufacturing (CAM) system, to companies with several dispersed sites and many hundreds of machines and systems.

CNC technology has the following advantages over NC technology:

1. Programs can be entered at the machine and stored into memory.

2. Programs are easier to edit, so part programming process design time is reduced.

3. There is greater flexibility in the complexity of parts that can be produced.

4. Three-dimensional geometric models of parts, stored in the computer, can be used to generate CNC part programs almost automatically, thus saving manual programming labor.

5. Computers can be connected to other computers worldwide either by direct modem connection or through a network, thereby allowing part programs to be transmitted directly to remote CNC machines.

The disadvantages of CNC are the following:

1. CNC is slightly more expensive, although today it would be rare to find an NC machine tool sold that is not CNC.

2. Possibly more training is required for the machine operator. This, however, depends on the complexity of the machine tool, since a CNC machine may actually require less training.

3. Maintenance costs may be greater.

MICRO COMPUTER TECHNOLOGY

The modern computer is an electronic machine that performs mathematical or logical calculations in accordance with a predetermined set of instructions. The computer itself is called the hardware; the programs that run on the computer are called software.

The three basic components of a computer are the following:

1. Central processing unit (CPU)

2. Memory

3. Input/output section

The CPU controls and sequences the activities of the computer components and performs the various arithmetic and logical operations. The memory is located in the computer and is used by the CPU for the manipulation of data. The input/output section interprets incoming and outgoing signals for the CPU.

There are also various peripheral devices associated with computers, including monitors, scanners, and printers.

The use of computers in industry is now an everyday occurrence. Cheaper and yet faster personal computers have allowed companies to introduce computers at all levels. There are various forms of computer-assisted programming for both shop floor control and numerical control programming.

COMPUTER BASICS

Although computers have enhanced NC to a great extent, certain rules still remain in affect. One rule that holds true today, but that is easier to live with is

Garbage In = Garbage Out

This rule, common in industry, was truer in the past than it is today. When writing NC programs using the old systems, programmers could check for errors only running the program. Incorrect data entered resulted in the machine not running as required or not running at all. Therefore the saying.

With today's more powerful computers and software, such as CNCez, syntax checking enables the programmer to verify programs without running them on a production CNC machine tool, hence lowering production time and overall costs.

NC APPLICATIONS

From the days of the first NC milling machine, there have been many applications for NC technology, ranging from milling, turning, electric discharge machining (EDM), punching and nibbling, forming, bending, grinding, inspection, and robotics.

Although aerospace is still one of the principal industries that require and use NC technology extensively, other industries have also embraced it. Because of the continuing advances and affordability of computers, the cost of NC technology has been dropping rapidly to the point where even small machine shops and small specialty industries have come to require it. Today you can find NC products in areas spanning metalworking and automotive, electronics, appliances, and furniture manufacturing.

Figure 1-1 GE Fanuc 18-T CNC control used on a Hardinge® CONQUEST® T42 CNC Lathe. Hardinge and CONQUEST are registered trademarks of Hardinge Brothers, Inc.

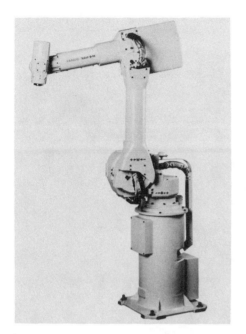
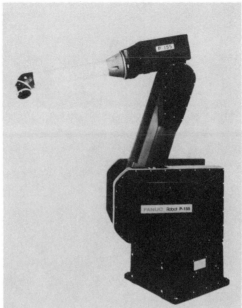

Figure 1-2 A) S-10 Material Handling Robot   B) P-155 Paint Robot
Courtesy of Fanuc Robotics North America, Inc.

Figure 1-3 25 VSP Vertical Machining Center with 8000 Series
Courtesy of Giddings & Lewis, Inc.

Figure 1-4 Hardinge® CONQUEST® T42 CNC Slant Bed Lathe with the GE Fanuc 18-T CNC Control Unit. Hardinge and CONQUEST are registered trademarks of Hardinge Brothers, Inc.

CNC CONTROLLERS

There are three major components in a CNC machine tool:

1. The machine tool itself, which as we described can be of many applications.

2. The motors and feedback mechanism, which are very important, since they are the link between the machine tool and the controller. Therefore the type, size, and resolution are very important considerations to the different applications.

3. The heart of the CNC machine tool—the controller or MCU.

Although standards exist and there are similarities among controllers, there are generally many differences between different controllers on the market. You may find that one manufacturer of controllers has more than a dozen different models and a dozen different variations of one model alone. Although the basic principal of controllers is easy to understand, one must realize that because there are thousands of variations of machine tools and applications, there will also be a requirement for different controllers. It is common to find two different machine tools using the same model controller with slightly different options.

Figure 1-5 A benchtop CNC milling machine used in classrooms to teach CNC technology.

CONTROLLER STANDARDS

To understand CNC, you must first understand both the differences and similarities of controllers on the market. The previous paragraph discussed why there may be differences in controllers based on the varied machine tools and applications. Other reasons for differences are the manufacturers and the standard they follow, if any, and how close they follow it.

EIA and ISO Standards

Two very similar standards are generally followed worldwide: the ISO 6983 and the EIA RS274. Some countries may have their own standards but most follow ISO and EIA. ISO (International Standardization Organization) and EIA (Electronic Industries Association) developed the main standard for NC, which uses simple programming instructions to enable a machine tool to carry out a particular operation. For example, the following lines of code will instruct a CNC milling machine that on executing line or block number 100, the tool is to cut relative to the origin point at a feedrate of 20 in./min along the X-axis 1.25 in. and the Y-axis 1.75 in.

```
N95 G90 G20
N100 G01 X1.25 Y1.75 F20
```

Axis designation on a machine tool and the coordinate system, both of which are covered in more detail in Chapter 2, are also standardized by the EIA in the EIA 267-C standard. This standard applies to all NC machine tools regardless of whether the controller follows a particular standard. This is equally, if not more important than the EIA RS274 standard, since it forms the link to CAD/CAM, which follow similar standards.

Conversational (Nonstandard)

An alternative method of programming is using the Conversational CNC Controller. These controllers generally do not follow any standard, are mostly proprietary, and are supposed to be easy to use, since you do not need to know how to program but only how to read and respond to the prompts on the controller screen. Generally, while simple machines that produce simple parts may use this system, more complex machines producing more complex parts may not. Therefore some CNC machines may offer both ISO/EIA standard programming and Conversational programming. Besides the nonstandardization of Conversational CNC Controllers, the other negative point is that communication from CAD/CAM becomes more difficult. In general, a machine that is standalone—that is, it does not require programs created through a CAD/CAM system and it will produce simple parts—is a good candidate for a Conversational Controller.

As you learn more about the CNC industry, you will soon discover there are several main controller manufacturers. Some of these are Fanuc, General Electric, and Bendix. However, some CNC machine tool companies, such as Cincinnati Milicron and Giddings and Lewis, may use their own proprietary controllers for their machine tools. In general, most of these companies follow the EIA/ISO standard, and with some modification, programs are quite portable between them.

As you work through the rest of this workbook and the CNC simulation software, keep in mind that standards used here follow as closely as possible EIA RS274 for basic three-axis NC Milling and two-axis NC Turning. Therefore programs developed with CNCez may require some modification for your machine tool. If you require more assistance, please consult the Technical Support section at the rear of this workbook.

THE CNC PROCESS

The process of CNC manufacturing is essentially identical in principal to conventional manufacturing methods. Conventionally, blueprints are generated by design engineers, who pass them to the machinists. The machinists then read the blueprints and mentally calculate toolpaths, cutter speeds and feeds, machining time, and so on.

CNC programming is much the same as conventional machining. The machinist still has sole responsibility for the machine's operation, although control is no longer via manual turning of the axis handwheels but through efficient CNC programming and the use of the controller.

This is not to say that most proficient machinists will be computer programmers. Early CNC machines required program specialists to input data as well as a machinist to oversee the setup and operation. With the G- and M-codes of today's CNC program languages, the computer specialist is no longer required.

FLOW OF CNC PROCESSING

1. Develop the part drawing.

2. Decide which machine will produce the part.

3. Choose the tooling required.

4. Decide on the machining sequence.

5. Do math calculations for the program coordinates.

6. Calculate the spindle speeds and feedrates required for the tooling and part material.

7. Write the CNC program.

8. Prepare setup sheets and tool lists.

9. Verify and edit the program using either a virtual machine simulator such as CNCez or on the actual machine tool.

10. Verify and edit the program on the actual machine and edit it if necessary.

11. Run the program and produce the part.

FLOW OF COMPUTER-AIDED CNC PROCESSING

1. Develop the three-dimensional geometric model of the part using CAD.

2. Decide which machining operations are required to produce the part (sometimes computer assisted).

3. Choose the tooling to be used (sometimes computer assisted).

4. Run a CAM software program to generate the CNC part program, including the setup sheets and list of tools.

5. Verify and edit the program using a virtual machine simulator such as CNCez.

6. Download the part program(s) to the appropriate machine(s) over the network. (Sometimes multiple machines will be used to fabricate a part.)

7. Verify the program(s) on the actual machine(s) and edit them if necessary.

8. Run the program and produce the part.

QUALITY CONTROL

As the operator uses the CNC machine tool and its controller, it will become evident to the operator which tools and machining procedures work best. This information should be documented, periodically reviewed, and used in all subsequent part programs for that particular machine. Doing this should enhance the efficiency of part programs and reduce runtime problems.

LAB EXERCISE

1. What is NC? _____
_____
_____
_____

2. How did CNC come to be developed? _____
_____
_____
_____
_____

3. What is DNC? _____
_____
_____
_____
_____

4. List the steps in the CNC process. _____
_____
_____
_____
_____

5. Name some of the advantages of CNC. _____
_____
_____
_____
_____

6. What are some of the characteristics that CNC produced parts should have?
_____
_____
_____
_____
_____

7. Describe in your own words the CNC process. _____
_____
_____
_____
_____

Chapter 2

CNC Fundamentals and Vocabulary

CHAPTER OBJECTIVES

After studying this chapter, the student should have knowledge of the following:

The Cartesian coordinate system

The motion directions of the CNC mill and lathe

The types of coordinate systems

Dimensioning theory

The CNC vocabulary

AXIS AND MOTION NOMENCLATURE

All CNC machine tools follow the same standard for motion nomenclature and the same coordinate system. This, as mentioned in Chapter 1, is defined as the EIA 267-C standard. The standard defines a machine coordinate system and machine movements so that a programmer can describe machining operations without worrying whether a tool approaches a workpiece or a workpiece approaches a tool.

Different machine tools have different machine motions, but they always use the same coordinate system. When describing a machine operation, the programmer always calculates tool movements relative to the coordinate system of the stationary workpiece. For example, you may have a CNC machine on which the tool is always stationary; however, the workpiece will move in various directions to achieve a finished part. In this example, when describing the tool motion or coordinate system you describe the tool moving relative to the workpiece.

THE RIGHT-HAND RULE OF COORDINATES

The machine coordinate system is described by the right-hand rectangular coordinate system, that is, the rectangular Cartesian system. Based on this system, the right-hand rule governs how the primary axis of a machine tool should be designated.

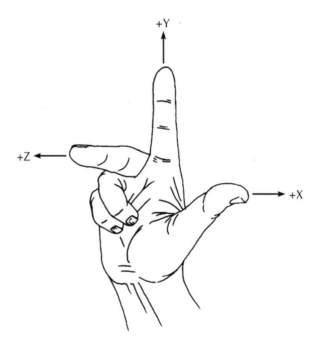

Figure 2-1 The Right-hand rule of machine tool coordinates

As shown in Fig. 2-1, you hold your right hand with the thumb, forefinger, and middle finger perpendicular to each other. The thumb represents the X-axis, the forefinger the Y-axis, and the middle finger the Z-axis. The other two fingers are kept closed.

The direction of each finger represents the positive direction of motion.

The axis of the main spindle is always Z, and the positive direction is into the spindle.

The longest travel slide is known as the X-axis and is always perpendicular to the Z-axis.

If you rotate your hand looking into your middle finger, the forefinger, which is perpendicular to it represents the Y-axis.

The base of your fingers are the start point or X0,Y0,Z0.

To determine the positive, or clockwise, direction about an axis, close your hand with the thumb pointing out, as shown in Fig. 2-2. The thumb may represent either X, Y, or Z axis direction and the curl of the fingers may represent the clockwise or positive rotation about each axis. These are known as A, B, and C and represent the rotary motions about X, Y, and Z, respectively.

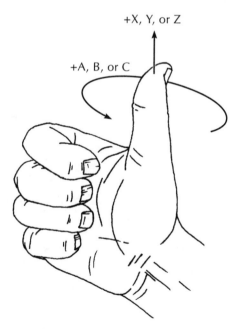

Figure 2-2 The Right-Hand Rule for determining the clockwise rotary motion about X, Y, and Z

See Figs. 2-3 through 2-5 for examples of axis designation on various machine tools.

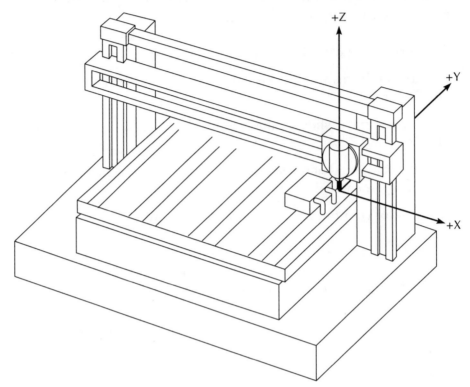

Figure 2-3 A typical CNC milling machine

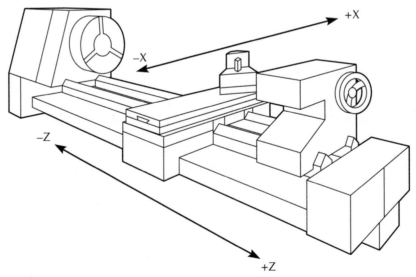

Figure 2-4 A typical CNC lathe

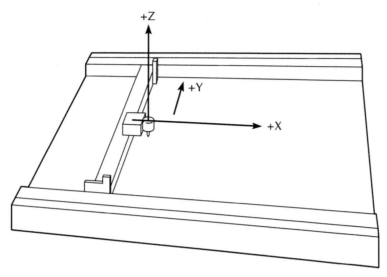

Figure 2-5 A plotter used in CAD applications

CNC MILLING FUNDAMENTALS

THE CARTESIAN GRAPH FOR CNC MILLING

Note from Figs. 2-6(a) and 2-6(b) the origin point (reference point) is at X0,Y0,Z0. The direction of travel will dictate the integer value for the axis coordinate. Measuring the distance to a location from a fixed origin is referred to as the absolute coordinate system and measuring the distance of a point relative to the last point is referred to as the incremental coordinate system. These are explained in more detail in the following sections.

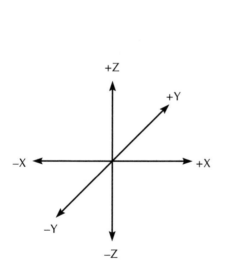

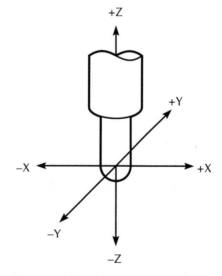

Figure 2-6(a) The Cartesian graph for CNC milling. It shows the three axes and the positive and negative directions.

Figure 2-6(b) The Cartesian graph as it pertains to the CNC machine tool.

Figure 2-7 shows the three planes in the Cartesian coordinate system: the XY plane, XZ plane, and YZ plane. The XY plane is the conventional standard.

There are two main reference points on a CNC machine from which to base all coordinates. The machine reference zero (MRZ) is a point on the actual machine. The part reference zero (PRZ) is a point on the actual part or workpiece.

All CNC machine tools require a reference point from which to base all coordinates. Although every CNC machine will usually have a MRZ, it is generally easier to use a point on the workpiece itself for reference, since the coordinates apply to the part anyway, hence, the PRZ. Since it makes sense to put reference points on prominent objects, so the lower left-hand corner and the top of the stock of each part is where the PRZ is defined.

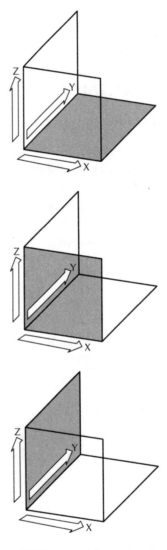

Figure 2-7 The three planes in the Cartesian coordinate system: XY, XZ, and YZ

Look at Fig. 2-8 to see why the PRZ (or the origin point) is at the lower left-hand top corner of the workpiece.

The advantages of having the PRZ at the lower left top corner of the workpiece are as follows:

1. Geometry creation is in the positive X-Y plane when using CAD/CAM systems.

2. The corner of the workpiece is easy to find.

3. All negative Z depths are below the surface of the workpiece.

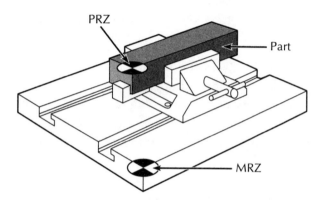

Figure 2-8 The PRZ is located at the lower left-hand top corner of the workpiece to allow for easier coordinate measurement.

ABSOLUTE COORDINATES FOR MILLING

Absolute coordinates use the origin point as the reference point. This means that any point on the Cartesian graph can be plotted accurately by measuring the distance **from the origin, to the point,** first in the X direction, then in the Y direction, then (if applicable) in the Z direction. Points are generally written (X(+)(−)__,Y(+)(−)__,Z(+)(−)__) e.g. (X3.25, Y−7.5, Z−0.5). Placing a positive sign before a number or a zero before a decimal point is usually optional.

Observe from Fig. 2-9 the following:

Point A: This point is 1.5 units along the X-axis from the origin point and 4.5 units along the Y-axis from the origin point. It is at (X1.5, Y4.5).

Point B: This point is 2 units along the X-axis and 3 units along the Y-axis from the origin point. It is at (X2,Y3).

Point C: Point C is 4 units along the X-axis and 1 unit from the Y-axis. It is at (X4,Y1).

With absolute coordinates, keep in mind that all coordinates are measured from X0,Y0 **to the point in question,** first in the X direction, then in the Y

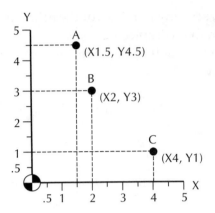

Figure 2-9 Cartesian graph with points A, B, and C

direction, and finally in the Z direction. (Note that if there is no Z coordinate, as on a two dimensional part, it need not be included.

Observe from the following example (Fig. 2-10) how the plus or minus values are derived. Remember, absolute coordinates are measured from the origin (0,0) to the point, first in the X direction, then in the Y direction, and finally (if applicable) in the Z direction.

Example A: From the origin point, point A is 3 units on the +X-axis, then down 2 units on the -Y-axis. Therefore (X3,Y-2).

Example B: From the origin point, point B is 4 units along the -X-axis, then down 3 units in the -Y-axis. Therefore (X-4,Y-3).

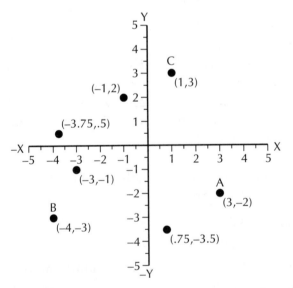

Figure 2-10 Several examples of absolute coordinates. Look at each point and the coordinate values attached to it. Notice how the coordinates for each point are measured first in the X direction, then the Y direction to that point.

Example C: From the origin point, point C is 1 unit along the +X-axis, then up 3 units in the +Y-axis. Therefore (X1,Y3).

INCREMENTAL COORDINATES FOR MILLING

Incremental coordinates use the present position as the reference point for the next movement. This means that any point in the Cartesian graph can be plotted accurately by measuring the distance between points, generally starting at the origin point.

It is important to remember that incremental coordinates are from point to point, always starting from a known reference point such as (0,0).

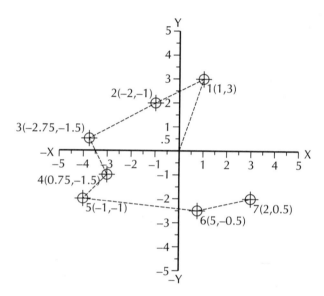

Figure 2-11 In this graph, point 1 is 1 unit in the +X direction from the origin point and up 3 units in the +Y direction, so the incremental coordinates for point 1 are (X+1,Y+3). Point 2 is 2 units in the –X direction and down 1 unit in the –Y direction. So the incremental coordinates for point 2 are (X–2,Y–1).

Example A: From Fig. 2-11, the incremental coordinates for points 3, 4, 5, 6, and 7 are as follows,

Point 3 is (X-2.75,Y-1.5) units from the previous point (point 2).

Point 4 is (X+.75,Y-1.5) units from the previous point (point 3).

Point 5 is (X-1,Y-1) units from the previous point (point 4).

Point 6 is (X+5,Y-.5) units from the previous point (point 5).

Point 7 is (X+2,Y+.5) units from the previous point (point 6).

You generally use incremental coordinates when plotting a large series of points that are clustered around a reference point. In this way, a programmer can use absolute coordinates to pinpoint the reference point (for example, a corner in a milled pocket), then use incremental coordinates to plot the points that are around it.

EXERCISES

To demonstrate an understanding of the characteristics and format of absolute and incremental coordinates, refer to Fig. 2-12 and complete the following exercises.

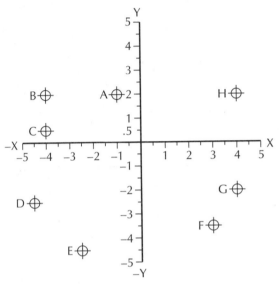

Figure 2-12 CNC milling coordinates

Exercise 1: Absolute Positioning
Fill in the X and Y chart with the appropriate absolute coordinates for the given points A through H.

A: X_____,Y_____   B: X_____,Y_____   C: X_____,Y_____

D: X_____,Y_____   E: X_____,Y_____   F: X_____,Y_____

G: X_____,Y_____   H: X_____,Y_____

Exercise 2: Incremental Positioning
Fill in the X and Y chart with the appropriate incremental coordinates for the given points A through H.

A: X_____,Y_____   B: X_____,Y_____   C: X_____,Y_____

D: X_____,Y_____   E: X_____,Y_____   F: X_____,Y_____

G: X_____,Y_____   H: X_____,Y_____

CNC TURNING FUNDAMENTALS

CNC lathes share the same two-axis coordinate system. This allows for the transfer of CNC programs among different machines, since all measurements are derived from the same reference points.

Basically in CNC turning there is a primary (horizontal) axis and a secondary (vertical) axis. Refer to Figs. 2-13, 2-14, and 2-15, where you can see that the primary axis is labeled Z and the secondary X.

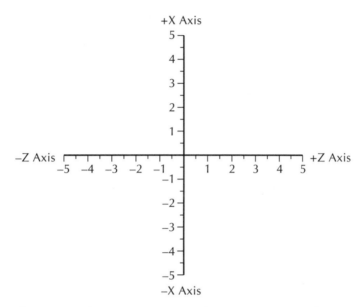

Figure 2-13 The XZ Cartesian coordinate system. Notice how the Z-axis is the horizontal and the X-axis is the vertical. The origin point is at X0,Z0 (the intersection of the X- and Z-axes). Also notice how each axis has a + and a – side. By taking the distance from (X0,Z0), and the direction (in the + or – direction), you can accurately locate any point in this graph.

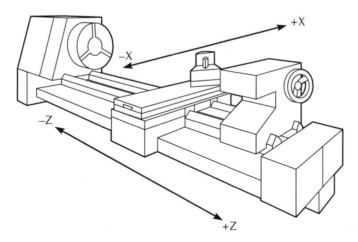

Figure 2-14 Relating the Cartesian graph to a CNC lathe. The major axis always runs through the spindle, so the Z-axis is the long one, while the X-axis is perpendicular to the Z-axis.

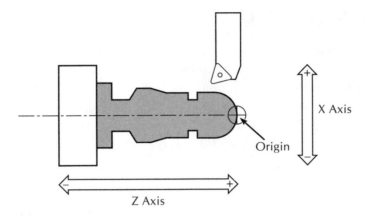

Figure 2-15 Merging the Cartesian graph with a lathe part. Notice how the Z-axis runs through the center of the part, while the X-axis is perpendicular. The origin point is at the intersection of the X- and Z-axes at the center of the end of the workpiece.

It is also important to remember that on most CNC machines, the lathe tool post is on the top, or backside, of the machine, unlike on a conventional lathe. This is why the tool is shown above the part.

When locating points on a profile, you need not use the entire four quadrant system. Any turned part is symmetrical about the Z-axis, so only its top half is required in a drawing. Compare Figs. 2-16 and 2-17 to see how the Cartesian graph is modified to better suit the lathe application.

When measuring X and Z coordinates, use a central reference point. Start all measurements at this reference point, the origin point (X0,Z0). For our

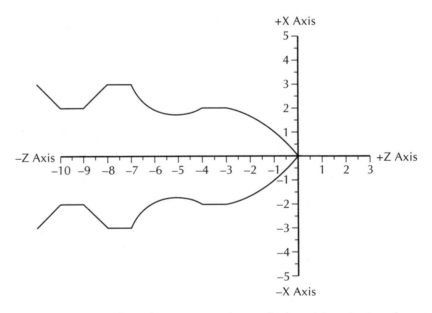

Figure 2-16 Notice how the part sits on the graph: the origin point is at the center of the end of the part. The Z-axis mirrors the part, so only the top half of the part is required. (We use the top half of the profile, since this is where the tool is.)

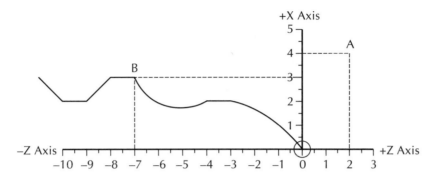

Figure 2-17 A typical lathe part drawing. Notice how the whole profile fits in one quadrant and how all X values are positive, while all Z values are negative.

purposes, the origin point is located at the center right-hand endpoint of the workpiece. Keep in mind that at times the center left-hand endpoint of the workpiece is used.

DIAMETER VERSUS RADIUS PROGRAMMING

Diameter programming relates the X-axis to the diameter of the workpiece. Therefore if the workpiece is 5 in. outside the diameter and you want to command an absolute move to the outside, you would program **X5**.

Radius programming relates the X-axis to the radius of the workpiece. Therefore with the same size workpiece of 5 in., you would program **X2.5** to move the tool to the outside.

Although many controllers can work in either mode, diameter programming is the most common and is the default with CNCez. To change to radius programming, edit the DIAMETER PROGRAMMING option to FALSE in the TURNING.CNF file in the TURNING directory. **Keep in mind that all samples and step-by-step examples are based on diameter programming.**

ABSOLUTE COORDINATES FOR TURNING

When measuring points on a profile, you will usually find it easier to relate each point to the origin point. Coordinates found in this way are called absolute coordinates, since all values are absolute (from the origin point). The following section explains how to find points using absolute coordinates (see Fig. 2-18).

Finding Absolute Coordinates

When plotting points using absolute coordinates, always start at the origin point (X0,Z0). Then travel along the Z-axis until you reach a point directly

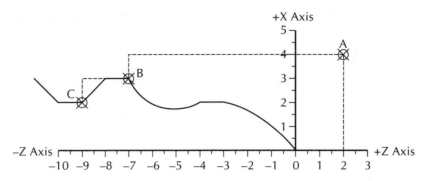

Figure 2-18 There are three points on this graph: A, B and C.

below the point you are trying to plot. Write down the Z value, then go up until you reach your point. Write down the X value. You now have the XZ coordinate for that point. Remember, travel left or right first along the Z-axis, then up or down X-axis.

Example: Find point A.

1. Start at (X0,Z0).

2. Travel right until you are below point A.

3. Move up to point A.

The diametrical XZ coordinates for point A are (X8,Z2).
The radial XZ coordinates for point A are (X4, Z2).

Example: Find point B.

1. Start at (X0, Z0).

2. Travel along the Z-axis to a point below point B.

3. Move up to point B.

The diametrical XZ coordinates for point B are (X6,Z-7).
The radial XZ coordinate for point B are (X3,Z-7)

Example: Find point C.

1. Start at (X0,Z0).

2. Travel along the Z-axis until you are below point C.

3. Move up the X-axis until you are at point C.

The diametrical XZ coordinates for point C are (X4,Z-9).
The radial XZ coordinates for point C are (X2,Z-9).

INCREMENTAL COORDINATES FOR TURNING

The second method for finding points in a Cartesian coordinate system is by using incremental coordinates. This method is used rarely.

Incremental coordinates use each successive point to measure the next coordinate. Instead of constantly referring back to the origin point, the incremental method refers to the previous point, like stepping stones across a lake. The following section explains how to find incremental coordinates (see Fig. 2-19).

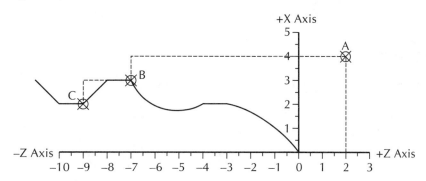

Figure 2-19 Incremental coordinate example. The start point is (X0,Z0).

FINDING INCREMENTAL COORDINATES

Starting with the origin point, each point in turn is the reference point for the next coordinate. This method is easier to use when you are plotting many closely placed points.

Keep in mind that some controllers use G90 and G91 to change the controller mode between absolute and incremental, while other controllers do not have G90 and G91 and instead use X and Z for absolute programming and U and W for incremental. To accommodate both standards, this controller will accept both methods of programming (G90 absolute is the default).

Example: Find point A.
1. Starting at the origin point, travel along the Z-axis until you are below point A.
2. Move up the X-axis until you reach point A.
  The diametrical XZ coordinates for point A are (X8,Z2).
  The radial XZ coordinates for point A are (X4,Z2).

Example: Find point B.
1. Starting at point A, travel along the X-axis until you are below (or above) point B.
2. Move up (or down) the X-axis until you are at point B.
  The diametrical XZ coordinates for point B are (X-2,Z-9).
  The radial XZ coordinates for point B are (X-1,Z-9).

Example: Find Point C.
1. Starting at point B, travel along the Z-axis until you are below (or above) point C.
2. Move up (or down) the X-axis to find the X coordinate.
   The radial XZ coordinates for point C are (X-2,Z-2)
   The radial XZ coordinates for point C are (X-1,Z-2)

EXERCISES

Refer to Fig. 2-20 to complete the following exercises.

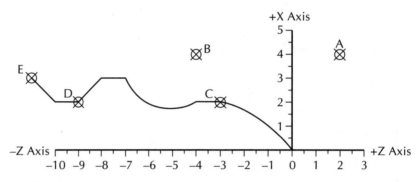

Figure 2-20

Exercise 1: Using Incremental Coordinates
Find the diametrical X and Z points A through E.

A: X____,Z____   B: X____,Z____   C: X____,Z____

D: X____,Z____   E: X____,Z____

Exercise 2: Using Absolute Coordinates
Find the X and Z coordinates for the given points A through E.

A: X____,Z____   B: X____,Z____   C: X____,Z____

D: X____,Z____   E: X____,Z____

LAB EXERCISE

1. What is the standard coordinate system called? _____

_____

_____

2. What are the three axes used on the CNC mill? _____

_____

_____

3. What are the two axes used on the CNC Lathe? _____

_____

_____

4. What are the two types of coordinate systems? Explain the difference
   between them. _____

_____

_____

_____

_____

_____

_____

5. Does the X-axis on a CNC milling machine run vertically or horizontally?

_____

_____

6. What are the three planes in the Cartesian coordinate system? _____

_____

_____

7. What is the PRZ? _____

_____

_____

8. Where do you find the PRZ on the following?

   Milling workpiece _____

_____

_____

   Turning workpiece _____

_____

_____

Chapter 3

Programming Concepts

CHAPTER OBJECTIVES

After studying this chapter, the student should have knowledge of the following:

Format of a CNC program

How to prepare to write CNC programs

Types of tool motion

Uses of canned cycles

Tooling

INTRODUCTION

Before you can fully understand CNC, you must first understand how a manufacturing company processes a job that will be produced on a CNC machine. The following is an example of how a company may break down the process of CNC.

FLOW OF CNC PROCESSING

1. Develop the part drawing.
2. Decide which machine will produce the part.
3. Choose the tooling required.
4. Decide on the machining sequence.
5. Do math calculations for the program coordinates.
6. Calculate the speeds and feeds required for the tooling and part material.
7. Write the NC program.
8. Prepare setup sheets and tool lists.
9. Send program to machine.
10. Verify the program.
11. Run the program if no changes are required.

PREPARING A PROGRAM

A program is a sequential list of machining instructions for the CNC machine to execute. These instructions are CNC code that contains all the information required to machine a part, as specified by the programmer.

CNC code consists of blocks (also called lines), each of which contains an individual command for a movement or specific action. Just as with conventional machines, one movement is made before the next one. This is why CNC codes are listed sequentially in numbered blocks.

Following is a sample CNC milling program. Notice how each block is numbered and usually contains only one specific command. Notice how the blocks are numbered in increments of 5 (this is the software default on startup). Each block contains specific information for the machine to execute in sequence.

Workpiece Size:	X4,Y3,Z1
Tool:	Tool #3, 3/8" Slot Drill
Tool Start Position:	X0,Y0,Z1

```
%                              (Program Start Flag)
:1002                          (Program #1002)
```

```
N5  G90 G20              (Block #5, Absolute in Inches)
N10 M06 T3               (Tool change to Tool #3)
N15 M03 S1250            (Spindle On CW at 1250rpm)
N20 G00 X1 Y1            (Rapid over to X1,Y1)
N25 Z0.1                 (Rapid down to Z0.1)
N30 G01 Z-0.125 F5       (Feed down to Z-0.125 at 5ipm)
N35 X3 Y2 F10            (Feed diagonally to X3,Y2 at 10ipm)
N40 G00 Z1               (Rapid up to Z1)
N45 X0 Y0                (Rapid over to X0,Y0)
N50 M05                  (Spindle Off)
N55 M30                  (Program End)
```

CNC CODES

There are two major types of CNC codes, or letter addresses, in any program. The major CNC codes are called G-codes and M-codes.

G-codes are preparatory functions, which involve actual tool moves (for example, control of the machine). These include rapid moves, feed moves, radial feed moves, dwells, and roughing and profiling cycles.

M-codes are miscellaneous functions, which include actions necessary for machining, but not those that are an actual tool movement (for example, auxiliary functions). These include spindle on and off, tool changes, coolant on and off, program stops, and other similar related functions.

Other *letter addresses* or variables are used in the G- and M-codes to make words. Most G-codes contain a variable, defined by the programmer, for each specific function. Each designation used in CNC programming is called a letter address. The letters used for programming are as follows;

N   Block number—specifies the start of a block

G   Preparatory function, as previously explained

X   X-axis coordinate

Y   Y-axis coordinate

Z   Z-axis coordinate

I   X-axis location of arc center

J   Y-axis location of arc center

K   Z-axis location of arc center

S   Sets the spindle speed

F Assigns a feedrate

T Specifies tool to be used

M Miscellaneous function, as previously explained.

The process of writing CNC programs is primarily the same as going through the steps involved with conventional machining. First, you must decide which units are to be used—metric or inch—and what type of coordinate system will be used—absolute or incremental. Next, a tool must be called up and the spindle turned on. Finally, the tool must rapid to a point close to the part to start the actual machining.

These steps are identical for both conventional and CNC machining. The two methods differ in that a CNC program has them programmed into each CNC file.

Without preparation, a beginner is virtually "doomed" from the start. To avoid this, remember that before you write your program you must develop a sequence of operations. Do all of the necessary math, then choose your tooling, units, and coordinate system.

THREE MAJOR PHASES OF A CNC PROGRAM

The following program shows the three major phases of a CNC program:

```
%
:1001
N5 G90 G20
N10 M06 T2
N15 M03 S1200
N20 G00 X1 Y1
N25 Z0.125
N30 G01 Z-0.125 F5
N35 G01 X2 Y2
N40 G00 Z1
N45 X0 Y0
N50 M05
N55 M30
```

1. Program setup

`%`	Program start flag
`:1001`	four digit program number
`N5 G90 G20`	Use absolute units, and inch programming.
`N10 M06 T2`	Stop for tool change, use Tool #2.
`N15 M03 S1200`	Turn the spindle on CW to 1200 rpm.

The program setup phase is virtually identical in every program. It always begins with the program start flag (% sign). Line two always has a program number (up to four digits, 0–9999).

Line three is the first that is actually numbered. Notice how it begins with N5 (N for Number, 5 for block number 5). You can use any number incrementing upwards. We use increments of 5 in our examples. Incrementing in this way enables you to insert up to 4 new lines between lines when you are editing the program. Some programmers use increments of 1 or 10. The software allows automatic numbering in increments specified by the user.

Block 5 tells the controller that all distances (X and Z coordinates) are absolute, that is, measured from the origin point. It also instructs the controller that all coordinates are measured in inch units.

The program setup contains all the instructions that prepare the machine for operation. The setup phase may also include such commands as coolant on, cutter compensation cancel, or stop for tool change.

2. Material Removal

`N20 G00 X1 Y1`	Rapid to (X1,Y1) from origin point.
`N25 Z0.125`	Rapid down to Z0.125.
`N30 G01 Z−0.125 F5`	Feed down to Z–0.125 at 5 ipm.
`N35 G01 X2 Y2`	Feed diagonally to (X2,Y2).
`N40 G00 Z1`	Rapid up to Z1.
`N45 X0 Y0`	Rapid to X0,Y0.

The material removal phase deals exclusively with the actual cutting feed moves. It contains all the commands that designate linear or circular feed moves, rapid moves, canned cycles such as grooving or profiling, or any other function required for that particular part.

3. System Shutdown

`N50 M05`	Turn the spindle off.
`N55 M30`	End of program

The system shutdown phase contains all those G- and M-codes that turn off all the options that were turned on in the setup phase. Functions such as coolant and spindle rotation must be shut off prior to removal of the part from the machine. The shutdown phase also is virtually identical in every program.

Example: Examine the program below to see how it is written.

This program shows how some G-code commands are *modal*. Modal means a code remains active once executed and until overridden by a different G-code command. See blocks N75 and N80.

You can also see how leading and trailing zeros are optional and do not effect the outcome of the program, only presentation. (Refer to blocks N20–N30.)

%	Program start flag
:1001	Program number
N5 G90 G20	Absolute coordinates and inch units
N10 M06 T1	Tool change, use Tool #1.
N15 M03 S1200	Turn spindle on CW at 1200 rpm.
N20 G00 X1 Y1	Rapid move to X1,Y1.
N25 Z0.125	Rapid down to Z0.125.
N30 G01 Z-0.125 F5.0	Feed down into the part 0.125 in. at 5 ipm.
N35 X3.0	Feed to X3 (the G01 is modal).
N40 Y2	Feed to Y2.
N45 X1	Feed back to X1.
N50 Y1	Feed back to Y1.
N55 Z-0.25	Feed down further to Z-0.25 in.
N60 X3	Feed across to X3.
N65 Y2	Feed to Y2.
N70 X1	Feed back to X1.
N75 Y1	Feed to start point at Y1.
N80 G00 Z1	Rapid to Z1.
N85 X0 Y0	Rapid tool to home position.
N90 M05	Turn spindle off.
N95 M30	End of program

USING A PROGRAMMING SHEET

You use the CNC programming sheet to prepare the CNC program. Using the program sheet simplifies the writing of the CNC program. Look at the sample sheet in Fig. 3-1 to see how it works. Each row contains all the data required to write one CNC block. Several blank programming sheets are included in Appendix C.

NC PROGRAMMING SHEET		PART NAME:				PROG BY:				
		MACHINE:				DATE:		PAGE:		
		SETUP INFORMATION:								

N SEQ	G Code	X Pos'n	Y Pos'n	Z Pos'n	I J K Pos'n	F Feed	R Radius or Retract	S Speed	T Tool	M Misc
5	20,90									
10									2	6
15								1200		3
20	0	0	0							
25				0.1						
30	1			-0.1		2				
35	1	1.5								

Figure 3-1 Sample programming sheet

BLOCK FORMAT

Block format is often more important than program format. It is vital that each block of CNC code be entered into the CPU correctly. Each block comprises different components, which can produce tool moves on the machine. Following is a sample block of CNC code. Examine it closely and note how it is written.

N135 G01 X1.0 Y1.0 Z0.125 F5

N135	Block number	Shows the current CNC block number
G01	G-Code	Tells the machine what it is to do, in this case, a Linear Feed move
X1.0 Y1.0 Z0.125	Coordinate	Gives the machine an end point for its move. X designates an X-axis coordinate, Y a Y-axis coordinate, and Z a Z-axis coordinate.
F5	Special function	Contains any special function or related parameter. In this case, a feed rate of 5 in/min is programmed.

There are some simple restrictions on CNC blocks, as follows:

- Each may contain only one tool move.

- Each may contain any number of non-tool move G-codes, provided they do not conflict between each other (for example, G42 and G43).

- Each may contain only one feedrate per block.

- Each may contain only one specified tool or spindle speed.

- The block numbers should be sequential.

- Both the program start flag and the program number must be independent of all other commands.

- The data within a block should follow the sequence shown in the above sample block.

PREPARING TO PROGRAM

Before you write a CNC program, you must first prepare to write it. The success of a CNC program is directly related to the preparation that you do before you write the CNC program.

You should do the following before you begin to write a program:

1. Develop an order of operations.

2. Do all the necessary math and complete a coordinate sheet.

3. Choose your tooling and calculate the speeds and feeds.

Develop an Order of Operations

Before you begin writing your program, you should plan it from start to finish, considering all operations that must be performed. Doing this will help you when you are writing your program.

Do All the Necessary Math and Complete a Coordinate Sheet

Do all the math that has to be done before you begin the program. You can mark up your part drawing and use a coordinate sheet (Fig. 3-2) if you find it helpful.

Coordinate Sheet

#	X	Z
1		
2		
3		
4		
5		
6		
7		
8		
9		
10		
11		
12		
13		
14		

Figure 3-2 Coordinate sheet sample

Choose Your Tooling and Calculate the Speeds and Feeds

Decide on which tools you are going to use and ensure the tools you have available will perform the required tasks. Also, calculate the required speeds and feeds that you will be using in your program. You can use a setup sheet

(Fig. 3-3)to help you choose your tools and to help you in the setup required before actual machining.

The CNC operator can also use a coordinate sheet and a setup sheet.

Example Setup Sheet				→
Cutting Tools:				
Stat #	Tool Description	Catalog Number	Insert	Comment:
1				
2				
3				
4				
5				
6				
7				
8				
9				
10				
11				
12				

Set Up Instructions:	Set Up Sketch:

Figure 3-3 Setup sheet sample

PROGRAM ZERO

Program zero allows the programmer to specify a position from which to start or to work. Once program zero is defined, all coordinates that go into a program will be referenced from this point. When you work from a constant program zero, you are using absolute programming as discussed in Chapter 2. In incremental programming, you have in effect a floating program zero that changes at all times. For most program samples in this book, absolute programming is used with a fixed program zero, or origin point. To specify absolute positions in the X direction, we use the X word. To specify absolute positions in the Y and Z, we use the Y and Z words, respectively. The position we select for milling is always the lower left-hand corner and top surface of the workpiece (see Fig. 3-4). The position we use for the lathe is always the center of the part in X and the right end of the finished workpiece in Z(see Fig. 3-5).

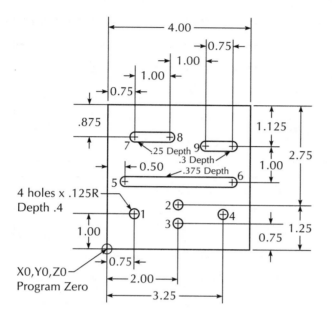

Coordinate Sheet

#	X	Y	Z
1			
2			
3			
4			
5			
6			
7			
8			
9			
10			

Figure 3-4 Milling zero

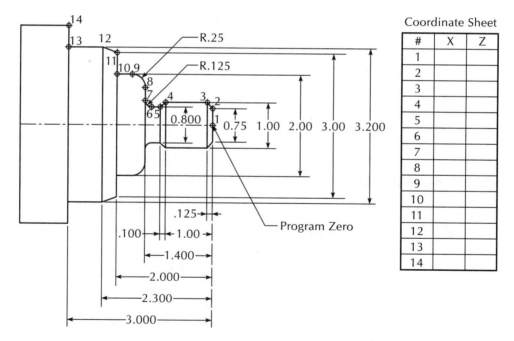

Coordinate Sheet

#	X	Z
1		
2		
3		
4		
5		
6		
7		
8		
9		
10		
11		
12		
13		
14		

Figure 3-5 Lathe zero

TOOL MOTION

There are only three types of tool motion used on a CNC machine. They are,

G00	Rapid tool move
G01	Straight line feedmove
G02/G03	Circular interpolation or arc feedmoves

All cycles such as G71 rough turning are either one of these types or a combination of these types of motion.

These motion commands are modal. That is, if you program one of these commands, you do not need to program the same code again until you want to change the type of tool motion. There are other codes in CNC programming which are modal. They will be identified as you learn the various commands.

The other codes are explained in detail in the following chapters.

USING CANNED CYCLES

Canned, or fixed program, cycles are programming aids that simplify programming. Canned cycles combine many standard programming operations and are designed to shorten the program length, minimize math calculations, and optimize cutting conditions to improve the production of the machine.

Examples of canned cycles on a mill are drilling; boring; spot facing; tapping, and so on; on a lathe, threading and pattern repeating cycles. On the lathe, canned cycles are also referred to as multiple repetitive cycles. You'll find examples of these cycles as you work through the milling and turning sections of this book. Quick examples you can refer to in each section are the G81 cycle in milling and the G71 cycle in turning found in Chapters 5 and 6.

All these cycles using canned cycles speeds up programming.

You should know that canned cycles your CNC control offers. Subroutines are also available on many CNC controllers. You can use these to make your own canned cycles.

TOOLING

Not all cutting operations can be performed with a single tool. Separate tools are used for roughing and finishing, and tasks such as drilling, slotting, and thread cutting require their own specific tools.

The correct cutting tool must be used at all times. The size and shape of the cutting tools you can use depend on the size and shape of the finished part. A tool manufacturers catalog will give you a complete listing of the various types of tools available and the applications of each. Remember that the depth of cut that can be taken depends on the workpiece material, the coolant, the type of tool, and the machine tool itself. The following considerations must be taken when choosing your tools:

Drilling   The most common tool for the making of holes is the fluted drill. Drills are made with two, three, or four cutting lips. The two-lip drill is used for drilling solid stock. The three- and four-lip drills are used for enlarging holes that have been previously drilled.

Milling   On a lathe, the cutting tool is fixed and the work rotates. In a milling machine, the cutter rotates and the work is fed against it. The rotating cutter, termed the milling cutter, has almost an unlimited variety of shapes and sizes for milling regular and irregular forms. The most common milling cutter is the endmill. Other tools that are often used are shell mills, face mills, and roughing mills. When milling, care must be taken not to take a cut that is deeper than the milling cutter can handle.

Endmills come in various shapes and sizes, each designed to perform a specific task. The three basic shapes of standard endmills are flat, ballnose, and bullnose. Fig. 3-6 shows the 3 basic endmills.

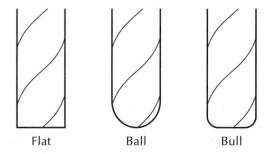

Flat   Ball   Bull

Figure 3-6 The three basic endmills

Lathe   In lathe operations, the tool is driven through the material to remove chips from the workpiece in order to leave geometrically true surfaces. The kind of surface produced by the cutting operation depends on the shape of the tool and the path it follows through the material. When the cutting edge of the tool breaks down, the surface finish becomes poor and the cutting forces rise. Vibration and chatter are definite signs of tool wear although many forces such as depth of cut, properties of materials, friction forces, and rubbing of the tool nose also affect tool vibration.

The following factors determine how a cutting tool performs:

The tool material

The shape of the tool point

The form of the tool

No one cutting material is best for all purposes. The principle materials used in NC tooling are carbon tool steel, high-speed steel, cast nonferrous alloys, carbides, sintered oxides, diamonds, artificial abrasives, and coated tooling.

Lathe tool shape and form should also be considered when you are choosing your tooling. The tool angles, relief angles, rake angles, cutting edge angles, and tool nose radius all affect the way metals are cut. (See Fig. 3-7.)

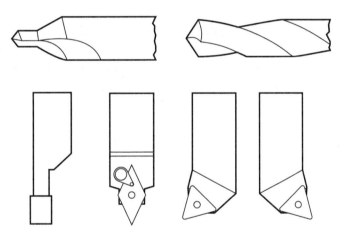

Figure 3-7 Sample turning tools

FEEDRATES, SPINDLE SPEEDS AND CUTTING FLUIDS

Every material differs in characteristics, from softer materials such as machinable wax to harder materials such as stainless steel. New tool technology has produced a wide range of tools that can be used at greater speeds and feeds for longer periods. It is very important that you fully understand the value of the correct spindle speed and feedrate. Too fast a speed or feedrate will result in early tool failure or poor surface finish. To slow a speed or feedrate will lead to increased machining time and, possibly to a greater part cost. A good surface finish and economical production rates require the proper use of spindle speeds and feedrates. The spindle speed and feedrates are influenced by the following conditions, as well as by the power and stability of your particular machine tool.

The spindle speed is the peripheral speed of the work passing the cutter (turning) or the rotating cutter passing the surface of the part (milling). Refer to Appendix B for detailed information on speeds and feedrates.

For milling, the correct speeds and feeds are determined in part by the diameter of the cutter, spindle RPM, number of teeth on the cutter, chip load per tooth, and surface feet per minute for a particular material.

Refer to the machinist's handbook to find the specific feeds and speeds for a particular material and cutter.

CUTTING FLUID

There are two main reasons for using cutting fluids, as follows:

1. To remove or reduce the heat being produced

2. To reduce cutting tool wear

Thus in most applications, fluids are used for cooling and lubrication, however in some cases they are used also to help in the removal of chips, prevent the production of dust or irritants, and dampen machine vibration. Remember to use the best cutting fluid for the job.

LAB EXERCISE

1. What do the following letter addresses stand for?

   X: _____

   Y: _____

   Z: _____

   F: _____

2. What are the basic definitions of the letter addresses?

   G: _____

   M: _____

3. What is a preparatory function? _____

   _____

   _____

   _____

   _____

   _____

   _____

4. What are two reasons for using cutting fluids? _____

   _____

   _____

   _____

   _____

   _____

   _____

5. What are the factors that affect how a cutting tool performs ? _____

   _____

   _____

   _____

   _____

   _____

6. Describe the PRZ for milling. _____

   _____

   _____

   _____

   _____

   _____

Chapter 4

Interactive Simulation Software

CHAPTER OBJECTIVES

After studying this chapter, the student should have knowledge of the following:

The user interface of the CNC simulation software

How to install the simulation software

How to use the interactive CNC editor

How to run a simple CNC simulation

INSTALLATION AND SETUP

Before attempting to install the software, ensure your workstation has the following:

- 8086, 80286, or higher processor

- MS-DOS 3.0 or higher

- EGA or VGA graphics monitor

- 1 MB hard disk space (minimum)

- 640K RAM

- 2- or 3-button mouse

INSTALLING AND OPENING THE PROGRAM

1. Insert the program disk into the appropriate disk drive.

   If your diskette is in drive A, type **A:INSTALL**

   If your diskette is in drive B, type **B:INSTALL**

2. Follow the installation options displayed on screen.
   The interactive simulation software will be installed onto your hard disk into the CNCEZ directory.
   The following directories and files will be set up.

   \CNCEZ\DEMOMILL - milling sample programs directory

   \CNCEZ\DEMOTURN - turning sample programs directory

   \CNCEZ\MILLING - milling executable files

   \CNCEZ\TURNING - turning executable files

   \CNCEZ\INIT.COM - initializer file

   \CNCEZ\MENU.COM - menu file

   In addition, the file CNCEZ.BAT will be placed in the root directory of the drive on which the software was installed. This batch file runs the simulation software.

3. After the installation is complete, run the program by typing CNCEZ at the DOS prompt and pressing Enter.

4. After CNCEZ.BAT is executed, the main options menu appears (Fig.4-1):

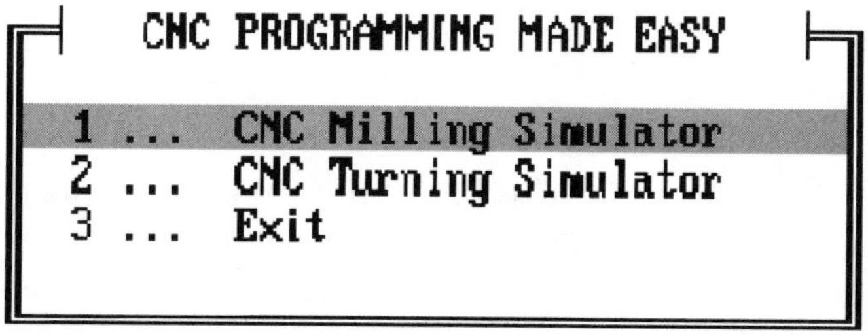

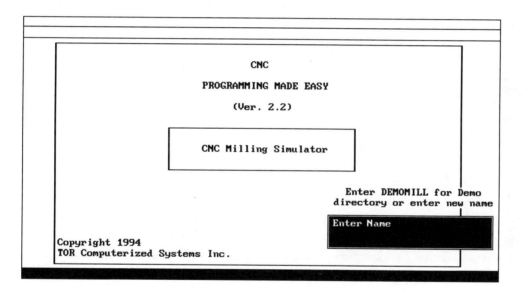

Figure 4-1 Main options menu

Choose the option required either by using the cursor keys to highlight it and then pressing Enter or by typing the number next to it and pressing Enter.

The main system screen should be displayed (Fig. 4-2):

Figure 4-2 Main system screen for milling

At this point, you can either select the data directory in which you want your CNC files and information to be stored or enter DEMOMILL or DEMOTURN, directories that contain all the sample programs and exercises used in this book. If you enter a new directory (for example, TEST), the system will ask you if you want to create a new directory. This directory will then be created and used until changed.

DEFAULT CONFIGURATION

Certain standards and modes are defaulted in this program for both milling and turning, for example, diametrical programming for turning. To change many of the defaults for either milling or turning, the following two files must be edited:

MILLING.CNF

TURNING.CNF

MILLING.CNF is in the \CNCEZ\MILLING subdirectory and TURNING.CNF is in the \CNC\TURNING subdirectory.

To edit either file, use an ASCII editor such EDIT.COM found in DOS. Simply type EDIT, press Enter, then change to the proper directory. Select the file and edit it, then save it before exiting the editor. You can then rerun CNCEZ to see the results of the changes.

Variables you may want to change are the following:

- The tool default start position

- The tool default reference position

- Default inch or millimeter programming

- Diametrical or radial programming

THE USER INTERFACE

The user interface is divided into different areas, each dedicated to a different function (see Fig. 4-3). As the program information is updated, so are the different screen areas.

The simulation environment has been developed to provide the user with the maximum amount of relevant program information without screen clutter and data overload. Each window displays current information about the program in real-time simulation. As the data is updated in a running program, the respective windows display the appropriate updated information.

The following describes the content of each screen area:

- Menu Bar

  Contains the pull-down menus that govern system operations. Use the cursor keys to move the cursor or the respective F-key to pull down a menu.

- Identification Line

  Displays the current file name and data drive, as well as current workpiece dimensions and units of measurement.

- Tool Display Window

  Displays a graphical representation of the tool currently in use.

- System Status Window

  Defaults (is factory set) to the settings shown below. All settings are user definable. When they are altered, the new setting is displayed.

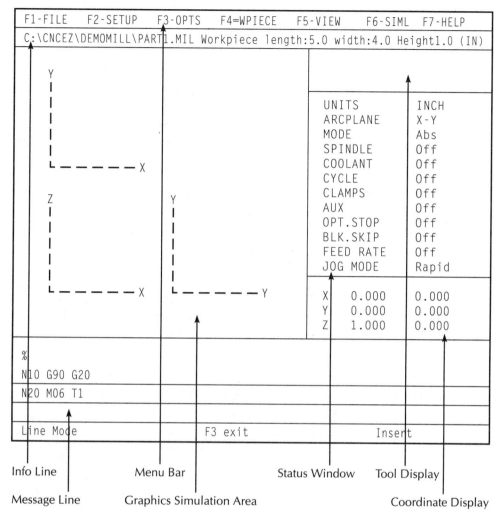

```
F1-FILE    F2-SETUP    F3-OPTS    F4=WPIECE    F5-VIEW    F6-SIML  F7-HELP
C:\CNCEZ\DEMOMILL\PART1.MIL Workpiece length:5.0 width:4.0 Height1.0 (IN)
```

	UNITS	INCH
	ARCPLANE	X-Y
	MODE	Abs
	SPINDLE	Off
	COOLANT	Off
	CYCLE	Off
	CLAMPS	Off
	AUX	Off
	OPT.STOP	Off
	BLK.SKIP	Off
	FEED RATE	Off
	JOG MODE	Rapid

X	0.000	0.000
Y	0.000	0.000
Z	1.000	0.000

```
%
N10 G90 G20
N20 M06 T1
```

```
Line Mode              F3 exit              Insert
```

Info Line Menu Bar Status Window Tool Display

Message Line Graphics Simulation Area Coordinate Display

Figure 4-3

UNITS	Inch (mm is optional)
ARC PLANE	XY (Can be changed to XZ or YZ)
MODE	Abs (Absolute. Incremental optional)
SPINDLE	Off (Can be switched ON)
COOLANT	Off (Can be switched ON)
CYCLE	(Displays current cycle, if any)
CLAMPS	Off (Can be switched ON)
AUX	Off (Can be switched ON)
OPT. STOP	Off (Can be switched ON)
BLK.SKIP	Off (Can be switched ON)
FEEDRATE	# displays programmed rate
JOG	Rapid (Can be changed to Feed or Step)

• Coordinate Display Window

Displays the current tool position. The left column shows absolute co-ordinates; the right column shows incremental coordinates.

• Graphics Simulation Window

Displays the program simulation. As each block is executed, the window displays the toolpath and material removal. Different views are available. (Refer to the VIEW menu)

• Message Line

Displays the block currently being executed, as well as a simple English translation of what the code means.

ACCESSING THE MENU OPTIONS

The entire program is controlled by the pull-down menus and the options within them, so you need to be able to access them. There are three ways of manipulating the cursor in order to access the menus and select an option:

1. Use the cursor keys (the arrow keys on your keyboard) to move the cursor around on screen. You can toggle the speed between fast and slow by pressing the Scroll-lock key.

   To access a pull-down menu with the cursor keys, move the cursor until it is directly over a menu. A pull-down menu will then appear.

2. Use the function keys on your keyboard. Notice how each pull-down menu in the menu bar has a function key number before it. By pressing the corresponding function key, you can access that particular menu; for example press F1 and the FILES menu will appear).

3. Use the mouse. Move the mouse around until the arrow overlaps the title of the desired menu. That menu will appear.

To select an option from within a pull-down menu, use one of the three methods described above to move the cursor until it highlights the selected option. When the option is highlighted, press Enter or the left mouse button.

You can access menu options by typing the first letter of that option; (for example, in the HELP menu, type I to select the INFO option.)

MENUS

F1- FILE

F1- FILE
NEW
OPEN
SAVE
SAVE AS
DELETE
EDIT
PRINT
QUIT

NEW Allows you to start a new part program. It clears the current part program from the memory buffers and resets the screen environment for a new part program. If the old part has not yet been saved, a screen prompt appears asking if you want to save it.

OPEN Retrieves an existing program from the current data directory on your data disk. Choose the file you want by clicking with the mouse or using the cursor keys and pressing Enter on the highlighted item. This will load the file for editing or simulating.

SAVE Saves the CNC code for the current part program, as well as the environment data. (Environment data is any information concerning the graphics, part dimensions, tool information, and so on.) These are saved as different files. The CNC code is saved as an ASCII text file with the .MIL or .TRN extension. The environment file is saved with a different extension but is non-readable. (**Note:** The DOS file extension for any CNC code may be changed. See the SETUP menu.)

SAVE AS Saves the current CNC file under a new name. After you select this option, you are prompted, "Enter File Name:". Enter a new name and press Enter. If you enter a name that already exists, you are prompted "File exists - Overwrite?," whereupon you select either Yes or No.

DELETE Deletes unwanted CNC files in the data directory. Select the file to be deleted by highlighting it, then pressing Enter. A double-check prompt will be displayed.

EDIT (The Editor) Puts you into the line editor (appears as three lines of a text window at the bottom of the screen) in which you can input and edit CNC codes. F1 toggles between the three-line screen and a full screen that displays much more of the current CNC file.

Cursor Movements

Left/Right Cursor Key	Moves the cursor left/right.
Up/Down Cursor Key	Moves the cursor up/down.
CTRL Left/Right	Moves the cursor one word left/right.
Page up/Page down	Moves the cursor five lines up/down.
Home/End (CTRL-F/CTRL-N)	Moves the cursor to the start/end of file.

Delete Functions

DEL	Deletes the character under the cursor.
BACKSPAC	Erases the character to the left.
CTRL-W	Deletes the entire word to the left.
CTRL-T	Deletes the entire word to the right.
CTRL-Y	Deletes the entire line.
CTRL-U	Restores the last deleted item.
ESC	Undoes the previous change.

Miscellaneous

INSERT	Toggles between insert/overwrite.
CTRL-I	Inserts a blank line after the current line.
F3	Exits the editor to the current line.

PRINT Prints the currently opened file to an Epson compatible printer (if one is connected). Prompts, "Are you sure - Y/N," before printing.

QUIT Quits you from the program and puts you back at the DOS prompt. If the file has been changed and not saved, you will be asked to save it first.

SETUP (F2)

Milling

F2-SETUP
TOOLS
OFFSET
UNITS
DRIVE
CH-DIREC
FILETYPE
LIBRARY

Turning

F2-SETUP
TOOLS
OFFSET
UNITS
CHUCK
DRIVE
CH-DIREC
FILETYPE
LIBRARY

TOOLS Allows you to view and modify the loaded tool library. On selecting Tools a window will be displayed showing two smaller windows. The tool library is shown in the larger window on the left and contains 24 standard tools. The tool turret, the smaller window on the right, can contain any of 12 tools from the library in any order, depending on program requirements.

To move a tool from the library into the turret, use the cursor to move the box until it rests on top of the desired tool. Press Enter to transfer the tool to the library and then move it to the desired turret location. Press Enter again.

When you use different tools in a program, it is the tool turrent that distinguishes between tools. It may be simpler to use the default tool turret, since the tools in it are preorganized.

OFFSET Opens the input box so you can input or edit the offset registers for the tools. The register values are used for the tool length and toolnose radius compensation in the CNC program. The same registers may be utilized by both the G41/G42 cutter radius compensation and the G43/G44 cutter length offset. The registers are preset to common values, but they may be altered. Refer to Chapters 5 and 6 for detailed explanations of how the offsets work.

Move the cursor to the desired register, then press Enter. A display prompt appears asking for the offset value for that register. Type in the new value and then press the Enter key. Remember, the offset values are in whatever units the system defaults to.

To exit the offset register, move the cursor to one side and press Enter.

UNITS Prompts for inch or metric (mm) programming with "INCH PROGRAMMING? Y/N". This unit default is for the system environment: the workpiece, offsets, and system default. The programming units may be switched within the program via the appropriate G-code.

CHUCK (Turning only) When selecting this option you are prompted to enter the length.

DRIVE Enables you to specify to which disk drive the CNC files are to be saved. To save to a floppy disk, type either A or B (depending on your systems configuration). To save to the hard disk, type the appropriate drive letter, for example, C. For network drives, type the letter of the network drive, for example, H.

CH-DIREC Changes the current user directory without your having to leave the user interface, for example, C:\CNCEZ\DEMOMILL to A:\PROGRAMS.

FILETYPE Allows you to input different types of CNC files simply by changing the DOS file extension. The default extension for CNCEZ milling files is .MIL and for CNCEZ turning files, .TRN. Other CNC files may require a .NC or .CNC extension.

LIBRARY Enables you to specify whether you want to use the inch tool library or the metric tool library. The libraries consist of 24 standard tools. The inch library is the default.

OPTIONS (F3)

Milling

F3-OPTS	
O. STOP	-
B. SKIP	-
DRY RUN	-
A NUMBER	+
JOG MODE	R
SHOWPATHS	-
REWIND	+

Turning

F3-OPTS	
O.STOP	-
B.SKIP	-
REWIND	+
A NUMBER	+
JOG MODE	R
SHOWPATHS	-

All menu prompts under the OPTIONS (F3) menu can be toggled on or off (+ or –) simply by selecting that option. The JOG MODE option has a sub-menu for optional Rapid, Feed, and Step.

O. STOP [– +] Toggle option that enables or disables program optional stop. If O. STOP is on (+), the simulation and controller will stop when it encounters an M01 command and until Enter is pressed. If O. STOP is off, the M01 command will be skipped.

B. SKIP [– +] Toggle option that enables or disables the block skip lines. A line with a block skip starts with a "/" (forward slash). If the block skip is on [+], the lines are not executed. When the block skip is off [–], these blocks are executed in the program. This toggle is also displayed in the status window of the screen. The default is off.

DRY RUN [– +] (milling only) Toggle option that enables or disables the dry-run mode. If DRY RUN is on [+], all the Z moves are ignored and the spindle will always be off. The default is off.

A NUMBER [– +] Toggle option that generates automatic block numbers during edit mode. A NUMBER [+] generates automatic block numbers with a block increment of 5. A NUMBER [–] generates no block numbers; you move to enter the block number. (If no block number is entered, the software will generate an error message.)The software allows you to enter a previously used block number. The default is on [+], with a block increment of 5. Upon choosing this option, you can change the block increment to any desired number.

JOG MODE [R F S] Selects the axis speed for movements in JOG. When you select this item, a pop-down menu gives you a choice of speeds required for JOG. The default is Rapid.

RAPID   Highest velocity

FEED   Current set feed

STEP   Smallest machine increment

The default is Rapid.

SHOW PATH (– +) Toggle option that generates a red graphics line that trails the tool center around the simulation screen. It is visible in all three views and provides some useful data regarding the tool's actual position. The default is off(–), rapid or positioning moves will be dashed lines, and feed or cutting moves will be solid lines.

REWIND (– +) Rewinds the program to the start of the CNC code, provided the option is on (+). The program prompts you for permission before rerunning the code. If REWIND is off (–), the program halts execution of the code.

WORKPIECE (F4)

Milling

F4-WPIECE
DEFINE
LOAD
SAVE

Turning

F4-WPIECE
WORKPIECE
PIPE
LOAD
SAVE

DEFINE (milling only) Prompts you to input workpiece dimensions by length, width and height. Press Enter after you enter each dimension. A display prompt tells you if the workpiece size is too small or too large for the simulation window.

WORKPIECE (turning only) Prompts you to input stock length and diameter. Press Enter after you enter each dimension A display prompt tells you if the workpiece size is too small or too large for the simulation window.

PIPE (turning only) Prompts you to input pipe length and external and internal diameters. Press Enter after you enter each dimension A display prompt tells you if the workpiece size is too small or too large for the simulation window.

LOAD Loads a previously saved workpiece. A pull-down menu of file names appears, as when opening a program from the data directory. Highlight the desired workpiece with the cursor, then press Enter.

SAVE Saves the current workpiece blank. When prompted, enter a file name. The workpiece is saved with a different DOS extension than the program has, so identical file names may be used. Or, use the dimensions as a file name, for example, 3X1.

VIEW (F5)

Milling	Turning
F5-VIEW	F5-VIEW
1ST ANGLE 3RD ANGLE PLAN SOLID DUMP	RESET GRID DUMP

1ST ANGLE (milling only) Displays the European standard projection: Side view, Front view, and Plan view.

3RD ANGLE (milling only) Displays the North American standard projection: Plan view, Side view, and Front view.

PLAN (milling only) Displays a Plan view of the part only. This is used when you are using small cutters or when more clarity is required. Shown at the edge of the simulation window is a "Depth Indicator"—a red bar that visually displays cutter depth relative to the part.

SOLID (milling only) Displays a solid three-dimensional view of the part after the program has been executed. The part appears as a solid block, with any modifications/material removal shown in different colors.

RESET (turning only) Restores the graphics to a clean state. Select RESET if the grid is no longer required or you want to refresh the screen.

GRID (turning only) Displays as a quick reference a small scale on the X- and Z-axes. This can help you in determining the tool moves.

DUMP Prints a screen dump of the graphics to an Epson compatible printer.

SIMULATE (F6)

Milling	Turning
F6-SIMUL	F6-SIMUL
JOG CYCLE STEP EDIT MDI ZERO AXIS	JOG CYCLE STEP EDIT MDI

JOG Appears as a panel in the lower portion of the simulation window. It simulates tool movement of the machine tool. The cursor keys control tool movement.

The default jog rate (Rapid, Feed, or Step) can be changed by exiting to the OPTIONS menu, then changing the jog rate. (Refer to the OPTIONS menu earlier in this chapter.)

CYCLE Executes the entire program. If there are any errors in the program, the system will stop and display the appropriate error message for each. Keep in mind that the simulation speed of the tool is not the actual tool feedrate.

STEP Simulates the current program line by line. It executes only one line at a time, initialized to continue when you press ENTER. Pressing Escape aborts the simulation.

EDIT Where all real-time CNC editing occurs. As each line is written and executed, the resulting actions are animated in the graphics simulation window. The tool status window and program status window keep track of system functions concurrently, constantly being updated. Using EDIT, you can edit your CNC program while you are actually executing it.

The system also checks for syntax while confirming all tool movements for feasibility. A display prompt informs you of any errors or impossible functions. To correct an incorrect block of CNC code, use the cursor keys to remove the bad line, then re-enter it with the correct information.

When editing the program, use the cursor keys to move up, down, left, and/or right. You can move around this way without triggering screen refresh. If you move around and also make a change, moving down a line will cause a refresh.

Edit mode also numbers the CNC blocks automatically in a standard 5-block increment (this increment amount may be modified via the OPTIONS menu) and saves the program in memory files.

MDI Simulates the Manual Data Input (MDI) function. Every block is treated and executed independently, not as a part program. MDI is used when you are moving or testing individual blocks.

MDI does not automatically number the lines, since they are not saved in memory. MDI commands are one-time executable.

ZERO AXIS (milling only) Used instead of the G92 command. Use the simulation JOG panel to move the tool to the new origin point location, then use ZERO AXIS. The system will reset the absolute coordinates to X0.0,Y0.0,Z0.0 This is the new origin point.

Note: Most programs require this tool to be in the tool home position (X0,Y0,Z1) prior to execution. When using ZERO AXIS, be sure to raise the tool prior to program execution.

ESC (Escape) Used during program simulation to stop the cycle. When using CYCLE, STEP, or LINE mode, pressing ESC will cause the simulation to stop after the current line has finished executing. A display prompt will ask the user: "CONTINUE? YES / NO."

HELP (F7)

F7-HELP
LIST
INFO

LIST Lists help topics. Each topic has nested subtopics. Picking an item displays a box of help text or a further submenu. The textbox has a scrolling bar (along the right-hand side of the blue box) so that you can see more text (if there is any) and a OUT button (top right-hand corner). Selecting OUT quits you from the help system.

Note: The HELP menu is the only menu that does not respond to first-letter input for menu access.

INFO Displays the program's version number and a copyright notice.

GETTING STARTED

This section deals with loading, editing, writing, and executing CNC programs using the simulation software. There are several sample procedures to follow, which are intended to be a beginner's guide to program manipulation. The more experienced user will explore the endless possibilities of the simulator and gain knowledge en route.

Loading and Running a Sample CNC File

1. If you have installed the software onto your hard disk, from the DOS prompt, type CNCEZ and press Enter. Then select either DEMOMILL for milling or DEMOTURN for turning.

2. You are prompted to enter a directory, DEMOMILL for milling, or DEMOTURN for turning. This sets up the user Data Directory and can be any eight alphanumeric character combination. The software is shipped with demonstration programs preloaded into these directories. The main simulation screen will now be displayed.

3. Access the FILES menu by pressing F1, then scroll down to and high-light the OPEN option. Press Enter.

4. A list of CNC programs is displayed in a pull-down menu. These are all sample files. Use the cursor keys to highlight a file name, then press Enter. The CNC file will be loaded into RAM, and the workpiece, dimensions, and file name will be displayed in the information bar.

5. To start the simulation, access the SIMULATION menu by pressing F6. Use the cursor keys to highlight the CYCLE option, then press Enter.
    The program is simulated on screen. (Be sure to watch the screen for any user prompts such as for a tool change.)

This entire procedure can be condensed into the following commands:

```
F1 FILE-OPEN...    <enter>
Pick File...
F6 SIMUL-Cycle.    <enter>
```

Editing an Existing Program

1. Once the CNC file has been opened and is residing in the simulation environment (to open a file, use F1 FILES-OPEN), access the FILE menu (press F1). Press E for EDIT (or cursor down and highlight the EDIT), then press Enter.

2. The CNC file is displayed in the Program Status Window that is at the bottom of the screen. This is the text editor. Notice how only three lines of text are displayed at once. Use the cursor keys to scroll up or down or press F1 to toggle the FULLSCREEN option on.

3. To exit the text editor, press F3, displayed at the bottom of the screen.

Note: It is important to realize that any changes to the program made in the text editor will be checked for syntax and errors to ensure correct CNC code. The program will only simulate each line in the SIMULATION menu.

Writing and Executing Your Own CNC Program

1. Access the FILE menu and choose NEW (highlight NEW, then press Enter).

2. When prompted, type in the eight-letter alphanumeric file name of the program you are about to write and press Enter.

3. To choose the UNITS option, access the SETUP menu (press F2). Type U for units (or cursor down and highlight the word UNITS), then press Enter. Answer the prompt, INCH PROGRAMMING? YES/NO.

4. To define a workpiece, access the WORKPIECE menu (press F4) and select the DEFINE option by highlighting it, then pressing Enter. When prompted for the length, type in the length of the blank workpiece, then press Enter. Type in the width and height of the workpiece when prompted to do so, pressing Enter after each entry each dimension. The workpiece will be defined in the same units defined in the SETUP menu.

5. To change the view, access the VIEW menu (press F5) and select a view. 3RD ANGLE is the default.

6. To begin writing the program, access the SIMULATE menu (press F6), then select the EDIT option.

7. Once you are in the text editor, you type in the program. Use one of the examples that are installed in the DEMOMILL or DEMOTURN directories to get a feel for how interactive graphics simulation works. Notice how each line of code is simulated when entered and how the status windows are also updated.

   If there is an error in the code, use the cursor keys to return to the flawed line, then edit it and press Enter.

8. To exit the interactive graphics editor, press F3 at the bottom of the screen.

9. To watch the entire program simulate, exit EDIT (press F3), then access the SIMULATION menu (press F6) and select the CYCLE option. The program currently in memory will be cycled through. Remember to watch for user input prompts (for example, tool change)

Saving a New CNC File

To save the current CNC file, access the FILE menu (press F1), then select the SAVE option. If the file does not have a name, you will be prompted to enter one. If the file name has been previously saved, you will be prompted to enter a different name. Press ESC to cancel out of the SAVE option.

Printing the Current File

To get a printer listing of the current CNC program, access the FILE menu (press F1). Choose the PRINT option, then answer the prompt, "PRINT CURRENT FILE? YES/NO." The computer must have an Epson compatible printer connected to its parallel port (printer port). The current CNC program will be printed.

Getting a Printer Dump of the Graphics

To dump the screen graphics to an Epson compatible printer, (that is, to print whatever is on the screen is printed out graphically), access the VIEW menu (press F5), then select the DUMP option. Be sure your printer is ready; the printed result fills a whole page.

Quitting the Simulator

To quit the simulator, access the FILE menu (press F1) and select the QUIT option. If the current file has not been saved, you will be prompted to save it. Selecting QUIT returns you to the initial menu.

Chapter 5

CNC Milling

CHAPTER OBJECTIVES

After studying this chapter, the student should have knowledge of the following:

Programming for milling operations

Linear and circular interpolation

Cutter diameter compensation

Letter address commands for the CNC mill

When working through Chapters 5 and 6, have the software running on your computer and enter the programs using the F6-SIMULATE (EDIT) or (MDI) options. Follow these steps when simulating programming codes or creating new programs:

1. Select NEW from the FILE menu.
   Enter a file name.

2. Change the tool library if required.

3. Select the WORKPIECE menu.
   Specify or load a new workpiece.

4. Select the SIMULATE menu.
   Use EDIT if you want to create a program and run it or MDI simply to test a code.

NOTE: The completed sample programs are in the DEMOMILL directory.

G-CODES

G-codes are preparatory functions, which involve actual tool moves (for example, control of the machine). These include rapid moves, feed moves, radial feed moves, dwells, and roughing and profiling cycles. Most G-codes described here are modal, meaning they remain active until cancelled by another G-code. The following codes are described in more detail in the following pages:

G00	Positioning In Rapid	Modal
G01	Linear Interpolation	Modal
G02	Circular Interpolation (CW)	Modal
G03	Circular Interpolation (CCW)	Modal
G04	Dwell	
G17	XY Plane	Modal
G18	XZ Plane	Modal
G19	YZ Plane	Modal
G20/G70	Inch Units	Modal
G21/G71	Metric Units	Modal

G28	Automatic return *to* reference point	
G29	Automatic return *from* reference point	
G40	Cutter Compensation Cancel	Modal
G41	Cutter Compensation Left	Modal
G42	Cutter Compensation Right	Modal
G43	Tool Length Compensation (Plus)	Modal
G44	Tool Length Compensation (Minus)	Modal
G49	Tool Length Compensation Cancel	Modal
G80	Cancel Canned Cycles	Modal
G81	Drilling Cycle	Modal
G82	Counter Boring Cycle	Modal
G83	Deep Hole Drilling Cycle	Modal
G90	Absolute Positioning	Modal
G91	Incremental Positioning	Modal
G92	Reposition Origin Point	
G98	Set Initial Plane default	
G99	Return to Retract (Rapid) Plane	

G00 POSITIONING IN RAPID

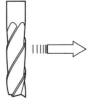

Format: `N_ G00 X_ Y_ Z_`

The G00 command is a *rapid tool move*. A rapid tool move is used when moving the tool in a linear motion from position to position without cutting any material. This command is **not** to be used for cutting any material, as to do so would seriously damage the tool and ruin the workpiece. It is modal.

On most CNC machine tools, it is standard to program a G00 rapid for an X,Y move and the Z move separately. See Figs. 5-1, 5-2, and 5-3.

Example: `N25 G00 X2.5 Y4.75`   (Rapid to X2.5,Y4.75)
   `N30 Z0.1`   (Rapid down to Z0.1)

Depending on where the tool is located, there are two basic rules to follow for safety's sake:

1. If the Z value represents a negative move, the X- and Y-axes should be executed first.

2. If the Z value represents a positive move, the X- and Y-axes should be executed last.

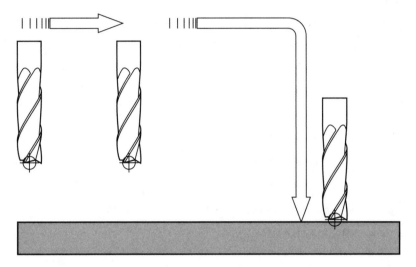

Figure 5-1 The G00 command is used to move the tool quickly from one point to another, without cutting, thus allowing for quick tool positioning.

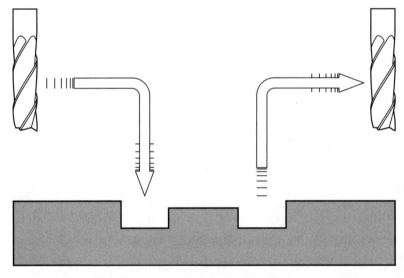

Figure 5-2 Notice that the G00 rapid move should have two distinct movements to ensure the vertical moves are always separate from the horizontal moves. The figure shows a typical rapid move towards the part. First, the tool rapids in the flat, horizontal XY plane. Then, it rapids down in the Z-axis. When rapiding out of a part, the G00 command always goes up in the Z-axis first, then laterally in the XY plane.

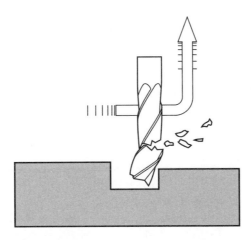

Figure 5-3 As this diagram shows, if the basic rules are not followed, an accident can result. Improper use of G00 often occurs because clamps are not taken into consideration. Following the basic rules will lesson any chance of error.

Sample Program G00EX1:

Workpiece Size:	X6,Y4,Z1
Tool:	Tool #2, 1/4" Slot Drill
Tool Start Position:	X0,Y0,Z1

For this example it may be helpful to toggle on the SHOWPATHS options (F3-OPTS).

%	(Program start flag)
:1001	(Program number 1001)
N5 G90 G20	(Absolute and inch programming)
N10 M06 T2	(Tool change, Tool #2)
N15 M03 S1200	(Spindle on CW, at 1200 rpm)
N20 G00 X1 Y1	**(Rapid over to X1,Y1)**
N25 Z0.1	**(Rapid down to Z0.1)**
N30 G01 Z-0.25 F5	(Feed move down to a depth of 0.25 in.)
N35 Y3	(Feed move to Y3)
N40 X5	(Feed to X5)
N45 X1 Y1 Z-0.125	(Feed to X1,Y1,Z–0.125)
N50 G00 Z1	**(Rapid up to Z1)**
N55 X0 Y0	**(Rapid over to X0,Y0)**
N60 M05	(Spindle off)
N65 M30	(End of program)

Notice how in the first rapid section N20,N25, the tool first moves in the horizontal plane and then down in the Z-axis. In the second rapid section

N50,N55, the tool first moved up and then over to X0,Y0, since the tool was into the part.

G01 LINEAR INTERPOLATION

Format: N_ G01 X_ Y_ Z_ F_

Linear interpolation is nothing more than straight-line feed moves. A G01 command is specifically for the linear removal of material from a workpiece, in any combination of the X-, Y- or Z-axis.

The G01 is modal and is subject to a user variable feedrate (designated by the letter F followed by a number). The G01 is not limited to one plane. Three-axis, simultaneous feed moves, where all three axes are used at the same time to cut different angles, are possible. (See Figs. 5-4 and 5-5.)

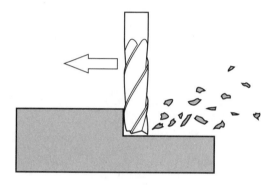

Figure 5-4 Linear interpolation, or straight-line feed moves, on the flat plane (no Z values are specified)

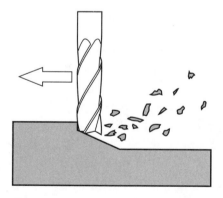

Figure 5-5 G01 command using multiaxis feed moves. All diagonal feed moves are a result of a G01 command, where two or more axes are used at once.

Sample Program G01EX2:

Workpiece Size:	X4,Y3,Z1
Tool:	Tool #3, 3/8" Slot Drill
Tool Start Position:	X0,Y0,Z1

```
%                          (Program start flag)
:1002                      (Program #1002)
N5 G90 G20                 (Block #5, absolute in inches)
N10 M06 T3                 (Tool change to Tool #3)
N15 M03 S1250              (Spindle on CW at 1250 rpm)
N20 G00 X1 Y1              (Rapid over to X1,Y1)
N25 Z0.1                   (Rapid down to Z0.1)
N30 G01 Z-0.125 F5         (Feed down to Z–0.125 at 5 ipm)
N35 X3 Y2 F10              (Feed diagonally to X3,Y2 at 10 ipm)
N40 G00 Z1                 (Rapid up to Z1)
N45 X0 Y0                  (Rapid over to X0,Y0)
N50 M05                    (Spindle off)
N55 M30                    (Program end)
```

In this sample program, several different examples of the G01 command are shown:

- The first G01 command (in N30) instructs the machine to feed down below the surface of the part by 0.125 in. at a feedrate of 5 in./min.

- N35 is a two-axis (X and Y) diagonal feed move, and the feedrate is increased to 10 ipm.

Note: Because there is contact between the cutting tool and the workpiece, it is imperative that the proper spindle speeds and feedrates be used. **It is the programmer's responsibility to ensure cutter speeds and feeds are acceptable.**

G02 CIRCULAR INTERPOLATION (CW)

Format: N_ G02 X_ Y_ Z_ I_ J_ K_ F_   (I, J, K specify the Radius)

or   N_ G02 X_ Y_ Z_ R_ F_   (R specifies the Radius)

Circular Interpolation is more commonly known as radial (or arc) feed moves. The G02 command is specifically for all clockwise radial feed moves, whether they are quadratic arcs, partial arcs, or complete circles, as long as they lie in any one plane.

The G02 command is modal and is subject to a user-definable feedrate.

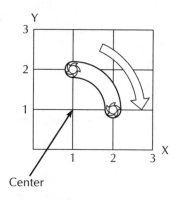

Figure 5-6 Shows cutter start point, end point and center point

Example: `G02 X2 Y1 I0 J-1`

The G02 command requires an endpoint and a radius in order to cut the arc. The startpoint of this arc is X1,Y2 and the endpoint is X2,Y1. To find the radius, simply measure the distance from the startpoint to the centerpoint. This radius is written in terms of the X and Y distance. To avoid confusion, these values are assigned variables, called I and J, respectively.

Example: `G02 X2 Y1 R1`

You can also specify G02 by entering the X and Y endpoints and then R for the radius.

Note that the use of an R value for the radius of an arc is limited to a maximum movement of 90 degrees.

An easy way to find the radius (the I and J values) is by making a small chart as follows. This will make it easier to determine the radius values.

Startpoint	X1	Y2
Centerpoint	X1	Y1
Radius	I0	J-1

`G02 X2 Y1 I0 J-1 F5`

Finding the I and J values is easier than it first seems. Follow these steps:

1. Write down the X and Y coordinates of the arc's startpoint.

2. Below these coordinates, write down the X and Y coordinates of the arc's centerpoint.

3. Draw a line below this to separate the two areas.

4. To find the I value, calculate the difference between the arc's startpoint and centerpoint in the X-axis. In this case, both X values are 1, and hence there is no difference between them, so the I value is 0!

To find the J value, calculate the difference between the arc's startpoint and centerpoint in the Y-axis. In this case, the difference between Y2 and Y1 is down 1 inch, so the J value is –1!

Sample Program G02EX3:

Workpiece Size:	X4,Y3,Z1
Tool:	Tool #2, 1/4" Slot Drill
Tool Start Position:	X0,Y0,Z1

```
%
:1003
N5 G90 G20
N10 M06 T2
N15 M03 S1200
N20 G00 X1 Y1
N25 Z0.1
N30 G01 Z-0.1 F5
N35 G02 X2 Y2 I1 J0 F20        (Arc feed CW, radius I1,J0 at
                                20 ipm)
N40 G01 X3.5
N45 G02 X3 Y0.5 R2             (Arc feed CW, radius 2)
N50 X1 Y1 R2                   (Arc feed CW, radius 2)
N55 G00 Z0.1
N60 X2 Y1.5
N65 G01 Z-0.25
N70 G02 X2 Y1.5 I0.25 J-0.25  (Full circle arc feed move CW)
N75 G00 Z1
N80 X0 Y0
N85 M05
N90 M30
```

G03 CIRCULAR INTERPOLATION (CCW)

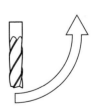

Format: N_ G03 X_ Y_ Z_ I_ J_ K_ F_   (I, J, K specify the Radius)

or   N_ G03 X_ Y_ Z_ R_ F_   (R specifies the Radius)

Circular interpolation is more commonly known as radial (or arc) feed moves. The G03 command is specifically for all counterclockwise radial feed moves, whether they are quadratic arcs, partial arcs, or complete circles, as long as they lie in any one plane. The G03 is modal and is subject to a user-definable feed rate.

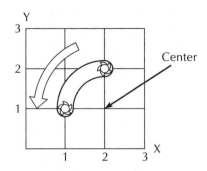

Figure 5-7 Shows arc start point, end point, and center point

Example: `G03 X1 Y1 I0 J-1`

The G03 command requires an endpoint and a radius in order to cut the arc. The startpoint of this arc is X2,Y2 and the endpoint is X1,Y1. To find the radius, simply measure the distance from the startpoint to the centerpoint of the arc. This radius is written in terms of the X and Y distance. To avoid confusion, these values are assigned variables, called I and J, respectively.

Example: `G03 X1 Y1 R1`

You can also specify G03 by entering the X and Y endpoints and then R for the radius.

Note that the use of an R value for the radius of an arc is limited to a maximum movement of 90 degrees.

An easy way to find the radius, (the I and J values) is to make a small chart as follows. This will make it easier to determine the radius values.

Startpoint	X2	Y2
Centerpoint	X2	Y1
Radius	I0	J-1

`G03 X1 Y1 I0 J-1`

Finding the I and J values is easier than it first seems. Follow these steps:

1. Write down the X and Y coordinates of the arc's startpoint.

2. Below these coordinates, write down the X and Y coordinates of the arc's centerpoint.

3. Draw a line below this to separate the two areas.

4. To find the I value, calculate the difference between the arc's startpoint and centerpoint in the X-axis. In this case, both X values are 2, and hence there is no difference between them, so the I value is 0!

   To find the J value, calculate the difference between the arc's startpoint and centerpoint in the Y-axis. In this case, the difference between Y2 and Y1 is down 1 inch, so the J value is –1!

Sample Program G03EX4:

Workpiece Size:	X4,Y4,Z0.25
Tool:	Tool #2, 1/4" Slot Drill
Tool Start Position:	X0,Y0,Z1

```
%
:1004
N5 G90 G20
N10 M06 T2
N15 M03 S1200
N20 G00 X2 Y0.5
N25 Z0.125
N30 G01 Z-0.125 F5
N35 X3 F15
N40 G03 X3.5 Y1 R0.5        (G03 arc using R value)
N45 G01 Y3
N50 G03 X3 Y3.5 I-0.5 J0    (G03 arc using I and J)
N55 G01 X2
N60 G03 X2 Y1.5 I0 J-1      (180-degree arc using I and J)
N65 G01 Y0.5
N70 G00 Z0.1
N75 X1.5 Y2.5
N80 G01 Z-0.25 F5
N85 G03 X1.5 Y2.5 I0.5 J0   (Full circle using I and J)
N90 G00 Z1
N95 X0 Y0
N100 M05
N105 M30
```

G04 DWELL

Format: N_ G04 P_

The G04 command is a nonmodal dwell command, which halts all axis movement for a specified time, while the spindle continues revolving at the specified rpm (see Fig. 5-8). A dwell is used largely in drilling operations .

Figure 5-8 The tool will pause for a short time only, rarely over several seconds. For a definite program pause, refer to the M00 and M01 commands. Being nonmodal, the G04 must be re-entered each time the dwell is to be executed.

This command requires a specified duration, denoted by the letter P and followed by the time in seconds.

Sample Program G04EX5:

Workpiece Size:	X3.5,Y2,Z0.5
Tool:	Tool #1, 1/8" Slot Mill
Tool Start Position:	X0,Y0,Z1

%	(Program start flag)
:1005	(Program #1005)
N5 G90 G20	(Absolute programming in Inch mode)
N10 M06 T1	(Tool change to Tool #1)
N15 M03 S1300	(Spindle on CW at 1300rpm)
N20 G00 X3 Y1 Z0.1	(Rapid to X3,Y1,Z0.1)
N25 G01 Z-0.125 F5	(Feed down to Z–0.125 at 5 ipm)
N30 G04 P0.5	**(Dwell for 0.5 sec)**
N35 G00 X2 Z0.1	(Rapid up to 0.1 and over to X2)
N40 G01 Z-0.125 F5	(Feed down to Z–0.125)
N45 G04 P0.5	**(Dwell for 0.5 sec)**
N50 G00 X0 Y0 Z1	(Rapid to X0,Y0,Z1)
N55 M05	(Spindle off)
N60 M30	(Program end)

G17 XY PLANE

Format: N_ G17

The G17 command sets the system to default to the XY plane as the main machining plane for specifying circular interpolation moves and/or cutter compensation.

On any three axis machine tool—X-axis, Y-axis, and Z-axis—there are two basic directions the tool can move: horizontally (in the X- or Y-axis) and vertically (in the Z-axis). On a simple two-dimensional part (for example, a milled pocket, or part, profile) the X- and Y-axes make up the main machining plane, which is horizontal. Here the Z-axis is secondary and works perpendicular to the XY plane. G17 is a system default, as it is the most common machining plane.

Sample Program G17EX6:

Workpiece Size:	X3,Y2,Z1
Tool:	Tool #4, 1/2" Slot Drill
Tool Start Position:	X0,Y0,Z1

```
%
:1006
N5  G90 G20 G17          (Set XY plane)
N10 M06 T4
N15 M03 S1200
N20 G00 X2 Y1
N25 Z0.125
N30 G01 Z-0.05 F5
N35 G02 X1 R1 F10
N40 G00 Z1
N45 X0 Y0
N50 M05
N55 M30
```

G18 XZ PLANE

Format: N_ G18

The G18 command sets the system to default to the XZ plane as the main machining plane for specifying circular interpolation moves and/or cutter compensation.

This command changes the default machining plane to the XZ plane, where the Y-axis is secondary, and works perpendicular to the XZ plane. In this plane, it is possible to cut convex or concave arcs using the G02 and G03 circular interpolation commands. It is important to note that because the X- and Z-axes are primary, the radius is no longer expressed in terms of I and J (remember, the distance from the start point to the center point; see G02 and G03), but rather I and K.

Remember, also, to determine the direction of travel look down at the two axes from the Y+ direction in the same way that you look down at the X-Y axis from the Z+ axis in the G17 plane.

When programming G02 and G03 commands, keep in mind that the primary and secondary axes are reversed. This means that the G02 will look

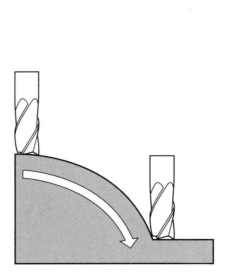

Figure 5-9(a) Shows a tool cutting an arc in XZ plane

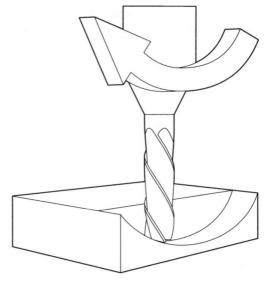

Figure 5-9(b) An example of an arc cut in the G18 XZ plane. Keep in mind that because the primary and secondary axes are reversed, this arc is actually a G03 command!

like a counterclockwise arc and the G03 will look like a clockwise arc. See the following example program to better understand this command.

Sample Program G18EX7:

Workpiece Size:	X2,Y1,Z1
Tool:	Tool #2, 1/4" Slot Drill
Tool Start Position:	X0,Y0,Z1

With this example, it is a good idea to toggle on the SHOWPATH option (under F3-OPTS).

```
%
:1007
N5 G90 G20 G17                    (G17 sets XY plane)
N10 M06 T2
N15 M03 S1200
N20 G00 X0 Y0
N25 Z1
N30 Z0.1
N35 G01 Z0 F5
N40 G18 G02 X2 Z0 I1 K0           (G18 sets XZ plane)
N45 G01 Y0.25
N50 G03 X0.5 Z0 I-0.75 K0
N55 G01 Y0.5 F10
```

```
N60 G02 X1.5 Z0 I0.5 K0
N65 G00 Z1
N70 X0 Y0
N75 M05
N80 M30
```

G19 YZ PLANE

Format: `N_ G19`

The G19 command sets the system to default to the YZ plane as the main machining plane for specifying circular interpolation moves and/or cutter compensation. See Fig. 5-10.

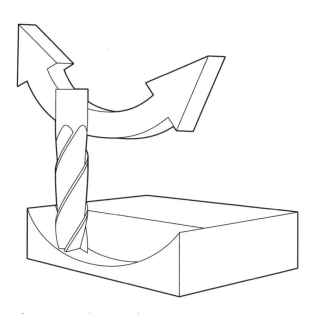

Figure 5-10 Shows tool-cutting arc in YZ plane

This command changes the default machining plane to the YZ plane, where the X-axis is secondary, and works perpendicular to the YZ plane. In this plane, it is possible to cut convex or concave arcs using the G02 and G03 circular interpolation commands. It is important to note that because the Y- and Z-axes are primary, the radius is no longer expressed in terms of I and J (remember, the distance from the start point to the center point), but rather J and K.

Remember, also, to determine the direction of travel look down at the two axes from the X+ direction in the same way that you look down at the XY axis from the Z+ axis in the G17 plane.

Sample Program G19EX8:

Workpiece Size:	X2,Y2,Z1
Tool:	Tool #2, 1/4" Slot Drill
Tool Start Position:	X0,Y0,Z1

With this example, it is a good idea to toggle on the SHOWPATH option (under F3-OPTS).

```
%
:1008
N5 G90 G20 G17                    (Set XY Plane)
N10 M06 T2
N15 M03 S1200
N20 G00 X0 Y0
N25 Z0.1
N30 G01 Z0 F5
N35 G19 G03 Y1 Z0 J0.5 K0     (Set YZ plane)
N40 G01 X1.5 Y2 F10
N45 G02 Y0 Z0 J-1 K0 F5
N50 G00 Z1
N55 X0 Y0
N60 M05
N65 M30
```

G20 OR G70 INCH UNITS

INCH

Format: N_ G20

The G20 command defaults the system to inch data units. When running a program and the G20 command is encountered, all coordinates are adopted as inch units.

This command is the CNCEZ system default and is modal, (see G21).

Sample Program G20EX9:

Workpiece Size:	X4,Y2,Z1
Tool:	Tool #2, 1/4" Slot Drill
Tool Start Position:	X0,Y0,Z1

```
%
:1009
N5 G90 G20          (Set inch mode)
N10 M06 T2
N15 M03 S1000
N20 G00 X1 Y1
```

```
N25 Z1
N30 G01 Z-0.125 F5
N35 X3.625 F15
N40 Y1.75
N45 G00 Z1
N50 X0 Y0
N55 M05
N60 M30
```

In this program, the system is using inch units, all coordinates are in inches, and feedrates are expressed as inches per minute (ipm).

G21 OR G71 METRIC UNITS

Format: N_ G21

METRIC

The G21 command defaults the system to metric data units (millimeters). After encountering this command, all coordinates are adopted as metric (mm) units.

This command is modal, (see G20). On most modern controls, it is possible to switch back and forth between metric and inch units within one program.

Sample Program G21EX10:

Workpiece Size:	X100,Y75,Z25
Tool:	Tool #2, 8mm Slot Drill
Tool Start Position:	X0,Y0,Z25.4
Select Metric units under Setup Menu	

```
%
:1010
N5 G90 G21                     (Set metric programming mode)
N10 M06 T2
N15 M03 S1200
N20 G00 X-5 Y5
N25 Z-8
N35 G01 X90 F300
N40 X95 Y20
N45 Y50
N50 G03 X75 Y65 R15
N55 G01 X40 Y50
N60 G02 X0 Y10 R40
N65 G00 Z25.4
N70 Y0
N75 M05
N80 M30
```

In this program, the system is using metric units, all coordinates are in millimeters, and all feedrates expressed as millimeters per minute.

G28 AUTOMATIC RETURN TO REFERENCE POINT

Format: N_ G28

   or   N_ G28 X_ Y_ Z_

The G28 command is used for automatic tool changing. It basically allows the existing tool to be positioned to the pre-defined reference point automatically via an intermediate position.

When using this command, it is advisable for safety reasons to cancel any tool offset or cutter compensation.

All axes are positioned to the intermediate point at the rapid traverse rate, and then from the intermediate point to the reference point (see Fig. 5-11).

The movement from the start point to the intermediate point and from the intermediate point to the reference point is the same as when using the G00 command.

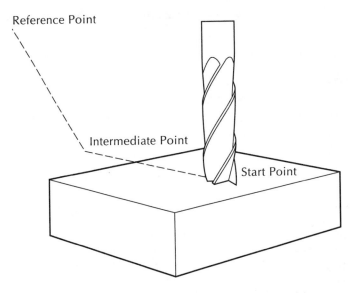

Figure 5-11 Shows cutter move on the G28 command from the start point to the intermediate point and finally to the reference point

Sample Program G28EX111:

Workpiece Size:	X4,Y4,Z1
Tool:	Tool #7, 1" Slot Drill
	Tool #10, 1/2" HSS Drill
Tool Start Position:	X0,Y0,Z1
Reference Point:	X0,Y0,Z5

```
%
:1111
N5 G90 G20
N10 M06 T7
N12 M03 S1000
N15 G00 X4.75 Y2
N20 Z-0.5
N25 G01 X2 F10
N30 G00 Z0.25
N35 G28 X0 Y2.5 Z1      (Return to reference via X0,Y2.5,Z1)
N40 M06 T10
N45 M03 S2000
N50 G29 X2 Y2 Z0.1
N55 G01 Z-1.25 F5
N60 G00 Z1
N65 X0 Y0
N70 M05
N75 M30
```

G29 AUTOMATIC RETURN *FROM* REFERENCE POINT

Format: N_ G29

   or   N_ G29 X_ Y_ Z_

The G29 command is used immediately after a G28 command to return the tool to a specified point via the intermediate point specified by the previous G28 command (see Fig. 5-12).

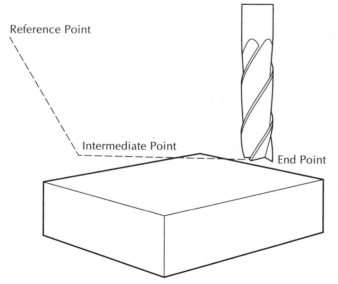

Figure 5-12 Shows cutter move on the G29 command from the reference point to the intermediate point and finally to the end point

Sample Program G29EX112:

Workpiece Size:	X4,Y4,Z1
Tool:	Tool #7, 1" Slot Drill
	Tool #10, 1/2" HSS Drill
Tool Start Position:	X0,Y0,Z1
Reference Point:	X0,Y0,Z5

```
%
:1112
N5 G90 G20
N10 M06 T7
N12 M03 S1000
N15 G00 X-0.75 Y2
N20 Z-0.5
N25 G01 X-0.5 F10
N30 G03 I2.5 J0
N35 G28 X-0.75 Y2 Z1
N40 M06 T10
N45 M03 S2000
N50 G29 X2 Y2 Z0.1      (Return from reference to X2,Y2,Z0.1)
N55 G01 Z-1.25 F5
N60 G00 Z1
N65 X0 Y0
N70 M05
N75 M30
```

G40 CUTTER COMPENSATION CANCEL

Format: N_ G40

The G40 command cancels any cutter compensation that was applied to the tool during a program and acts as a safeguard to cancel any cutter compensation applied to a previous program.

Cutter compensation is used whenever tool centerline programming is rather difficult. It can also be used to compensate for significant tool wear.

Normally, CNC programs are written so that the tool center follows the toolpath. When it is necessary to offset this either left or right, cutter compensation is used. However, cutter compensation is modal, so it must be cancelled once it is no longer required. This is the sole function of the G40.

Sample Program G40EX11:

Workpiece Size:	X4,Y3,Z1
Tool:	Tool #4, 1/2" Slot Drill

Register: D11 is 0.25"
Tool Start Position: X0,Y0,Z1

```
  %
:1011
N5 G90 G20 G17 G40          (G40 Compensation Cancel)
N10 T04 M06
N15 M03 S1500
N20 G00 X-0.5 Y-0.5
N25 Z-0.5
N30 G01 G42 X0 Y0 D2        (Compensation Right)
N35 X3 F10
N40 Y3
N45 X0
N50 Y0
N55 G00 G40 X-0.5 Y-0.5     (G40 Compensation Cancel)
N60 Z1
N65 X0 Y0
N70 M05
N75 M30
```

G41 CUTTER COMPENSATION LEFT

Format: `N_ G41 D_`

The G41 command compensates the cutter a specified distance to the **left-hand** side of the programmed tool path (see Fig. 5-13). It is used when compensating for excessive tool wear or when profiling a part.

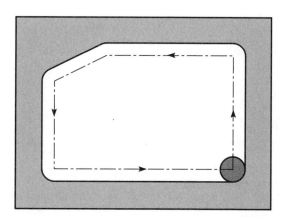

Figure 5-13 Shows cutter on the left-hand side of cutting line

This command refers to the offset registers to determine the correct compensation distance. When you set the offset registers prior to program execution, the MCU is able to refer to them when required. Each numbered register is accessed by the letter address D for CNC milling. To set up the offset registers, refer to Chapter 4 (see the SETUP menu).

The G41 command is modal, so it compensates each successive tool move the same specified distance, until it is overridden by a G40 command or receives a different offset.

Because the G41 command compensates the tool on the left-side of the programmed toolpath, it must first know how long the actual feed move is. It is for this reason that the compensation "lags behind" by one command during program cycles. When a program is executed, the compensation cycle must follow on the left-side of the programmed tool path. When the toolpath changes direction, the tool must compensate itself the appropriate distance from this new direction. Review the following program to understand the execution of a program using the G41 command.

Sample program G41EX12:

Workpiece Size:	X5,Y4,Z1
Tool:	Tool #2, 1/4" Slot Drill
Register:	D11 is 0.25"
Tool Start Position:	X0,Y0,Z1

```
%
:1012
N5 G90 G20 G40 G17 G80        (Cutter compensation cancel)
N10 T01 M06                   (Tool change to Tool #1)
N15 M03 S2000
N20 G00 X0.5 Y0.5
N25 Z0.1
N30 G01 Z-0.25 F5             (First profile)
N35 X2 F15
N40 X2.5 Y1
N45 Y2
N50 G03 X2 Y2.5 R0.5
N55 G01 X0.5
N60 Y0.5                      (End of first profile)
N65 G00 Z1
N70 X0 Y0
N75 T04 M06                   (Tool change to Tool #4))
N80 M03 S1000
N85 G00 X0.75 Y1
N90 Z0.125
N95 G01 Z-0.25 F5             (Second profile begins)
```

```
N100 G41 X0.5 Y0.5 D11 F20    (Compensation left)
N105 X2
N110 X2.5 Y1
N115 Y2
N120 G03 X2 Y2.5 R0.5
N125 G01 X0.5
N130 Y0.5
N135 G40 X0.75 Y0.75          (Compensation cancel)
N140 G00 Z1
N145 X0 Y0
N150 M05
N155 M30
N140
```

In this program, the default value for register number 11 is 0.25 in. Notice how the G41 works. It is specified, then the offset register number is, then the toolpath is programmed as usual.

G42 CUTTER COMPENSATION RIGHT

Format: N_ G42 D_

The G42 command compensates the cutter a specified distance to the **right-hand** side of the programmed tool path (see Fig. 5-14). It is used when compensating for excessive tool wear or when profiling a part. (Sometimes it is easier to compensate the tool rather than calculate new arc moves.)

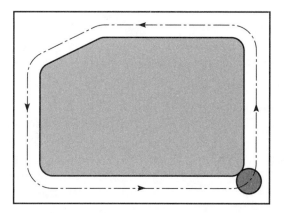

Figure 5-12 Shows cutter on the right-hand side of the cutting line

The G42 command refers to the offset registers to determine the correct compensation distance. By setting the offset registers prior to program execution, the MCU is able to refer to them when required. Each numbered register is accessed by the letter address D for CNC milling. To set up the offset registers, refer to Chapter 4 (see the SETUP menu).

The G42 command is modal, so it compensates each successive tool move the same specified distance, until it is overridden by a G40 command or receives a different offset.

Because the G42 command compensates the tool on the right-hand side of the programmed toolpath, it must first know how long the actual feed move is. It is for this reason that the offset "lags behind" by one command during program cycles. When a program is executed, the compensation cycle must follow on the right-hand side of the programmed toolpath. When the toolpath changes direction, the tool must compensate itself the appropriate distance from this new direction. Review the following program to understand the execution of a program using G42 command.

Sample Program G42EX13:

Workpiece Size:	X4,Y4,Z1
Tool:	Tool #2, 1/4" Slot Drill
Tool Start Position:	X0,Y0,Z1

```
%
:1013
N5 G90 G20 G40 G17 G80        (Setup defaults)
N10 T01 M06                   (Tool change to Tool #1)
N15 M03 S2000
N20 G00 X0.5 Y0.5
N25 Z0.1
N30 G01 Z-0.25 F5             (1st profile begins with no comp.)
N35 X2 F15
N40 X2.5 Y1
N45 Y2
N50 G03 X2 Y2.5 R0.5
N55 G01 X0.5
N60 Y0.5
N65 G00 Z1                    (End of 1st profile)
N70 X0 Y0
N75 T04 M06                   (Tool change to Tool #4)
N80 M03 S1000
N85 G00 X-0.5
N90 Z-0.5
N95 G01 G42 X0.5 Y0.5 Z-0.5 D11 F15    (2nd profile with
                                        comp.)
N100 X2
N105 X2.5 Y1
N110 Y2
```

```
N115  G03  X2  Y2.5  R0.5
N120  G01  X0.5
N125  Y0
N130  G01  G40  Z0.25              (G40 compensation cancel))
N135  G00  Z1
N140  X0  Y0
N145  M05
N150  M30
```

The default value for register number 11 is 0.25 in. The actual value of __D11__ does not influence the direction of the compensation (left or right), only the offset distance. Notice how the G42 command can be an integral part of a feed move command. The G42 cycle "lags behind" program execution by one block of CNC code so that the tool moves can be calculated.

G43 TOOL LENGTH COMPENSATION (PLUS)

Format: N_ G43 H_

The G43 command compensates for tool length in a positive direction (see Fig. 5-15). It is important to realize that different tools will have varying lengths, and when tools are changed in a program, any variation in tool length will throw the origin point out of zero. To prevent this, the tools can now be compensated for the difference in length for either shorter or longer tools.

This command uses the offset registers found in the SETUP menu. The letter address H is used to call up the particular register.

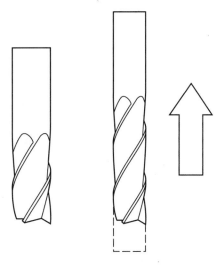

Figure 5-15 The G43 command is used when the new tool is longer than the reference tool. The tool must be offset higher so that the endpoints are the same actual height.

When offsetting cutters for different lengths, the difference between the two must first be accurately measured, then this value entered into the offset registers. Failure to properly measure the tool variation will result in unqualified tools and the possibility of machine, workpiece, or personal damage.

Sample Program G43EX14:

Workpiece Size:	X4,Y3,Z1
Tool:	Tool #12, 3/8" HSS Drill, 2" length
	Tool #10, 3/8" HSS Drill, 1.5" length
Tool Start Position:	X0,Y0,Z1
Register:	Number 13 0.5"

```
%
:1014
N5 G90 G20 G40 G49
N10 M06 T12
N15 M03 S2000
N20 G00 X1 Y1.5
N25 Z0.1
N30 G01 Z-0.5 F5
N35 G00 Z0.1
N40 X2
N45 G01 Z-0.5
N50 G00 Z0.1
N55 X3
N60 G01 Z-0.5
N65 G00 Z1
N70 X0 Y0
N75 M06 T10
N80 M03 S1000
N85 G43 H13            (Cutter compensation 0.25")
N90 G00 X-1.125
N95 Z-0.25
N100 G01 X5.125 F15
N105 G00 Y3
N110 G01 X-1.125
N115 G00 Z1
N120 X0 Y0
N125 G49 M05
N130 M30
```

In this example, register number 13 has a default value of 0.5 in. This means there is a difference of 0.5 in. between the two tools.

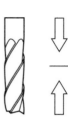

G44 TOOL LENGTH COMPENSATION (MINUS)

Format: N_ G44 H_

The G44 command compensates for tool length in a minus direction (see Fig 5-16). It is important to realize that different tools will have varying lengths, and when tools are changed in a program, any variation in tool length will throw the origin point out of zero. To prevent this, the tools can now be compensated for the difference in length. This command uses the offset registers found in the SETUP menu, and the letter address H is used to call a particular register.

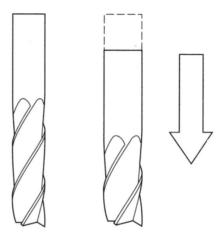

Figure 5-16 This is a typical scenario for a G44 command. The new tool is shorter than the original one, so the new one must be offset by the difference in their lengths. In this way, the end points of both tools are located at the same point.

Sample Program G44EX15:

Workpiece Size:	X4,Y3,Z1
Tool:	Tool #4, 1/2" Slot Drill, 1.75" length
	Tool #12, 1/2" HSS Drill, 2" length
Tool Start Position:	X0,Y0,Z1
Register:	Number 11 0.25"

```
%
:1015
N5 G90 G49 G20
N10 M06 T12
N15 M03 S1200
N20 G00 X1 Y1.5
N25 Z0.25
```

```
N30 G01 Z-0.5 F5
N35 G00 Z1
N40 X0 Y0
N45 M06 T4
N50 G44 H11                    (Compensate Tool #4 — 0.25")
N55 G00 X1 Y1.5
N60 Z-0.5
N65 G02 X3 R1.5 F20
N70 X1 R1.5
N75 G01 X3
N80 G00 Z1
N85 X0 Y0
N90 G49 M05
N95 M02
```

OK

G49 TOOL LENGTH COMPENSATION CANCEL

Format: N_ G49

The G49 command cancels all previous cutter length offset commands. Because the G43 and G44 commands are modal, they will remain active until cancelled by the G49 command. It is important to keep this in mind, or you may forget that a tool has been offset and so crash the cutter into the workpiece.

When cycling programs containing cutter length offsets, it is a good idea to include a G49 command in the program setup, as well as a G49 to cancel the offsets when they are no longer required.

Sample Program G49EX16:

Workpiece Size:	X4,Y3,Z1
Tool:	Tool #4, 1/2" Slot Drill, 1.75" length
	Tool #12, 1/2" HSS Drill, 2" length
Tool Start Position:	X0,Y0,Z1
Register:	Number 11 0.25"

```
%
:1016
N5 G90 G49 G20                 (Cutter compensation cancel)
N10 M06 T12
N15 M03 S1200
N20 G00 X1 Y1.5
N25 Z0.25
N30 G01 Z-0.5 F5
N35 G00 Z1
```

```
N40 X0 Y0
N45 M06 T4
N50 G44 H11                    (Compensate Tool #4 — 0.25")
N55 G00 X1 Y1.5
N60 Z-0.5
N65 G02 X3 R1.5 F20
N70 X1 R1.5
N75 G01 X3
N80 G00 Z1
N85 X0 Y0
N90 G49 M05                    (Cutter compensation cancel)
N95 M02
```

G80 CANCEL CANNED CYCLES

Format: N_ G80

The G80 command cancels all previous canned cycle commands. Because the canned cycles are modal (refer to the canned cycles on the following pages), they will remain active until cancelled by the G80 command.

Canned cycles include tapping, boring, spot facing, and drilling.

When creating programs containing canned cycles, it is a good idea to include a G80 command in the program setup at the beginning as well as after the drill cycle is completed.

Sample Program G80EX17:

Workpiece Size:	X4,Y3,Z1
Tool:	Tool #5, 5/8" HSS Drill
Tool Start Position:	X0,Y0,Z1

```
%
:1017
N5 G90 G80 G20            (Canned cycle cancel)
N10 M06 T5
N15 M03 S1450
N20 G00 X1 Y1
N25 G81 Z-0.5 R0.125
N30 X2
N35 X3
N40 G80 G00 Z1            (Canned cycle cancel)
N45 X0 Y0
N50 M05
N55 M30
```

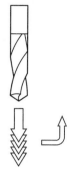

G81 DRILLING CYCLE

Format: N_ G81 Z_ R_ F_

The G81 command invokes a drill cycle at specified locations. The G81 drill cycle can be used for bolt holes, drilled patterns, and mold sprues among others. The G81 command is modal, and so remains active until overridden by another move command or cancelled by the G80 command.

The G81 cycle involves several different Z heights:

1. Z initial plane

2. Z depth

3. Z retract plane

Review the following example and Figs. 5-17(a)–(c) to better understand how a G81 cycle operates. Remember, the previous Z height before the G81 command (last Z value) is the Z initial plane.

Example:

```
N5 G00 X0 Y0 Z1
N10 X1 Y1 Z0.5
N15 G81 Z-0.25 R0.125 F5
```

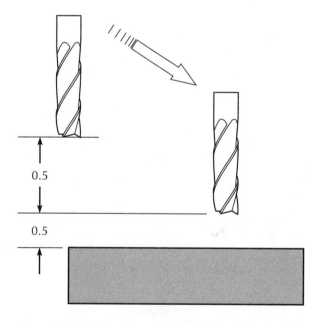

Figure 5-17(a) The first move establishes the Z initial plane. The Z initial plane is the height the tool is at before the G81 cycle (0.5 in.) It is a good idea to move the tool an intermediate distance from the part so that less time is wasted rapiding in and out. The tool will rapid back to the initial plane after each hole is drilled.

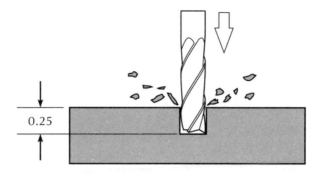

Figure 5-17(b) The tool rapids from the Z initial plane to the retract plane (0.125 in.). Starting at the Z retract plane (0.125 in.) the tool feeds down to the Z depth (–0.25 in.) at the specified feedrate.

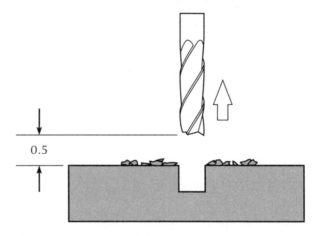

Figure 5-17(c) The tool then rapids up to the Z initial plane (0.5 in.). At this point, it would go on to the next hole.

Execute the following sample program to better understand the G81 drill cycle. Remember, the G81 command follows a certain sequence.

Sample Program G81EX18:

Workpiece Size:	X4,Y3,Z1
Tool:	Tool #6, 3/4" HSS Drill
Tool Start Position:	X0,Y0,Z1

```
%
:1018
N5 G90 G80 G20
N10 M06 T6
N15 M03 S1300
N20 G00 X1 Y1
N25 Z0.5
```

```
N30 G81 Z-0.25 R0.125 F5        (Drill cycle invoked)
N35 X2
N40 X3
N45 Y2
N50 X2
N55 X1
N60 G80 G00 Z1                   (Cancel canned cycles)
N65 X0 Y0
N70 M05
N75 M30
N80
```

G82 COUNTER BORING CYCLE

Format: N_ G82 Z_ R_ P_ F_

The G82 counter boring cycle follows the same operating procedures as the G81 drilling cycle does, with the addition of a dwell. The dwell is a pause in which the Z-axis stops moving, but the spindle continues rotating (see Fig 5-18).

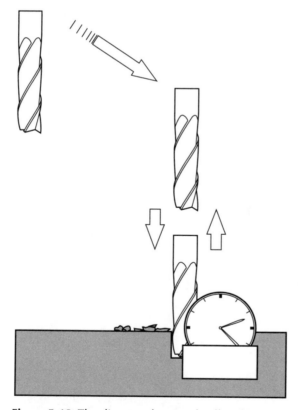

Figure 5-18 The diagram shows a dwell at the bottom of the cycle.

This pause allows for chip clearing and a finer finish on the hole. The dwell time is measured in seconds.

The dwell is initialized by the letter address P, followed by the dwell time in seconds.

Remember, the same Z levels apply to the G82 cycle as to the G81 cycle.

Sample Program G82EX19:

Workpiece Size:	X4,Y3,Z1
Tool:	Tool #6, 3/4" HSS Drill
Tool Start Position:	X0,Y0,Z1

```
%
:1019
N5 G90 G80 G20
N10 M06 T6
N15 M03 S1300
N20 G00 X1 Y1
N25 Z0.5
N30 G82 Z-0.25 R0.125 P1 F5   (Invoke G82)
N35 X2
N40 X3
N45 Y2
N50 X2
N55 X1
N60 G80 G00 Z1
N65 X0 Y0
N70 M05
N75 M30
```

In this program, the following key points occur:

1. The tool rapids from the Z position to the Z initial plane (see N25).

2. The tool rapids from the Z initial plane (0.5 in.) to the Z retract plane (0.125 in.). This is automatic in the drill cycle.

3. The tool feeds down to the Z depth (–0.25 in.) at the specified feedrate (5 ipm).

4. At this point, the dwell is executed (P1 specifying a 1 second dwell).

5. The tool returns from the Z depth (–0.25 in.) to the Z retract plane (0.125 in.) at the specified feedrate (F5).

6. The tool rapids up to the Z initial plane (0.5 in.), where it is ready to go on to the next hole. To have it rapid to another plane other than the Z initial plane, see the G98 and G99 commands.

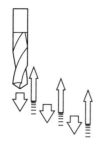

G83 DEEP HOLE DRILLING CYCLE

Format: `N_ G83 Z_ R_ Q_ F_`

The G83 command involves individual peck moves in each drilling operation. When this command is implemented, the tool positions itself as in a standard G81 drill cycle. The peck is the only action that distinguishes the deep hole drilling cycle from G81's cycle.

When pecking, the tool feeds in the specified distance (peck distance or depth of cut is specified by the letter address Q, followed by the incremental depth of cut), then rapids back out to the Z Retract plane. The next peck takes the tool deeper, and it rapids out of the hole. This process is repeated until the final Z depth is reached. Remember Q is the incremental depth of cut.

Follow the example below to better understand the G83 command.

Sample Program G83EX20:

Workpiece Size:	X4,Y3,Z1
Tool:	Tool #3, 3/8" HSS Drill
Tool Start Position:	X0,Y0,Z1

```
%
:1020
N5 G90 G80 G20
N10 M06 T3
N15 M03 S1200
N20 G00 X1 Y1
N25 G83 Z-0.75 R0.125 Q0.0625 F5     (Invoke G83 cycle)
N30 X2
N35 X3
N40 Y2
N45 X2
N50 X1
N55 G80 G00 Z1
N60 X0 Y0
N65 M05
N70 M30
```

G90 ABSOLUTE POSITIONING

Format: `N_ G90`

The G90 command defaults the system to accept all coordinates as absolute coordinates. Remember that absolute coordinates are those measured from a fixed origin point (X0,Y0,Z0) and expressed in terms of the X-axis, Y-axis, and Z-axis distances.

This command is found at the beginning of most programs to default the system to absolute coordinates. On some machines it is possible to change between absolute and incremental coordinates within a program (see G91). Remember that the system status window tells you the current coordinate system.

Sample Program G90EX21:

Workpiece Size:	X4,Y3,Z1
Tool:	Tool #2, 1/2" Slot Drill
Tool Start Position:	X0,Y0,Z1

```
%
:1021
N5 G90 G20               (Set to absolute mode)
N10 M06 T2
N12 M03 S1200
N15 G00 X1 Y1
N20 Z0.125
N25 G01 Z-0.125 F5
N30 X3
N35 Y2
N40 X1
N45 Y1
N50 G00 Z1
N55 X0 Y0
N60 M05
N65 M30
```

G91 INCREMENTAL POSITIONING

Format: N_ G91

The G91 command defaults the system to accept all coordinates as incremental coordinates. Remember that incremental coordinates are measured from the previous point and are expressed in terms of the X-axis, Y-axis, and Z-axis distances.

This command is found at the beginning of some programs to default the system to incremental coordinates. It is possible to flip between incremental and absolute coordinates within a program (see G90). Remember that the system status window tells you the current coordinate system.

Sample Program G91EX22:

Workpiece Size:	X4,Y3,Z1
Tool:	Tool #2, 1/4" Slot Drill
Tool Start Position:	X0,Y0,Z1

```
%
:1022
N5 G90 G20
N10 M06 T2
N15 M03 S1200
N20 G00 X1 Y1
N25 Z0.125
N30 G01 Z-0.125 F5
N35 G91 X1 Y1          (Set to incremental mode)
N40 Y-1
N45 X1
N50 Y1
N55 G90 G00 Z1
N60 X0 Y0
N65 M05
N70 M30
```

G92 REPOSITION ORIGIN POINT

Format: N_ G92

The G92 command is used to reposition the origin point. The origin point is not a physical spot on the machine tool, but rather a reference point to which the coordinates relate. Generally, the origin point is located at a prominent point or object (for example, front left corner of the part) so that it is easier to measure from.

Sometimes the origin point must be moved. If the operator is to cut several identical parts out of one workpiece, the origin point can be shifted, and the program rerun. Doing this will produce a second part identical to the first, but shifted over beside it.

Remember, once the origin point is moved it will remain there until you move it back!

Sample Program G92EX23:

Workpiece Size:	X3.5,Y2.5,Z0.75
Tool:	Tool #2, 1/4" Slot Drill
Tool Start Position:	X0,Y0,Z1

```
%
:1023
N5 G90 G20
N10 M06 T2
N15 M03 S1200
N20 G00 X0.5 Y0.5
N25 Z0.1
N30 G01 Z-0.25 F5
N35 G02 X0.5 Y0.5 I0.25 J0.25 F25
N40 G00 Z0.125
N45 X1.5 Y1.5
N50 G92 X0.5 Y0.5              (Reposition origin point)
N55 G01 Z-0.25 F5
N60 G02 X0.5 Y0.5 I0.25 J0.25 F20
N65 G00 Z0.1
N70 X1.5 Y-0.5
N75 G92 X0.5 Y0.5              (Reposition origin point)
N80 G01 Z-0.25 F5
N85 G02 X0.5 Y0.5 I0.25 J0.25 F15
N90 G00 Z1
N95 X-2 Y0
N100 G92 X0 Y0                (Reposition origin point)
N105 M05
N110 M30
```

G98 SET INITIAL PLANE RAPID DEFAULT

Format: N_ G98

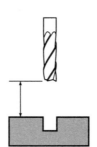

The G98 command forces the tool to return to the Z initial plane after a drilling operation (see Fig. 5-19). This forces the tool up and out of the workpiece. The G98 return to Z initial plane command is used on workpieces that have clamps or obstacles that could interfere with the tool movement. The G98 command is also the system default.

Sample Program G98EX24:

Workpiece Size:	X3,Y3,Z1
Tool:	Tool #3, 3/8" HSS Drill
Tool Start Position:	X0,Y0,Z1

```
%
:1024
N5 G90 G80 G20
```

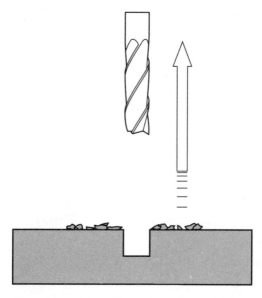

Figure 5-19 When this tool rapids out of the part during a drill cycle, it will rapid straight up to the Z initial plane.

```
N10  M06  T3
N15  M03  S1200
N20  G00  X1  Y1
N25  Z0.5
N30  G98  G81  Z-0.25  R0.25  F3      (Set initial plane to Z0.5)
N35  X2
N40  Y2
N45  X1
N50  G80  G00  Z1
N52  X0  Y0
N55  M05
N60  M30
```

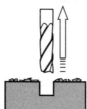

G99 RAPID TO RETRACT PLANE

Format: N_ G99

The G99 command forces the tool to return to the retract plane after a drilling operation. This forces the tool up and out of the workpiece, overriding the system default. This command is used on workpieces that do **not** have surface obstacles. They are quicker when executed, since the tool is only moving to the retract plane.

Sample Program G99EX25:

Workpiece Size:	X3,Y3,Z1
Tool:	Tool #3, 1/2" HSS Drill
Tool Start Position:	X0,Y0,Z1

```
%
:1025
N5 G90 G80 G20
N10 M06 T3
N15 M03 S1200
N20 G00 X1 Y1
N25 Z0.5
N30 G99 G81 Z-0.25 R0.25 F3     (Set rapid to retract plane)
N35 X2
N40 Y2
N45 X1
N50 G80 G00 Z1
N55 X0 Y0
N60 M05
N65 M30
```

When the tool retracts out of the hole, it stops at the Z retract level. It then rapids to the next X,Y hole location.

M-CODES

M-codes are miscellaneous functions, which include actions necessary for machining, but not those that are actual tool movements. That is, they are auxiliary functions, such as spindle on and off, tool changes, coolant on and off, program stops, and other similar related functions. The following codes are described in more detail in the following pages:

M00	Program Stop
M01	Optional Program Stop
M02	Program End
M03	Spindle On Clockwise
M04	Spindle On Counterclockwise
M05	Spindle Stop

M06	ToolChange
M08	Coolant On
M09	Coolant Off
M10	Clamps On
M11	Clamps Off
M30	Program End, Reset to Start

M00 PROGRAM STOP

Format: `N_ M00`

The M00 command is a temporary program stop function. When it is executed, all functions are temporarily stopped, and will not restart unless and until prompted by user input.

The following screen prompt will be displayed with CNCEZ: "PROGRAM STOP. ENTER TO CONTINUE." The program will not resume unless and until Enter is pressed. The wording of this prompt will vary by machine tool.

This command can be used in lengthy programs to stop the program in order to clear chips, take measurements, or adjust clamps, coolant hose, and so on.

Sample Program M00EX1:

Workpiece Size:	X4,Y3,Z1
Tool:	Tool #2, 1/4" Slot Drill
Tool Start Position:	X0,Y0,Z1

```
%
:1001
N5 G90 G20
N10 M06 T2
N15 M03 S1200
N20 G00 X1 Y1
N25 Z0.1
N30 G01 Z-0.125 F5
N35 M00                    (Program stop envoked)
N40 G01 X3
N45 G00 Z1
N50 X0 Y0
N55 M05
N60 M30
```

M01 OPTIONAL PROGRAM STOP

Format: N_ M01

The M01 command is an optional stop command and halts program execution only if the M01 switch is set to ON. If the M01 switch is set to OFF, the program will ignore any M01 commands it encounters in a program and no optional stop will be executed.

The M01 optional stop switch is listed in the OPTIONS (F3) menu and is called O.STOP. A + beside O.STOP indicates it is on. A - indicates it is off. Highlighting the option and pressing Enter toggles the switch on or off.

The M00 Program Stop command is not affected by the Optional Stop switch.

The optional stop is used in the following program. Cycle this program once with the switch off, then turn it on and cycle the program a second time.

Sample Program M01EX2:

Workpiece Size:	X4,Y3,Z1
Tool:	Tool #2, 1/4" Slot Drill
Tool Start Position:	X0,Y0,Z1
Optional Stop (F3):	On

```
%
:1002
N5 G90 G20
N10 M06 T2
N15 M03 S1200
N20 G00 X1 Y1
N25 Z0.1
N30 G01 Z-.125 F5
N35 M01                (Stop program)
N40 G01 X3
N45 G00 Z1
N47 X0 Y0
N50 M05
N55 M30
N60
```

M02 PROGRAM END

Format: N_ M02

The M02 command indicates an end of the main program cycle operation. Upon encountering the M02 command, the MCU switches off all machine operations (for example, spindle, coolant, all axes, and any auxiliaries), and the program is terminated.

This command is found by itself on the last line of the program.

Sample Program M02EX3:

Workpiece Size:	X4,Y3,Z1
Tool:	Tool #2, 1/4" Slot Drill
Tool Start Position:	X0,Y0,Z1

```
%
:1003
N5 G90 G20
N10 M06 T2
N15 M03 S1200
N20 G00 X1 Y1
N25 Z0.1
N30 G01 Z-.125 F5
N35 X3 F15
N40 G00 Z1
N45 X0 Y0
N50 M05
N55 M02            (Program end)
```

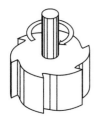

M03 SPINDLE ON CLOCKWISE

Format: N_ M03 S_

The M03 command switches the spindle on in a clockwise rotation. The spindle speed is designated by the letter address S, followed by the spindle speed in revolutions per minute.

The spindle speed is shown during program simulation in the program status window. Its on/off status is shown in the system status window. (CW, CCW, or OFF)

Sample Program M03EX4:

Workpiece Size:	X4,Y3,Z1
Tool:	Tool #2, 1/4" Slot Drill
Tool Start Position:	X0,Y0,Z1

```
%
:1004
N5 G90 G20
N10 M06 T2
```

```
N15 M03 S1200                          (Spindle on clockwise)
N20 G00 X1 Y1
N25 Z0.25
N30 G01 Z-0.1 F5
N35 X3 F20
N40 X1 Y2 Z-0.5
N45 G19 G02 Y1 Z-0.1 J-0.5 K0.2
N40 G17 G00 Z1
N45 X0 Y0
N50 M05
N55 M30
```

M04 SPINDLE ON COUNTERCLOCKWISE

Format: N_ M04 S_

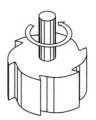

The M04 command switches the spindle on in a counterclockwise rotation. The spindle speed is designated by the letter address S, followed by the spindle speed in revolutions per minute.

The spindle speed is shown during program simulation in the program status window. Its on/off status is shown in the system status window. (CW, CCW, or OFF)

Sample Program M04EX4:

Workpiece Size:	X4,Y3,Z1
Tool:	Tool #4, 1/2" Slot Drill
Tool Start Position:	X0,Y0,Z1

```
%
:1005
N5 G91 G20
N10 M06 T4
N15 M04 S1000                    (Spindle on counterclockwise)
N20 G00 X1 Y2
N25 Z-0.75
N30 G01 Z-0.5 F5
N35 X0.5 F20
N40 G03 X0.5 Y0.5 R0.5
N45 X0.5 Y-0.5 R0.5
N50 G01 X0.5
N55 Y-0.25
N60 X-2
N65 Y-0.25
```

```
N70 X2
N75 Y-0.25
N80 X-2
N85 Y-0.25
N90 X2
N95 Y-0.25
N100 X-2
N105 G00 Z1.25
N110 G90 X0 Y0
N115 M05
N120 M02
```

M05 SPINDLE STOP

Format: N_ M05

The M05 command turns the spindle off. Although other M-codes turn off all functions (for example, M00 and M01), this command is dedicated to shutting the spindle off. The M05 command is found at the end of a program.

Sample Program M05EX5:

Workpiece Size:	X4,Y3,Z1
Tool:	Tool #2, 1/4" Slot Drill
Tool Start Position:	X0,Y0,Z1

```
%
:1005
N5 G90 G20
N10 M06 T2
N15 M03 S1200
N20 G00 X1 Y0.5
N25 Z0.1
N30 G01 Z-0.25 F5
N35 G03 X1 Y2.5 I0 J1 F25
N40 X3 I1 J0
N45 Y0.5 I0 J-1
N50 X1 I-1 J0
N55 G00 Z1
N60 X0 Y0
N65 M05                          (Spindle stop command)
N70 M30
```

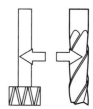

M06 TOOLCHANGE

Format: `N_ M06 T_`

The M06 command halts all program operations for a tool change. It is actually a two-fold command. First, it stops all machine operations—for example, the spindle is turned off and oriented for the tool change, and all axes motion stops—so that it is safe to physically change the tool. Secondly, it actually changes the tool. Look in the tool display window; the new tool will be changed.

For program operation to continue after the tool change, the user must respond to the prompt "M06 TOOLCHANGE-ENTER TO CONTINUE." The program will not continue until the user presses Enter.

Sample Program M06EX6:

Workpiece Size:	X4,Y3,Z1
Tool:	Tool #8, 3/4" HSS Drill
	Tool #9, 3/4" End Mill
Tool Start Position:	X0,Y0,Z1

```
%
:1006
N5 G90 G20
N10 M06 T8               (Tool change to Tool #8 end mill)
N15 M03 S1000
N20 G00 X0.75 Y1.5
N25 Z0.1
N30 G01 Z-0.5 F2.5
N35 G00 Z0.1
N40 X2.5
N45 G01 Z-0.5
N50 G00 Z1
N55 X0 Y0
N60 M06 T9               (Tool change to Tool #9 3/4" end mill)
N65 X0.75 Y1.5
N70 Z0.1
N75 G01 Z-0.5 F5
N80 G02 I0.375 J0 F15
N85 G00 Z0.1
N90 X2.5
N95 G01 Z-0.5 F5
N100 G02 I0.375 J0 F15
N105 G00 Z1
```

```
N110 X0 Y0
N115 M05
N120 M30
N125
```

The M06 command halts all functions until Enter is pressed. The new tool is shown in both the simulation window and the tool display window.

M08 COOLANT ON

Format: N_ M08

The M08 command switches on the coolant flow. Its status is shown in the system status window.

Sample Program M08EX7:

Workpiece Size:	X4,Y3,Z1
Tool:	Tool #2, 1/4" Slot Drill
Tool Start Position:	X0,Y0,Z1

```
%
:1008
N5 G90 G20
N10 M06 T2
N15 M03 S1200
N20 M08                 (Coolant on)
N25 G00 X1 Y1
N30 Z0.1
N35 G01 Z-.25 F5
N40 X3 F20
N45 Y2
N50 X1
N55 Y1
N60 G00 Z1
N65 M09                 (Coolant off)
N70 G00 X0 Y0
N75 M05
N80 M30
```

M09 COOLANT OFF

Format: N_ M09

The M09 command shuts off the coolant flow. The coolant should be shut off prior to tool changes or when rapiding the tool over long distances. Refer to the system status window to check on the status of the coolant flow.

Sample Program M09EX8:

Workpiece Size: X4,Y3,Z1
Tool: Tool #2, 1/4" Slot Drill
Tool Start Position: X0,Y0,Z1

```
%
:1009
N5 G90 G20
N10 M06 T2
N15 M03 S1200
N20 M08                    (Coolant on)
N25 G00 X1 Y1
N30 Z0.1
N35 G01 Z-.25 F5
N40 X3 F20
N45 Y2
N50 X1
N55 Y1
N60 G00 Z1
N65 M09                    (Coolant off)
N70 G00 X0 Y0
N75 M05
N80 M30
```

M10 CLAMPS ON

Format: N_ M10

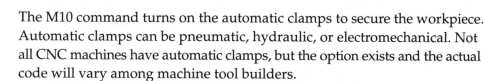

The M10 command turns on the automatic clamps to secure the workpiece. Automatic clamps can be pneumatic, hydraulic, or electromechanical. Not all CNC machines have automatic clamps, but the option exists and the actual code will vary among machine tool builders.

This command is normally in the program setup section of a CNC program. The system status window shows the status of the clamps.

Sample Program M10EX9:

Workpiece Size: X4,Y3,Z1
Tool: Tool #12, 1" End Mill
Tool Start Position: X0,Y0,Z1

```
%
:1010
N5 G90 G20
N10 M06 T12
N15 M10                    (Clamp workpiece)
N20 M03 S1000
N25 G00 X-0.75 Y1
N30 Z-0.375
N35 G01 X0 F10
N40 G03 Y2 I0 J0.5
N45 G01 X2 Y3
N50 X4 Y2
N55 G03 Y1 I0 J-0.5
N60 G01 X2 Y0
N65 X0 Y1
N70 G00 Z1
N75 X0 Y0
N80 M05
N85 M11                    (Unclamp workpiece)
N90 M30
```

M11 CLAMPS OFF

Format: N_ M11

The M11 command releases the automatic clamps so that the workpiece may be removed and the next blank inserted. The automatic clamps may be pneumatic, hydraulic, or electromechanical, depending on the application. The system status window shows the clamps status.

Sample Program M11EX10:

Workpiece Size: X4,Y3,Z1
Tool: Tool #12, 1" End Mill
Tool Start Position: X0,Y0,Z1

```
%
:1011
N5 G90 G20
```

```
N10 M06 T12
N15 M10                 (Clamp workpiece)
N20 M03 S1000
N25 G00 X-0.75 Y1
N30 Z-0.375
N35 G01 X0 F10
N40 G03 Y2 I0 J0.5
N45 G01 X2 Y3
N50 X4 Y2
N55 G03 Y1 I0 J-0.5
N60 G01 X2 Y0
N65 X0 Y1
N70 G00 Z1
N75 X0 Y0
N80 M05
N85 M11                 (Unclamp workpiece)
N90 M30
```

M30 PROGRAM END, RESET TO START

Format: N_ M30

The M30 command indicates the end of the program data. It means that there are no more program commands following it. This is a remnant of the older NC machines, which could not differentiate between one program and the next, so an End of Data command was developed. Now the M30 is used to end the program and reset it to the start.

Sample Program M30EX13:

Workpiece Size:	X4,Y3,Z1
Tool:	Tool #2, 1/4" Slot Drill
Tool Start Position:	X0,Y0,Z1

```
%
:1012
N5 G90 G20
N10 M06 T2
N15 M03 S1200
N20 G00 X0.5 Y1.25
N25 Z0.1
N30 G01 Z-0.25 F5
N35 G91 G02 X0.5 Y-0.5 R0.5 F15
N40 X0.5 Y-0.5 R0.5
```

```
N45 X1 I0.5
N50 X0.5 Y0.5 I0.5
N55 X0.5 Y0.5 I0.5
N60 G03 X-3 I-1.5
N60 G00 Z1
N65 X0 Y0
N70 M05
N75 M30                    (Program end, reset to start)
```

LETTER ADDRESS LISTING

Letter addresses are variables used in the different G- and M-codes. Most G-codes contain a variable, defined by the programmer, for each specific function. Each letter used in conjunction with G-codes or M-codes are called words. The letters used for programming are as follows:

D   Diameter offset register number

F   Assigns a feedrate

G   Preparatory function

H   Height offset register number

I   X-axis location of arc center

J   Y-axis location of arc center

K   Z-axis location of arc center

M   Miscellaneous function

N   Block number (specifies the start of a block)

P   Dwell time

R   Retract distance used with G81, 82, 83
    Radius when used with G02 or G03

S   Sets the spindle speed

T   Specifies the tool to be used

X   X-axis coordinate

Y   Y-axis coordinate

Z   Z-axis coordinate

The specific Letter Addresses are described in more detail next.

Character	Address For
D	Offset register number. Used to call the specified offset register for cutter diameter compensation.
F	Feedrate function. Specifies a feedrate in inches per minute or millimeters per minute.
G	Preparatory function. Specifies a preparatory function. Allows for various modes (for example, rapid and feed) to be set during a program.
H	Offset register number. Used to call the specified offset register for cutter tool length compensation.
I	Circular interpolation. Used in circular motion commands (see G02 and G03) to specify X distance and direction from the startpoint to the centerpoint of the arc.
J	Circular interpolation. Used in circular motion commands (see G02 and G03) to specify Y distance and direction from the startpoint to the centerpoint of the arc.
K	Circular interpolation. Used in circular motion commands (see G02 and G03) to specify Z distance and direction from the startpoint to the centerpoint of the arc.
M	Miscellaneous Function. Programmable on/off switches for various machine tool functions, as covered in the following section of this chapter.
N	Block number. Used for program line identification. Allows the programmer to organize each line and is helpful while you are editing. In TORSIM, increments by five to allow extra lines to be inserted if needed during editing.
P	Dwell time. Used to specify the length of time in seconds in a dwell command (see G04).
R	Retract distance. The Z retract distance in drilling operations.
	Radius, when used with G02 or G03. Can also be used in circular movement commands (see G02 and G03) to provide an easier way to designate the radius of the circular movement.
S	Spindle speed function. Specifies the spindle speed in revolutions per minute.
T	Tool number select function. Specifies the turret position of the current tool.
X	X-axis definition. Designates a coordinate along the X-axis.
Y	Y-axis definition. Designates a coordinate along the Y-axis.
Z	Z-axis definition. Designates a coordinate along the Z-axis.

STEP-BY-STEP MILLING EXAMPLES

Work through each of the following examples step by step. In the first example, each step is described in more detail than it is in the remaining examples, so be sure to work through it.

If you have any difficulties with the programs or simply want to test and see them without entering them in first, they can be found in the **/CNCEZ/ DEMOMILL** directory.

For each of the following examples, assume the PRZ is located at the lower left-hand corner at top. When entering the programs into CNCEZ, the tool will start at X0,Y0,Z1 relative to the PRZ.

EXAMPLE 1: I-PART1.MIL

This program introduces you to the Cartesian coordinate system and absolute coordinates. There are only single-axis, linear feed moves to show the travel directions of the X, Y, and Z axes. The completed part is shown in Fig. 5-20.

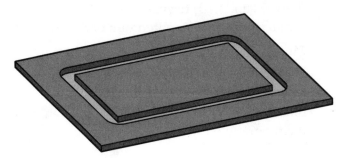

Figure 5-20 The finished part: a 5 in. × 4 in. block with a 4 in. × 3 in. slot.

Workpiece Size:	X5,Y4,Z1
Tool:	Tool #3, 3/8" End Mill
Tool Start Position:	X0,Y0,Z1 (Relative to workpiece)

```
%
:1001
N5 G90 G20
N10 M06 T3
N15 M03 S1200
N20 G00 X1 Y1
N22 Z0.125
N25 G01 Z-0.125 F5
N30 X4 F20
```

```
N35 Y3
N40 X1
N45 Y1
N50 G00 Z1
N52 X0 Y0
N55 M05
N60 M30
```

STEP 1: Execute the batch file CNCEZ.BAT located in the root directory.

```
C:\CNCEZ  [Enter]
```

The following opening menu appears on your screen (Fig. 5-21).

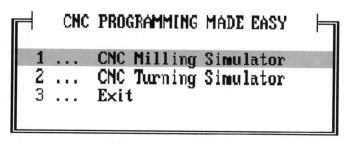

Figure 5-21 Opening menu for CNC Programming Made Easy

STEP 2: Choose the milling option either by using the cursor keys to highlight the required option and then pressing Enter or by typing the appropriate menu number option and pressing Enter.

The main system screen appears (Fig. 5-22).

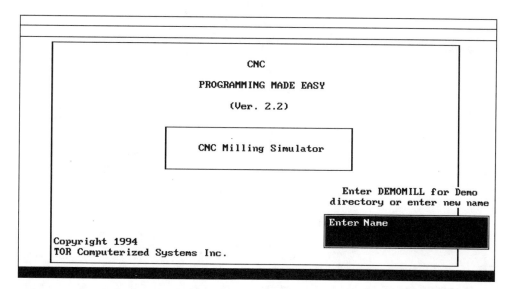

Figure 5-22 Main system screen for CNC Milling Simulator

STEP 3: You are prompted to enter DEMOMILL (for the default directory) or enter the name of a new directory. In this example, you will create a new directory to store all your files. Call this directory **PROJECTS**.

Enter DEMOMILL directory or enter new name: **PROJECTS [Enter]**
At the "Create New Directory" prompt, select **YES**.

The CNC graphical user interface is displayed (Fig. 5-23).

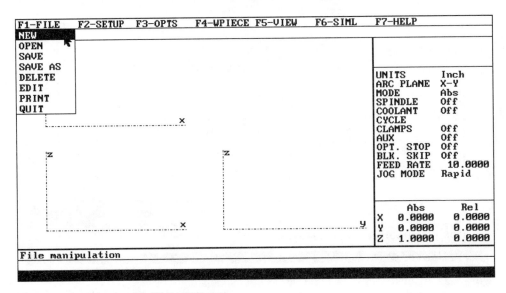

```
F1-FILE    F2-SETUP  F3-OPTS   F4-WPIECE F5-VIEW   F6-SIML   F7-HELP

 y
                                                    UNITS       Inch
                                                    ARC PLANE   X-Y
                                              ▶     MODE        Abs
                                                    SPINDLE     Off
                                                    COOLANT     Off
                      x                             CYCLE
                                                    CLAMPS      Off
                                                    AUX         Off
 z                        z                         OPT. STOP   Off
                                                    BLK. SKIP   Off
                                                    FEED RATE   10.0000
                                                    JOG MODE    Rapid

                                                        Abs       Rel
                                                    X   0.0000    0.0000
            x                              y        Y   0.0000    0.0000
                                                    Z   1.0000    0.0000
```

Figure 5-23 The CNC milling graphical user interface

STEP 4: Create a new file called **I-PART1.**

Move the pointer to the menu bar and select F1-FILE.
Select **NEW** (Fig. 5-24).
Enter the file name: **I-PART1 [Enter]** ((Fig.5-25).

```
F1-FILE    F2-SETUP  F3-OPTS   F4-WPIECE F5-VIEW   F6-SIML   F7-HELP
NEW
OPEN    ▲
SAVE
SAVE AS
DELETE                                              UNITS       Inch
EDIT                                                ARC PLANE   X-Y
PRINT                                               MODE        Abs
QUIT                                                SPINDLE     Off
                                                    COOLANT     Off
                      x                             CYCLE
                                                    CLAMPS      Off
                                                    AUX         Off
 z                        z                         OPT. STOP   Off
                                                    BLK. SKIP   Off
                                                    FEED RATE   10.0000
                                                    JOG MODE    Rapid

                                                        Abs       Rel
                                                    X   0.0000    0.0000
            x                              y        Y   0.0000    0.0000
                                                    Z   1.0000    0.0000
File manipulation
```

Figure 5-24 Selecting F1-FILE NEW option

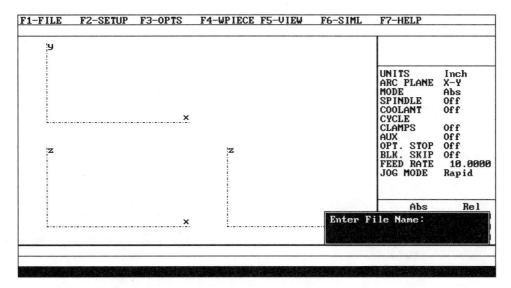

Figure 5-25 I-PART1 file name entered

STEP 5:   Set up the workpiece (stock material) for this program.

From the Menu Bar, select **F4-WPIECE**.
Select **Define** (Fig. 5-26).
Workpiece Length (in): **5** (Fig. 5-27)
Workpiece Width (in): **4**
Workpiece Height (in): **1**

The workpiece appears in the graphics simulation window in 3rd angle projection, showing the top view, front view, and right-hand side view (Fig. 5-28). You may change views by using the F5 VIEW option.

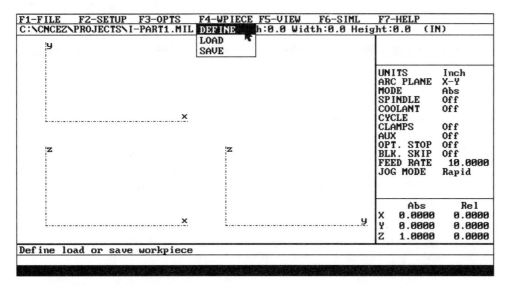

Figure 5-26 F4-WPIECE menu

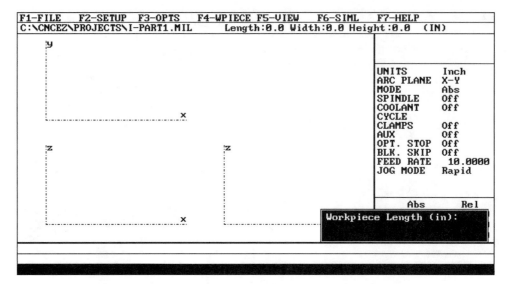

Figure 5-27 Prompt for Length input the bottom right-hand corner.

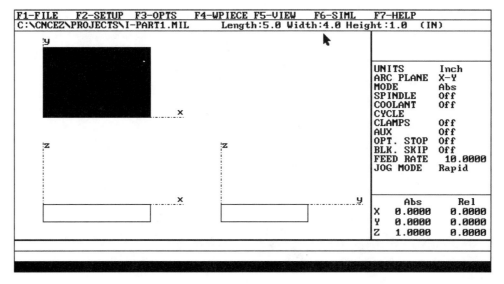

Figure 5-28

STEP 6: This CNC program will use the default tool library that is shipped with the software. The program uses Tool #3, which is defaulted in the turret to be a 3/8-in. slot drill. Look at the tool library at Tool #3.

From the Menu Bar, select **F2-SETUP**.
Select **TOOLS**.
Move the pointer over Tool #3 and click on it
Move the pointer over the #3 entry in the next table and click on it.
You have now set the library (Fig. 5-29).

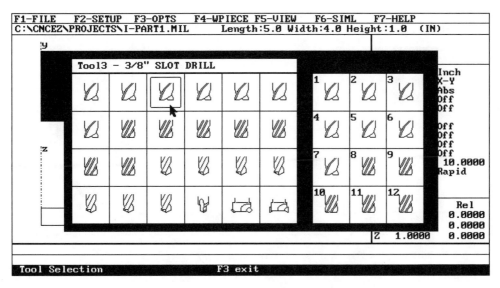

Figure 5-29 The tool library, which can be modified

STEP 7: Begin entering the program and simulate the cutter path. Use the SIMULATE/EDIT option.

From the Menu Bar, select **F6-SIML**.
Select **EDIT** (Fig. 5-30).

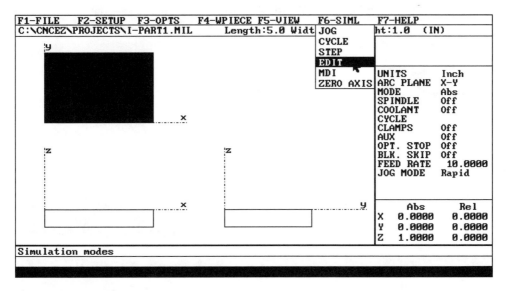

Figure 5-30 F6-SIML menu

STEP 8: Program setup phase. You must enter all the setup parameters before you can enter the actual cutting moves (Figs. 5-31, 5-32, and 5-33).

>% [Enter]   Program Start Flag
>:1001 [Enter]   Program Number

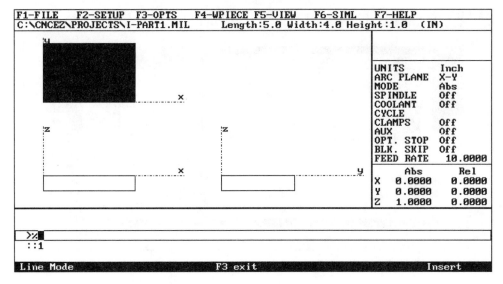

Figure 5-31 Prompt at lower left-hand corner, next to % sign

>N5 G90 G20 [Enter]   Absolute coordinates and inch
>N10 M06 T3 [Enter]   Tool change and tool #3
>N15 M03 S1200 [Enter]   Spindle on CW at 1200 rpm

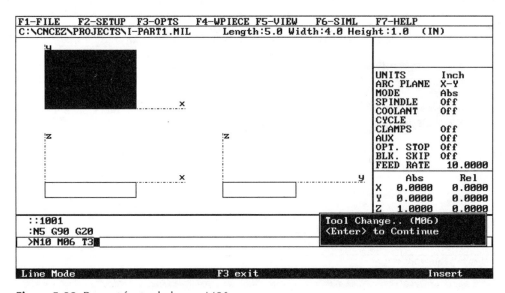

Figure 5-32 Prompt for tool change M06

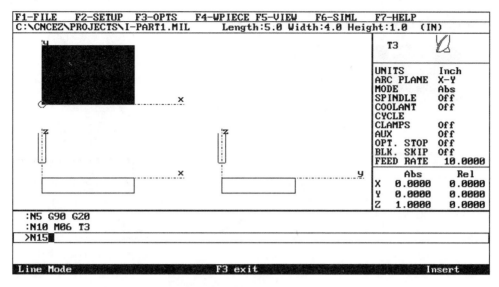

Figure 5-33 The tool at home position (X0,Y0,Z1)

STEP 9: Material removal phase. Begin cutting the workpiece using G00 and G01.

>**N20 G00 X1 Y1 [Enter]**

>**N22 Z0.125 [Enter]**   Rapid move to X1,Y1,Z0.125 (Fig. 5-34)

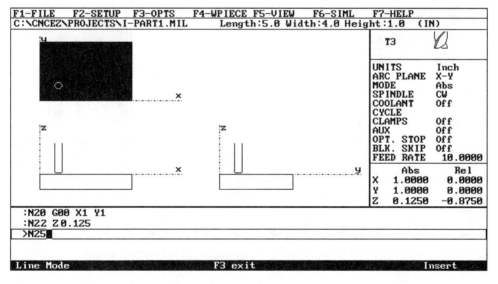

Figure 5-34 After rapid move, the tool is at (X1,Y1,Z0.125).

>**N25 G01 Z-0.125 F5 [Enter]**   Feed into part 0.125 at 5 ipm
(Fig. 5-35)

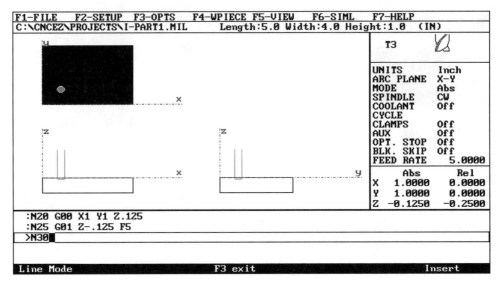

Figure 5-35 The cutter drilling in by 0.125 in.

>**N30 X4 F20 [Enter]**   Feed across to 4 inches at 20ipm
                                           (Fig. 5-36)

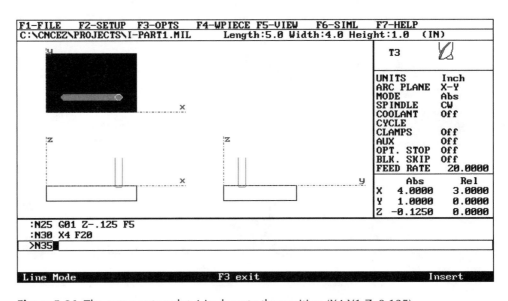

Figure 5-36 The cutter cuts a slot 4 in. long to the position (X4,Y1,Z–0.125).

Note the status area and the X,Y,Z absolute and incremental position.

>**N35 Y3 [Enter]**   Feed up 3 inches (Fig. 5-37)

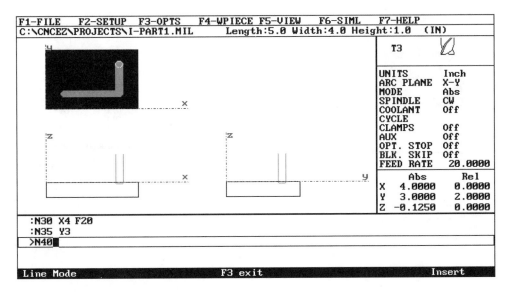

Figure 5-37 G00 cutter move to Y3

Note on the status window that the feedrate remains the same. Also note that the G01 is modal and remains in effect until cancelled by another code.

>**N40 X1 [Enter]**   Feed back 4 inches (Fig. 5-38)
>**N45 Y1 [Enter]**   Feed down 3 inches (Fig. 5-38)

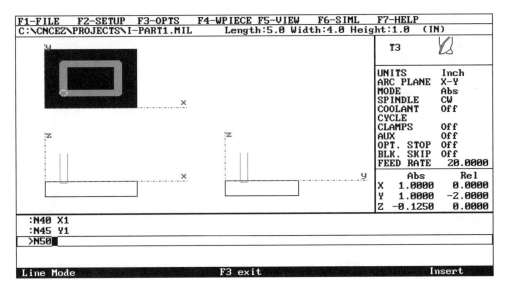

Figure 5-38 The completed slot

>**N50 G00 Z1 [Enter]**
>**N52 G00 X0 Y0 [Enter]**   Rapid to home position (Fig. 5-39)

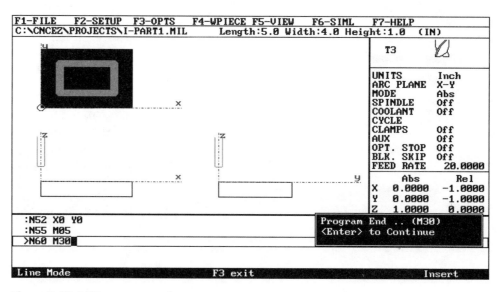

```
F1-FILE    F2-SETUP   F3-OPTS    F4-WPIECE F5-VIEW    F6-SIML    F7-HELP
C:\CNCEZ\PROJECTS\I-PART1.MIL       Length:5.0 Width:4.0 Height:1.0  (IN)
                                                      T3

                                              UNITS        Inch
                                              ARC PLANE    X-Y
                                              MODE         Abs
                                              SPINDLE      CW
                                              COOLANT      Off
                                              CYCLE
                                              CLAMPS       Off
                                              AUX          Off
                                              OPT. STOP    Off
                                              BLK. SKIP    Off
                                              FEED RATE    20.0000
                                                   Abs        Rel
                                              X  0.0000    -1.0000
                                              Y  0.0000    -1.0000
                                              Z  1.0000     0.0000
  :N50 G00 Z1
  :N52 X0 Y0
  >N55
Line Mode                        F3 exit                        Insert
```

Figure 5-39 Cutter rapids to Z1 and X0,Y0.

STEP 10: Program shutdown phase. Turn off the spindle and program end (Fig. 5-40).

> **N55 M05 [Enter]** Turns spindle off
> **N60 M30 [Enter]** End of program
> **N65 Press F3** Exit from Simulate/Edit mode

```
F1-FILE    F2-SETUP   F3-OPTS    F4-WPIECE F5-VIEW    F6-SIML    F7-HELP
C:\CNCEZ\PROJECTS\I-PART1.MIL       Length:5.0 Width:4.0 Height:1.0  (IN)
                                                      T3

                                              UNITS        Inch
                                              ARC PLANE    X-Y
                                              MODE         Abs
                                              SPINDLE      Off
                                              COOLANT      Off
                                              CYCLE
                                              CLAMPS       Off
                                              AUX          Off
                                              OPT. STOP    Off
                                              BLK. SKIP    Off
                                              FEED RATE    20.0000
                                                   Abs        Rel
                                              X  0.0000    -1.0000
                                              Y  0.0000    -1.0000
                                              Z  1.0000     0.0000
  :N52 X0 Y0                             Program End .. (M30)
  :N55 M05                               <Enter> to Continue
  >N60 M30
Line Mode                        F3 exit                        Insert
```

Figure 5-40 M30 program end prompt

STEP 11: The program is now complete. Rerun the program using the SIMULATE/CYCLE option.

From the Menu Bar, select **F6-SIML**.
Select **CYCLE** (Fig. 5-41).

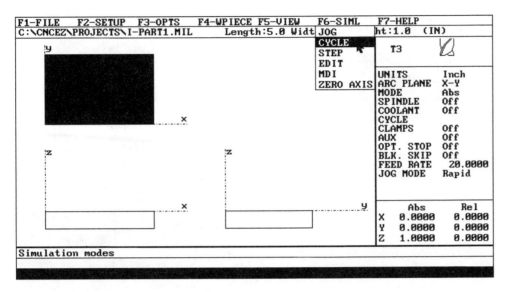

Figure 5-41 Selection of SIMULATE/EDIT option

Note the program stops at M06 and prompts you for a tool change (Fig. 5-42). Press Enter to continue (Fig. 5-43).

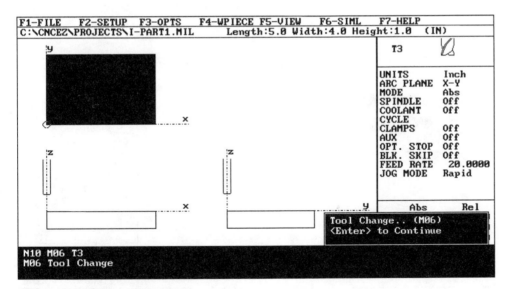

Figure 5-42 Prompt for tool change

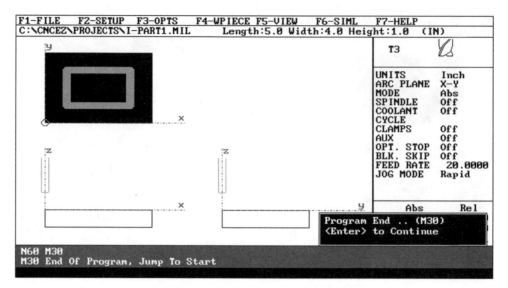

Figure 5-43 End of program cycle

STEP 12: Display the three-dimensional solid using the F5-VIEW/SOLID option.

From the pull-down menu, select **F5-VIEW**.
From the F5-VIEW menu ,select **SOLID** (Fig. 5-44).

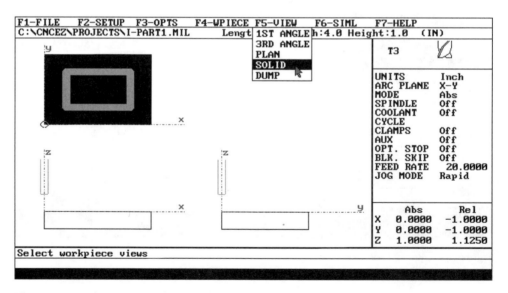

Figure 5-44 Selecting F5-VIEW/SOLID

The final result is shown in Fig. 5-45.

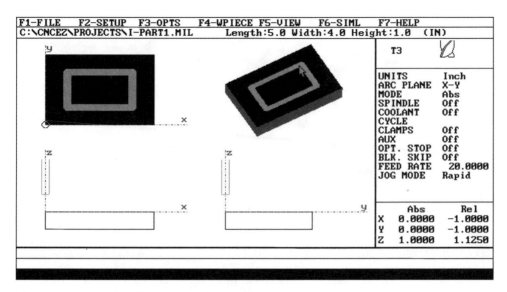

Figure 5-45 Completed part with solid isometric view

STEP 13: End of program.

EXAMPLE #2: I-PART2.MIL

This program introduces the user to diagonal linear feedmoves, where both the X-axis and the Y-axis are traversing. See Fig. 5-46.

Workpiece Size:	X5,Y4,Z1
Tool:	Tool #2, 1/4" End Mill
Tool Start Position:	X0,Y0,Z1 (Relative to workpiece)

```
%
:1002
N5 G90 G20
N10 M06 T2
N15 M03 S1200
N20 G00 X1 Y1
N22 Z0.125
N25 G01 Z-0.125 F5
N30 X4 F10
N35 Y3
N40 X1 Y1
N45 Y3
N50 X4 Y1
N55 G00 Z1
N57 X0 Y0
N60 M05
N65 M30
```

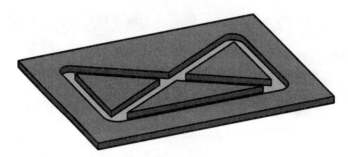

Figure 5-46 The finished part. Notice how two axes combined in a G01 feed move results in a diagonal cut. Line 35 is an example of a single-axis feed move, while line 40 is an example of a multiaxis feed move.

STEP 1: Create a new file called **I-PART2**.

Move the pointer to the Menu Bar and select **F1-FILE**.
Select **NEW**.
Enter the file name: **I-PART2 [Enter]**.

STEP 2: Set up the workpiece (stock material) for this program.

From the Menu Bar, select **F4-WPIECE**.
Select **Define**.
Workpiece Length (in): **5**
Workpiece Width (in): **4**
Workpiece Height (in): **1**

STEP 3: Begin entering the program and simulate the cutter path. Use the SIMULATE/EDIT option.

From the Menu Bar, select **F6-SIML**.
Select **EDIT**.

STEP 4: Program setup phase. You must enter all the setup parameters before you can enter all the actual cutting moves.

>% [Enter]	Program start flag
>:1002 [Enter]	Program number
>N5 G90 G20 [Enter]	Absolute coordinates and inch
>N10 M06 T3 [Enter]	Tool change and Tool #3
>N15 M03 S1200 [Enter]	Spindle on CW at 1200 rpm

STEP 5: Material removal phase. Begin cutting the workpiece using G00 and G01.

>N20 G00 X1 Y1 [Enter]	Rapid to X1,Y1
>N22 Z0.125 [Enter]	Rapid to Z0.125

>N25 G01 Z-0.125 F5 [Enter]   Feed move Z–.125", at 5 ipm
>N30 G01 X4 F10 [Enter]   Feed move to X4, at 10 ipm
>N35 Y3 [Enter]   Feed move, at 10 ipm
>N40 X1 Y1 [Enter]   Diagonal feed move to X1,Y1
(Fig. 5-47)

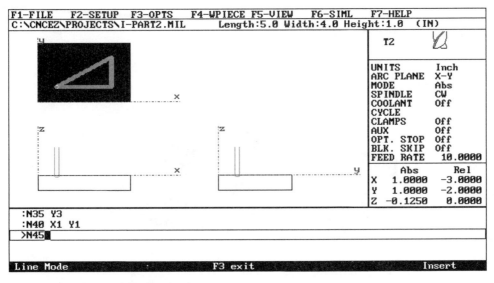

Figure 5-47 Diagonal feed move from X4,Y3 to X1,Y1

>N45 Y3 [Enter]   Feed move to Y3, at 10 ipm
>N50 X4 Y1 [Enter]   Feed move to X4,Y1 (Fig. 5-48)

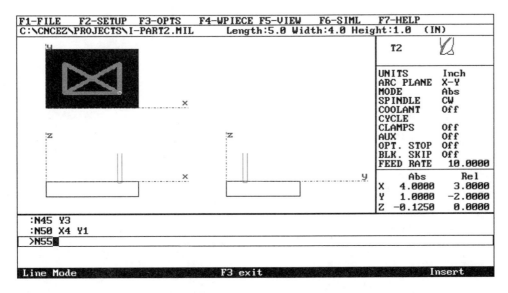

Figure 5-48 Last cutter move to X4,Y1

>N55 G00 Z1 [Enter]   Rapid to Z1
>N57 X0 Y0 [Enter]   Rapid to X0,Y0

STEP 6: Program shutdown phase. Turn off the spindle and program end.

>**N60 M05 [Enter]**   Turn off spindle
>**N65 M30 [Enter]**   End of program

STEP 7: End of program

EXAMPLE #3: I-PART3.MIL

This program introduces arcs: G02 (clockwise) and G03 (counterclockwise). These are all simple quarter quadrant arcs with a 1-in. radius.

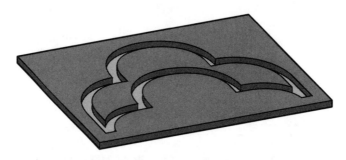

Figure 5-49 The completed part.

Workpiece Size:	X5,Y4,Z1
Tool:	Tool #2, 0.25" Slot Mill
Tool Start Position:	X0,Y0,Z1 (Relative to workpiece)

```
%
:1003
N5 G90 G20
N10 M06 T2
N15 M03 S1200
N20 G00 X0.5 Y0.5
N22 Z0.25
N25 G01 Z-0.25 F5
N30 G02 X1.5 Y1.5 I1 J0 F10
N35 X2.5 Y2.5 R1
N40 X3.5 Y1.5 I0 J-1
N45 X4.5 Y0.5 R1
N50 G01 Y1.5
N55 G03 X3.5 Y2.5 R1
N60 X2.5 Y3.5 I-1 J0
N65 X1.5 Y2.5 R1
N70 X0.5 Y1.5 I0 J-1
N75 G01 Y0.5
```

```
N80 G00 Z1
N82 X0 Y0
N85 M05
N90 M30
```

STEP 1:   Create a new file called **I-PART3**.

Move the pointer to the Menu Bar and select **F1-FILE**.
Select **NEW**.
Enter the file name: **I-PART3 [Enter]**.

STEP 2:   Set up the workpiece (stock material) for this program.

From the Menu Bar, select **F4-WPIECE**.
Select **Define**.
Workpiece Length (in): **5**
Workpiece Width (in): **4**
Workpiece Height (in): **1**

STEP 3:   Change the view to Plan view using F5-VIEW/PLAN.

From the Menu Bar, select **F5-VIEW**.
Select **PLAN**, as shown in Fig. 5-50.

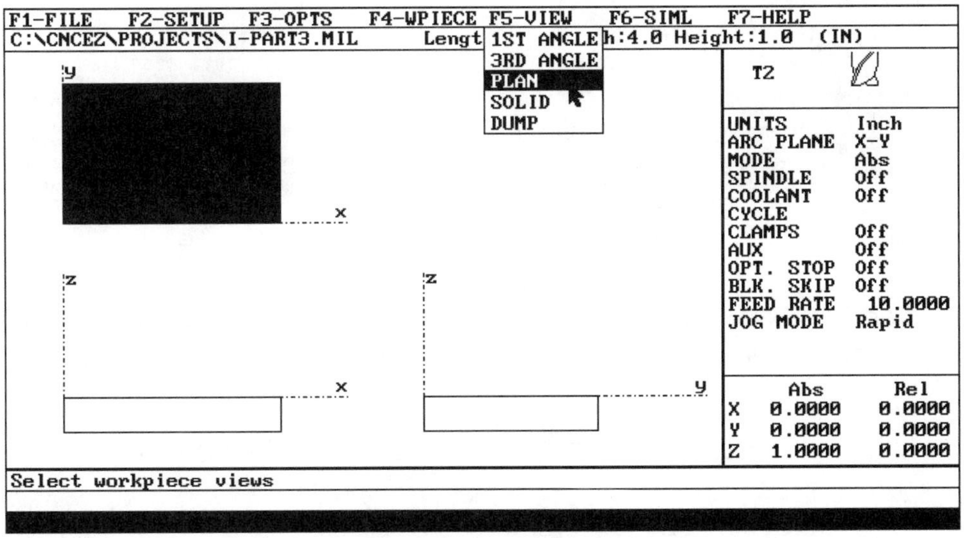

Figure 5-50 Selecting Plan view from the F5-VIEW menu.

STEP 4:   Begin entering the program and simulate the cutter path. Use the SIMULATE/EDIT option.

From the Menu Bar, select **F6-SIML**.
Select **EDIT**.

STEP 5: Program setup phase. You must enter all the setup parameters before you can enter all the actual cutting moves.

>% [Enter]	Program start flag
>:1003 [Enter]	Program number
>N5 G90 G20 [Enter]	Absolute coordinates and inch
>N10 M06 T3 [Enter]	Tool change and Tool #3
>N15 M03 S1200 [Enter]	Spindle on CW at 1200 rpm

STEP 6: Material removal phase. Begin cutting the workpiece using G00, G01, G02, and G03.

>N20 G00 X0.5 Y0.5 [Enter]	Rapid to X0.5,Y0.5
>N22 Z0.25 [Enter]	Rapid to Z0.25
>N25 G01 Z-0.25 F5 [Enter]	Feed down to –0.25 at 5 ipm
>N30 G02 X1.5 Y1.5 I1 J0 F10 [Enter]	Circular interpolation (Fig. 5-51)

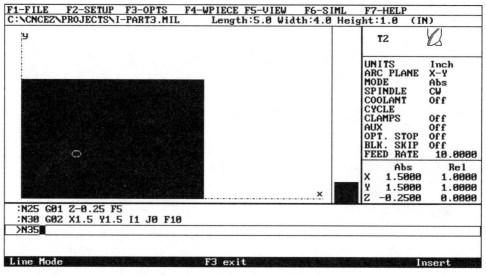

Figure 5-51 G02 Circular interpolation clockwise

>N35 X2.5 Y2.5 R1 [Enter]	G02 command using Radius value (Fig. 5-52)
>N40 X3.5 Y1.5 I0 J-1 [Enter]	G02 command using I and J
>N45 X4.5 Y0.5 R1 [Enter]	G02 command using R value
>N50 G01 Y1.5 [Enter]	G01 feed to Y1.5 (Fig. 5-53)
>N55 G03 X3.5 Y2.5 R1 [Enter]	G03 arc using R value
>N60 X2.5 Y3.5 I-1 J0 [Enter]	G03 arc using I and J values
>N65 X1.5 Y2.5 R1 [Enter]	G03 arc using R value
>N70 X0.5 Y1.5 I0 J-1 [Enter]	G03 arc using I and J values

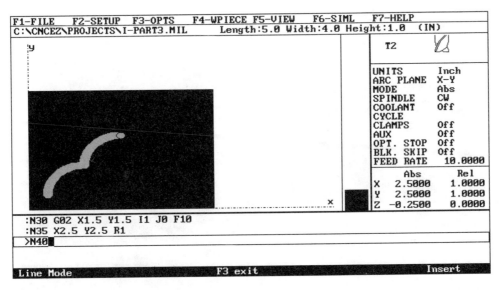

Figure 5-52 G02 move using R1 rather then I1,J0

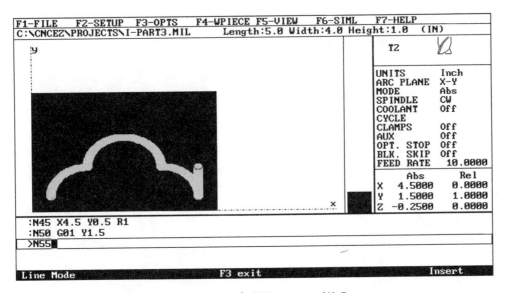

Figure 5-53 Completed G02 operation with G01 move to Y1.5

>**N75 G01 Y0.5 [Enter]** G01 feed move to Y0.5
>**N80 G00 Z1 [Enter]** G00 rapid move to Z1
>**N82 X0 Y0 [Enter]** G00 rapid move to X0,Y0 (Fig. 5-54)

STEP 7: Program shutdown phase. Turn off the spindle and program end.

>**N85 M05 [Enter]** Turn off spindle
>**N90 M30 [Enter]** End of program

STEP 8: End of program

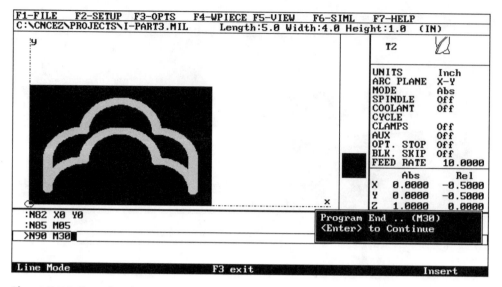

Figure 5-54 Completed part.

EXAMPLE #4: I-PART4.MIL

This program cuts several G02 and G03 arcs (clockwise and counterclockwise) in semicircles and full circles (see finished part in Fig. 5-55).

Workpiece Size:	X4,Y4,Z2
Tool:	Tool #4, 0.5" Slot Mill
Tool Start Position:	X0,Y0,Z1 (Relative to workpiece)

```
%
:1004
N5 G90 G20
N10 M06 T4
N15 M03 S1200
N20 G00 Z0.25
N25 G01 Z0 F5
N30 G18 G02 X4 Z0 I2 K0
N35 G19 G03 Y4 Z0 J2 K0
N40 G18 G03 X0 Z0 I-2 K0
N45 G19 G02 Y0 Z0 J-2 K0
N50 G00 X1 Y2 Z0.25
N55 G01 Z-0.25
N60 G17 G02 I1 J0 F10
N65 G00 Z1
N67 X0 Y0
N70 M05
N75 M30
```

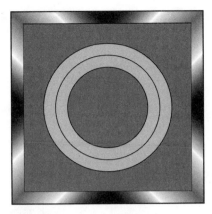

Figure 5-55 The finished part

STEP 1:   Create a new file called **I-PART4**.

Move the pointer to the Menu Bar and select **F1-FILE**.
Select **NEW**.
Enter the file name: **I-PART4 [Enter]**.

STEP 2:   Set up the workpiece (stock material) for this program and save the workpiece as a stock part.

From the Menu Bar, select **F4-WPIECE**.
Select **Define**.
Workpiece Length (in): **4**
Workpiece Width (in): **4**
Workpiece Height (in): **2**
From the Menu Bar, select **F4-WPIECE**.
Select **SAVE**, (Fig. 5-56).
Enter the file name: **4X4X2-IN [Enter]** (Fig. 5-57).

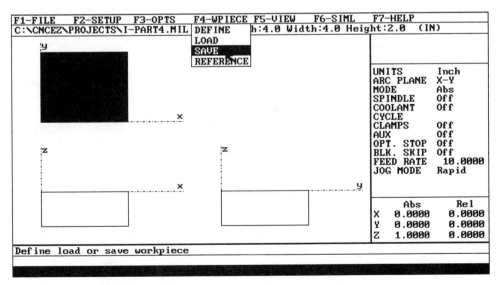

Figure 5-56 Selecting SAVE from F4-WPIECE menu

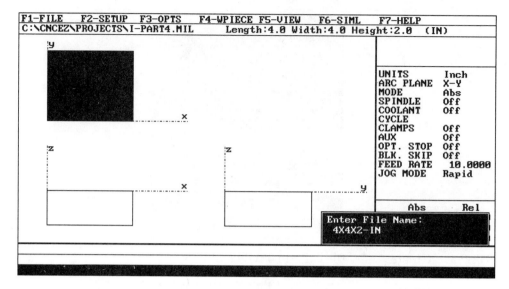

Figure 5-57 Entering the workpiece file name

STEP 3: Turn SHOWPATHS on in order to show the centerline moves.

From the Menu Bar, select **F3-OPTN**.
From the OPTIONS menu, select **SHOWPATH** (Fig. 5-58).

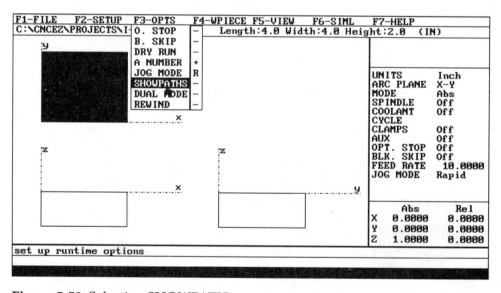

Figure 5-58 Selecting SHOWPATH

STEP 4: Begin entering the program and simulate the cutter path. Use SIMULATE/EDIT.

From the Menu Bar, select **F6-SIML**.
Select **EDIT**.

STEP 5: Program setup phase. You must enter all the setup parameters before you can enter all the actual cutting moves.

>% [Enter]   Program start flag
>:1004 [Enter]   Program number
>N5 G90 G20 [Enter]   Absolute coordinates and inch
>N10 M06 T4 [Enter]   Tool change and Tool #4
>N15 M03 S1200 [Enter]   Spindle on CW at 1200 rpm

STEP 6: Material removal phase. Begin cutting the workpiece using G00, G01, G02, and G03.

>N20 G00 Z0.25 [Enter]   Rapid to Z0.25
>N25 G01 Z0 F5 [Enter]   Feed down to Z0 at 5 ipm
>N30 G18 G02 X4 Z0 I2 K0 [Enter]   Circular interpolation using
                                   G18 on the X and Z arc plane
                                   (Fig. 5-59)

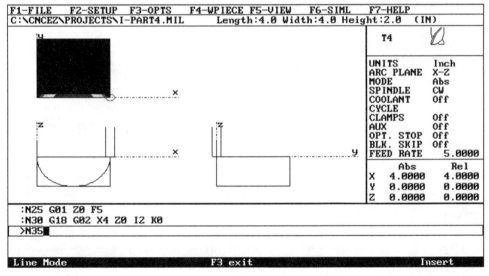

Figure 5-59 Part after G18 and G02 arc move

>N35 G19 G03 Y4 Z0 J2 K0 [Enter]   Circular interpolation using
                                   G19 in the Y and Z arc plane
                                   (Fig. 5-60)

>N40 G18 G03 X0 Z0 I-2 K0 [Enter] Circular interpolation using
                                   G18 in the X and Z arc plane
                                   (Fig. 5-61)

>N45 G19 G02 Y0 Z0 J-2 K0 [Enter] Circular interpolation using
                                   G19 in the Y and Z arc plane
                                   (Fig. 5-61)

142 CNC MILLING

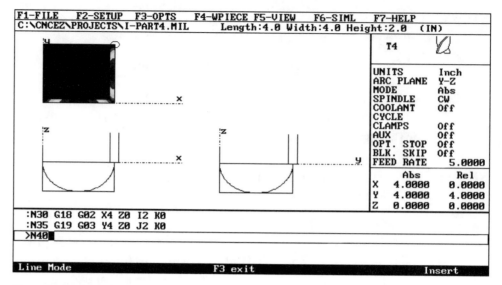

Figure 5-60 Part after G19 and G03 arc feed move

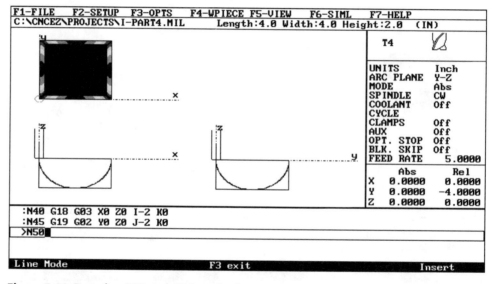

Figure 5-61 Part after G19 and G02 arc feed move

>N50 G00 X1 Y2 Z0.25 [Enter]　　Rapid up to X1,Y1,Z0.25
>N55 G01 Z-0.25 [Enter]　　Feed in to Z–0.25 at 5 ipm
>N60 G17 G02 I1 J0 F10 [Enter]　　Circular interpolation in the X and Y arc plane using G17 (Fig. 5-62)

Note that the G17 command is required, otherwise the G19 would still be in force.

>N65 G00 Z1 [Enter]　　Rapid to Z1
>N67 X0 Y0 [Enter]　　Rapid to X0,Y0

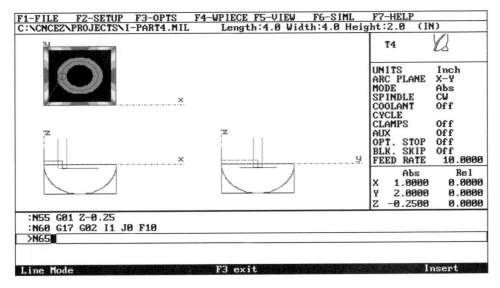

Figure 5-62 Part after G17 and G02 arc feed move

STEP 7: Program shutdown phase. Turn off the spindle and program end.

>**N70 M05 [Enter]**   Turn off spindle
>**N75 M30 [Enter]**   End of program

STEP 8: End of Program

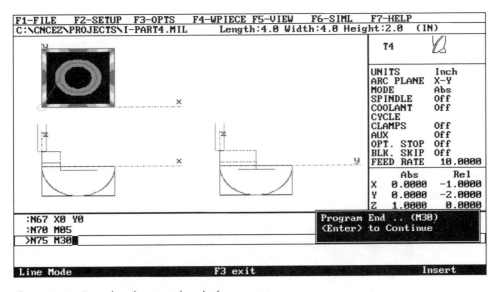

Figure 5-63 Completed part and end of program

EXAMPLE #5: I-PART5.MIL

This program involves a simple drilling cycle with a defined retract plane. Once the G-code for the drill cycle is executed, only the X and/or Y location of the remaining holes need to be defined (see finished part in Fig. 5-64).

Workpiece Size:	X5,Y4,Z1
Tool:	Tool #7, 3/8" HSS Drill
Tool Start Position:	X0,Y0,Z1 (Relative to workpiece)

```
%
:1005
N5 G90 G20
N10 M06 T7
N15 M03 S1000
N20 G00 X1 Y1
N22 Z0.25
N25 G98 G81 X1 Y1 Z-0.25 R0.25 F3
N30 Y2
N35 Y3
N40 X2
N45 Y2
N50 Y1
N55 X3
N60 X4
N65 Y2
N70 Y3
N75 X3
N80 Y2
N85 G00 Z1
N87 X0 Y0
N90 M05
N95 M30
```

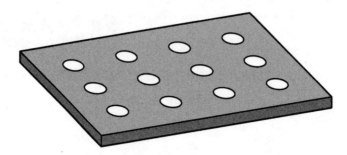

Figure 5-64 The finished part

STEP 1: Create a new file called **I-PART5**.

Move the pointer to the Menu Bar and select **F1-FILE**.
Select **NEW**.
Enter the file name: **I-PART5 [Enter]**.

STEP 2: Set up the workpiece (stock material) for this program and save the workpiece as a stock part.

From the Menu Bar, select **F4-WPIECE**.
Select **Define**.
Workpiece Length (in): **5**
Workpiece Width (in): **4**
Workpiece Height (in): **1**

STEP 3: Turn SHOWPATHS on in order to show the center line moves.

From the Menu Bar, select **F3-OPTN**.
From the OPTIONS menu, select **SHOWPATH**.

STEP 4: Begin entering the program and simulate the cutter path. Use SIMULATE/EDIT.

From the Menu Bar, select **F6-SIML**.
Select **EDIT**.

STEP 5: Program setup phase. You must enter all the setup parameters before you can enter all the actual cutting moves.

>% **[Enter]**	Program start flag
>:1005 **[Enter]**	Program number
>N5 G90 G20 **[Enter]**	Absolute coordinates and inch
>N10 M06 T7 **[Enter]**	Tool change and Tool #7
>N15 M03 S1000 **[Enter]**	Spindle on CW at 1000 rpm

STEP 6: Material removal phase

>N20 G00 X1 Y1 **[Enter]**	Rapid to X1,Y1
>N22 Z0.25 **[Enter]**	Rapid to Z0.25
>N25 G98 G81 X1 Y1 Z-0.25 R0.25 F3 **[Enter]**	G81 drill cycle with the first hole at X1,Y1,Z–0.25 and the retract at Z0.25, (Figs. 5-65 and 5-66)

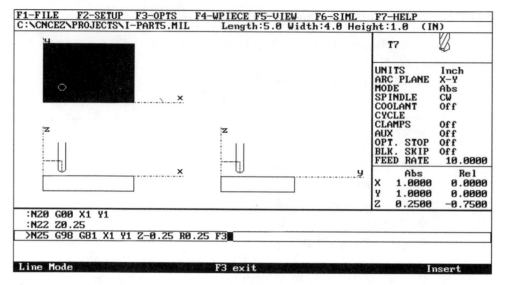

Figure 5-65 The workpiece before the drill cycle

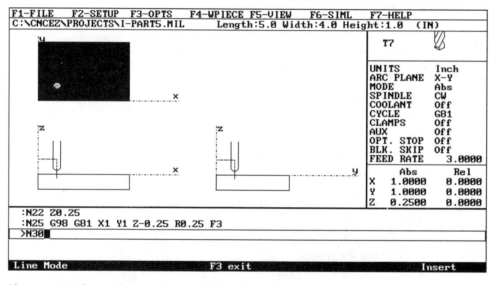

Figure 5-66 The workpiece after the drill cycle

>N30 Y2 [Enter]	The drill moves to Y2 and drills in –0.25 and then retracts back to Z0.25 (Fig 5-67)
>N35 Y3 [Enter]	Part of drill cycle (Fig. 5-68)
>N40 X2 [Enter]	Fig. 5-68
>N45 Y2 [Enter]	Fig. 5-68
>N50 Y1 [Enter]	Fig. 5-68
>N55 X3 [Enter]	Fig. 5-68
>N60 X4 [Enter]	Fig. 5-68
>N65 Y2 [Enter]	Fig. 5-68
>N70 Y3 [Enter]	Fig. 5-68

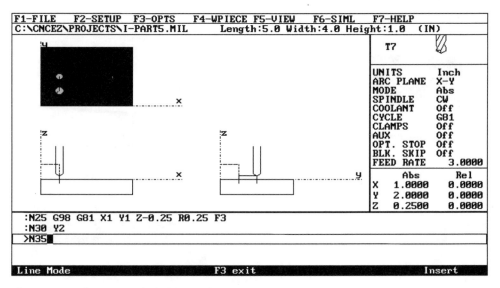

Figure 5-67 The second hole by simply entering Y2

>**N75 X3 [Enter]**   Fig. 5-68
>**N80 Y2 [Enter]**   Fig. 5-68

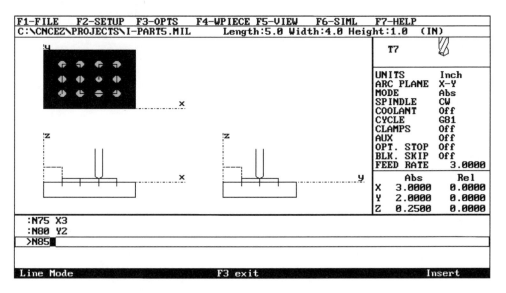

Figure 5-68 Shows all holes drilled

>**N85 G00 Z1 [Enter]**   Rapid to Z1
>**N87 X0 Y0 [Enter]**   Rapid to X0,Y0

STEP 7: Program shutdown phase. Turn off the spindle and program end.

>**N90 M05 [Enter]**   Turn off spindle
>**N95 M30 [Enter]**   End of program (Fig. 5-69)

STEP 8: End of program

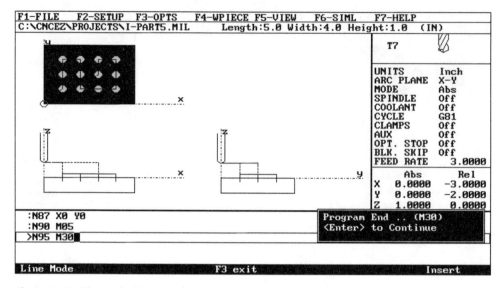

Figure 5-69 The end of the program

EXAMPLE #6: I-PART6.MIL

This program involves a drilling cycle with a dwell and incremental coordinates (see finished part in Fig. 5-70).

Workpiece Size:	X5,Y4,Z1
Tool:	Tool #8, 3/4" HSS Drill
Tool Start Position:	X0,Y0,Z1 (Relative to workpiece)

```
%
:1006
N5 G90 G20
N10 M06 T8
N15 M03 S500
N20 G00 X1 Y1
N22 Z0.25
N25 G91 G98 G82 Z-0.5 R0.25 P1
N30 X1
N35 X2
N40 Y1
N45 Y1
N50 X-2
N55 X-1
N60 Y-1
N65 X1
```

```
N70 G80 G90 G00 Z1
N72 X0 Y0
N75 M05
N80 M30
```

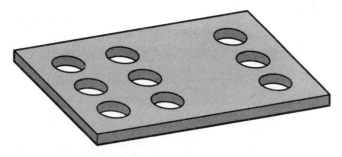

Figure 5-70 The finished part

STEP 1: Create a new file called **I-PART6**.

Move the pointer to the Menu Bar and select **F1-FILE**.
Select **NEW**.
Enter the file name: **I-PART6 [Enter]**.

STEP 2: Load the workpiece (stock material) for this program.

From the Menu Bar, select **F4-WPIECE**.
Select **LOAD**.
Select the file: **5X4X1-IN** (Figs. 5-71 and 5-72).

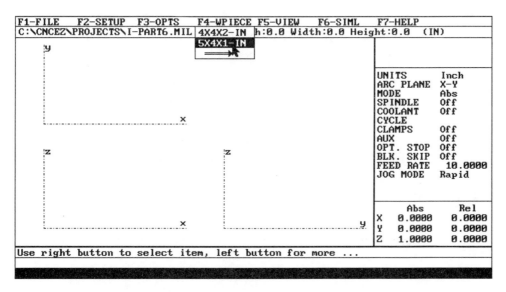

Figure 5-71 Selecting stock material workpiece

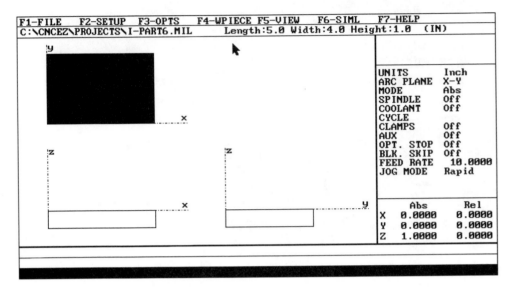

Figure 5-72 After selecting stock workpiece

STEP 3: Turn SHOWPATHS on in order to show the center line moves.

From the Menu Bar, select **F3-OPTN**.
From the OPTIONS menu, select **SHOWPATH**.

STEP 4: Begin entering the program and simulate the cutter path. Use SIMULATE/EDIT.

From the Menu Bar, select **F6-SIML**.
Select **EDIT**.

STEP 5: Program setup phase. You must enter all the setup parameters before you can enter all the actual cutting moves.

>% [Enter]	Program start flag
>:1006 [Enter]	Program number
>N5 G90 G20 [Enter]	Absolute coordinates and inch
>N10 M06 T8 [Enter]	Tool change and Tool #8
>N15 M03 S500 [Enter]	Spindle on CW at 500 rpm

STEP 6: Material removal phase

>N20 G00 X1 Y1 [Enter]	Rapid to X1,Y1
>N22 Z0.25 [Enter]	Rapid to Z0.25 (Fig. 5-73)

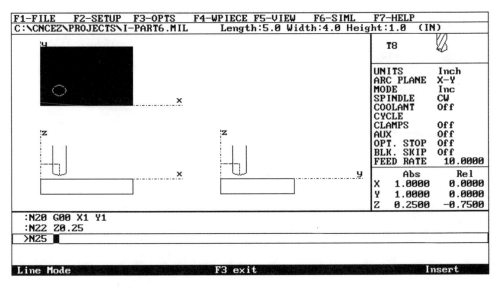

Figure 5-73 Rapid to Z0.25

>**N25 G91 G98 G82 Z-0.5 R0.25 P1 [Enter]** Cutter will drill in
−0.25 in., perform a
one-second dwell,
and retract to 0.25
above part (Fig. 5-74)

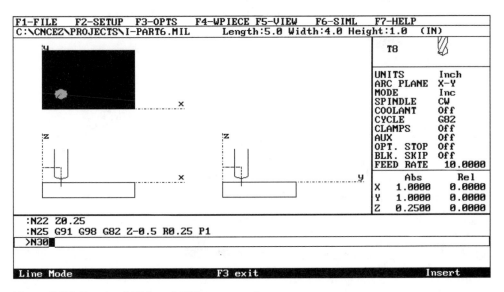

Figure 5-74 Result of G98 and G82 commands

>**N30 X1 [Enter]** Drill will move 1 in. to the right, drill in −0.25
in., perform a one-second dwell, and retract to
0.25 above part (Fig. 5-75)

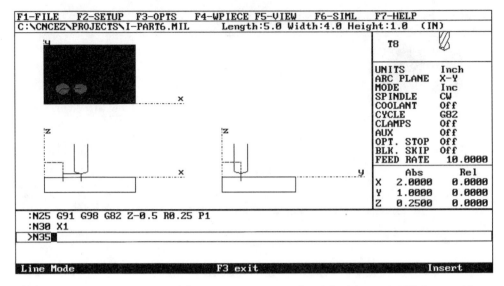

Figure 5-75 Entering X1 caused the cutter to move to the right 1 in. and drill down with a dwell and finally return to the retract plane.

>**N35 X2 [Enter]**   Drill will move 2 in. to the right, drill in –0.25 in., perform a one-second dwell, and retract to 0.25 above part (Fig. 5-76)

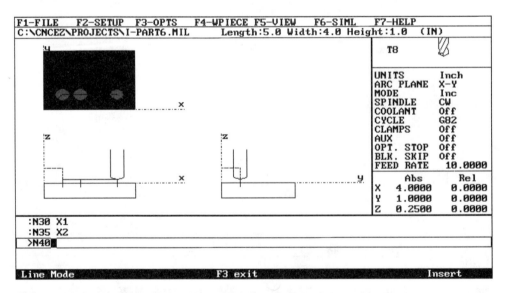

Figure 5-76 Result after entering X2 on N35

>**N40 Y1 [Enter]**   Drill will move 1 in. on the Y-axis, drill in –0.25 in., perform a one-second dwell, and retract to 0.25 above part

>**N45 Y1 [Enter]**   Drill will move 1 in. on the Y-axis, drill in –0.25 in., perform a one-second dwell, and retract to 0.25 above part (Fig. 5-77)

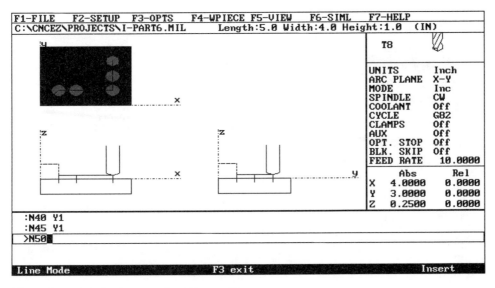

Figure 5-77 Result after entering Y1 on N45

>N50 X-2 [Enter]
>N55 X-1 [Enter]
>N60 Y-1 [Enter]
>N65 X1 [Enter]   (Fig. 5-78)

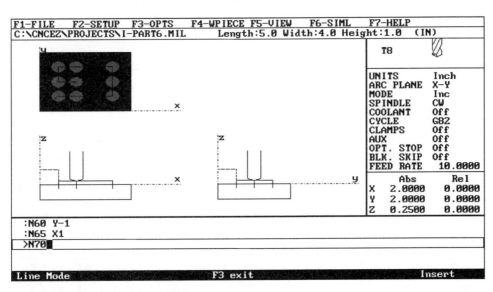

Figure 5-78 Result after final drill on N65

>N70 G80 G90 G00 Z1 [Enter]   Cancels the drill cycle and returns
                                to absolute programming
>N72 X0 Y0 [Enter]   (Fig. 5-79)

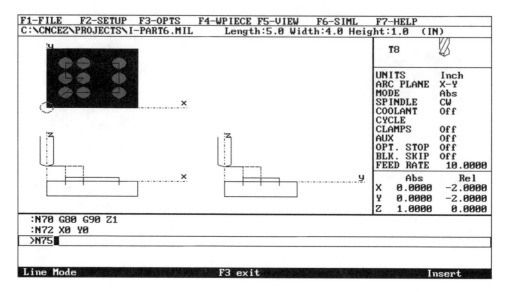

Figure 5-79 Result after entering the drill cycle cancel and G90 absolute with a rapid move

STEP 7: Program shutdown phase. Turn off the spindle and program end.

>N75 M05 [Enter]   Turn off spindle
>N80 M30 [Enter]   End of program (Fig. 5-80)

STEP 8: End of program

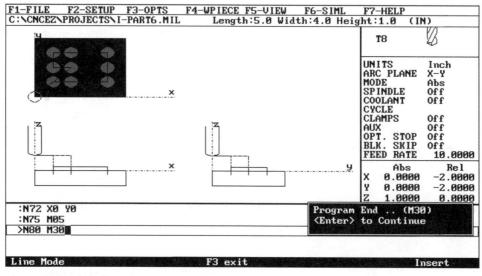

Figure 5-80 End of program message

LAB EXERCISE

1. What does the preparatory function G01 command do ? _____

   _____

   _____

   _____

2. How are tool length offsets called? _____

   _____

   _____

   _____

3. Give an example of a positioning rapid in move. _____

   _____

   _____

   _____

4. What does the letter address F stand for when a G01 command is
   programmed? _____

   _____

   _____

   _____

   _____

5. What plane does a G18 command specify? _____

   _____

   _____

   _____

6. Which G-code and additional letter address call up cutter compensation
   left? _____

   _____

   _____

   _____

   _____

7. Write out an example start line for a G81 drilling cycle. _____

   _____

   _____

   _____

8. Which M-code specifies program end, reset to start? _____

   _____

   _____

   _____

Chapter 6

CNC Turning

CHAPTER OBJECTIVES

After studying this chapter, the student should have knowledge of the following:

Programming for turning operations

Linear and circular interpolation

Tool nose radius compensation

Word address commands for the NC lathe

Use of multiple repetitive cycles

When working through this chapter, have the software running on your computer and enter the programs using the F6-SIMULATE (EDIT) or (MDI) options. Follow these following steps when simulating programming codes or creating new programs,

1. Select NEW from FILE menu.

   Enter a file name.

2. Change the tool library if required.

3. Select the WPIECE menu.

   Specify or load a new workpiece.

4. Select the SIMULATE menu.

   Use either EDIT if you want to create a program or run it or MDI simply to test a code.

Note: The completed sample programs are in the DEMOTURN directory.

G-CODES

G-codes are preparatory functions, which involve actual tool moves (for example, control of the machine). These include rapid moves, feed moves, radial feed moves, dwells, and roughing and profiling cycles. Most G-codes described here are modal, meaning that they remain active until cancelled by another G-code. The following codes are described in more detail in the following pages:

G00	Positioning In Rapid	Modal
G01	Linear Interpolation	Modal
G02	Circular Interpolation (CW)	Modal
G03	Circular Interpolation (CCW)	Modal
G04	Dwell	
G20	Inch Units	Modal
G21	Metric Units	Modal
G28	Automatic Zero Return	
G29	Return from Zero Return Position	
G40	Tool Nose Radius Compensation Cancel	Modal
G41	Tool Nose Radius Compensation Left	Modal

G42	Tool Nose Radius Compensation Right	Modal
G70	Finishing Cycle	Modal
G71	Turning Cycle	Modal
G72	Facing Cycle	Modal
G74	Peck Drilling Cycle	Modal
G75	Grooving Cycle	
G76	Threading Cycle	
G90	Absolute Programming	Modal
G91	Incremental Programming	Modal
G98	Linear Feedrate Per Time	Modal
G99	Feedrate Per Revolution	Modal

G00 POSITIONING IN RAPID

Format: `N_ G00 X_ Z_`

The G00 command is used primarily to move the tool to and from a cutting position. It is used most often before and after a G01, G02, and G03 command. It can also be used to position the tool for a tool change.

This command causes the tool to move at its fastest possible rate. This rate may vary among machines, but it will be the fastest possible. With G00, you can control one or two axes on one block of code. When programming two axes on one line, keep in mind that some controllers will move the tool in a straight line to the end point, whereas other will move each motor at its fastest possible rate and thereby cause the motion to be at a 45-degree angle and then straight.

Example: `N15 G90 G00 X1 Z0`

In this example the tool positions in rapid mode from its present location to a point at X1,Z0, as shown in Fig. 6-1.

Sample Program G00EX0:

Workpiece Size:	Length 4", Diameter 2"
Tool:	Tool #2, Right-hand Facing Tool
Tool Start Position:	X2,Z3

```
%
:1000
N5 G20 G40
```

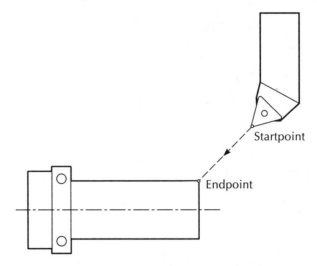

Figure 6-1 G00 causes the tool to move to the endpoint

```
N10  T0101
N15  M03
N20  G00 X1.9                    (Rapid to X1.9)
N25  Z0.1 M08                    (Rapid to Z0.1)
N30  G01 Z-1.25 F0.012
N35  G00 X4 Z3 M09               (Rapid to X4 and Z3)
N40  T0100 M05
N45  M30
```

Note: For safety and for good programming practice, you should never let the tool be rapid moved to the workpiece.

G01 LINEAR INTERPOLATION

Format: N_ G01 X_ Z_ F_

The G01 command executes all movement along a straight line at a particular feedrate. These straight-line feed moves may cut in one or two axes simultaneously. This command can be used for turning, facing, and tapering.

It is specified by G01 command, followed by the end point of the move, and then a specified feedrate.

Example: G01 Z-2.5 F0.01

In this example, the tool cuts a straight line from its present location to a point at Z–2.5 at a rate of 0.01 ipr (see Fig. 6-2).

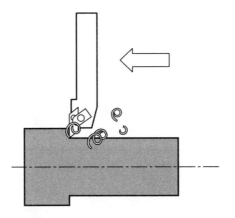

Figure 6-2 Tool cutting along the
Z-axis

Sample Program G01EX1:

Workpiece Size:	Length 4", Diameter 2.5"
Tool:	Tool #1, Right-hand Facing Tool
Tool Start Position:	X2,Z3

```
%
:1001
N5 G20 G40
N10 T0101
N15 M03
N20 G00 X2.375 M08
N22 Z0.1
N25 G01 Z-2.0 F0.015      (Feed to Z-2.0 at a feedrate of 0.015 ipr)
N30 G00 X2.5
N35 Z0.1
N40 X2.25
N45 G01 Z-1.75           (Feed to Z-1.75 at same feedrate)
N50 G00 X2.375
N55 Z0.1
N60 X2.125
N65 G01 Z-1.5            (Feed to Z-1.5 at same feedrate)
N70 G00 X2.25
N75 Z0.1
N80 X1.875
N85 G01 Z0              (Feed to 0 at same feedrate)
N90 X2.125 Z-0.125      (Feed to X2.125,Z-1.125 at same feedrate)
N95 G00 X4 M09
N100 Z3
N105 T0100 M05
N110 M30
```

G02 CIRCULAR INTERPOLATION (CW)

Format: N_ G02 X_ Z_ I_ K_ F_
   or N_ G02 X_ Z_ R_ F_

The G02 command executes all circular or radial cuts in a clockwise motion. It is specified by the G02 command, followed by the end point for the move, then the radius (the distance from start point to the center point) and a feedrate. Therefore the three requirements for cutting arcs are the following:

1. The end point

2. The radius R or I and K values that represent the distance and direction from the start point to the center

3. The feedrate

The radius is specified by defining the distance and direction from the arc's start point to center point, on both the X- and Z-axes. These values are identified by I and K variables, respectively. The R word, the value of the radius of the arc, can also be used.

Example: N05 G01 X2 Z-1 F0.012
              N10 G02 X0 Z0 I-1 K0
   or   N10 G02 X0 Z0 R0.5

In this example, the tool cuts a clockwise arc from its present location X2,Z-1 at a feedrate of 0.012 ipr (see Fig. 6-3). The tool cuts an arc from X2,Z–1 to the specified end point at X0,Z0. There is a change of 1 in. in the X from the arc's start point to its center point, so the I value is –1. There is no change in the Z from the start point to the center point, so the K value is 0.

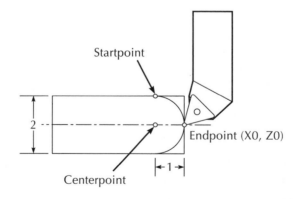

Figure 6-3 G02 example

Sample Program G02EX2:

Workpiece Size:	Length 4", Diameter 2"
Tool:	Tool #1, Right-hand Facing Tool
Tool Start Position:	X2,Z3

```
%
:1002
N5 G20 G40
N10 T0202
N15 M03
N20 G00 X1.7
N22 Z0.1 M08
N25 G01 Z-0.5 F0.012
N30 G00 X2
N35 Z0.1
N40 X1.4
N45 G01 Z-0.25
N50 G00 X2.1
N55 Z-1
N60 G01 X2
N65 G02 X0 Z0 I-1 K0        (90-degree CW arc feed move)
N70 G00 X2.1
N75 Z-1
N80 G01 X2
N85 G02 X2 Z-2 I0.5 K-0.5   (Partial CW arc feed move)
N90 G00 X4 Z3 M09
N95 T0200 M05
N100 M30
```

G03 CIRCULAR INTERPOLATION (CCW)

Format: N_ G03 X_ Z_ I_ K_ F_
  or   N_ G03 X_ Z_ R_ F_

The G03 command executes all radial cuts in a counterclockwise motion. It is specified by the G03 command, followed by the end point for the move, then the radius (the distance from the start point to the center point) and a feedrate.

The radius is specified by defining the distance and direction from the arc's start point to its center point on both the X- and Z-axes. These values are identified by I and K variables respectively. The R word, the value of the radius of the arc, can also be used.

Example: `G03 X2 Z-1 I0 K-1 F0.012`

In this example, the tool cuts a counterclockwise arc from its present position to X2,Z–1 at a feedrate of 0.012 ipr (see Fig. 6-4). There is no change in the X from the start point to the center point, so the I value is 0. There is a –1 difference between the arc's start point and its center point on the Z-axis, so the K value is –1.

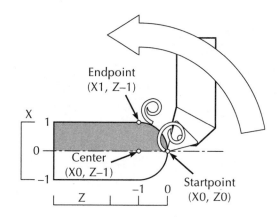

Figure 6-4 The tool cuts an arc from X0,Z0 to the diametrical point X2,Z–1.

Sample Program G03EX3:

Workpiece Size:	Length 4", Diameter 2"
Tool:	Tool #2, Right-hand Facing Tool
Tool Start Position:	X2,Z3

```
%
:1003
N5 G20 G40
N10 T0202
N15 M03
N20 G00 X1.7
N22 Z0.1 M08
N25 G01 Z-0.5 F0.012
N30 G00 X2
N35 Z0.1
N40 X1.4
N45 G01 Z-0.25
N50 G00 X1.5
N55 Z0.1
N60 X0
N65 G01 Z0
N70 G03 X2 Z-1 I0 K-1      (90-degree CCW arc feed move)
```

```
N75 G01 Z-2
N80 G03 X2 Z-1 I0.5 K0.5     (Partial CCW arc feed move)
N85 G00 X4 Z3 M09
N90 T0200 M05
N95 M30
```

G04 DWELL

Format: `N_ G04 P_`

The G04 command designates a period of time the tool is to wait in one particular position. It is used most frequently in drilling operations.

It is specified by the G04 command, followed by the letter address P, which defines the period of time in seconds.

Upon encountering a G04 command, the MCU halts all axes movement. The spindle, coolant, and other auxiliaries will continue to operate.

Example: `G04 P2`

In this example, the tool pauses at its current location for a period of 2 sec (Fig. 6-5).

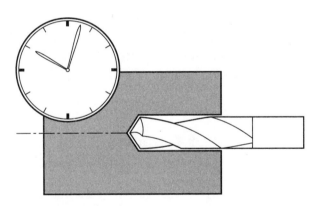

Figure 6-5 The drill pauses at its current location for a period of 2 sec. As only the tool motion is affected by the dwell, the spindle will continue to rotate.

Sample Program G04EX4:

Workpiece Size: Length 4", Diameter 2"
Tool: Tool #8, 1" Diameter Drill
Tool Start Position: X2,Z3

```
%
:1004
N5 G20 G40
```

```
N10  T0808
N15  M03
N20  G00  X0
N25  Z0.125
N30  G01  Z-2.0  F0.015
N35  G04  P0.5            (Dwell for 0.5 seconds)
N40  G00  Z3
N45  X4
N50  T0800  M05
N55  M30
```

G20 INCH UNITS

Format: N_ G20

The G20 command sets the system to accept all data in inch units.

Example: N15 G20

In this example, the MCU accepts any and all data as standard inch units. All decimals are indicated by a decimal point and trailing or leading zeros are optional.

This command may be placed on the same line as other system setting commands (for example, G90, G20, and G40).

In this controller, it rounds all figures to 0.0001 in.

Sample Program G20EX20:

Workpiece Size: Length 4", Diameter 1"
Tool: Tool #1, Right-hand Facing Tool
Tool Start Position: X2,Z3

```
%
:1020
N5   G90
N10  G20                        (All data in inch units)
N15  T0101
N20  M03
N25  G00  Z0.1
N30  X0.5
N35  G01  Z0  F0.015
N40  G03  X1  Z-0.25  I0  K-0.25
N45  G00  X4  Z3
```

```
N50 T0100 M05
N55 M30
```

Block N10 will switch the system to accept all data as inch units. As a result, block N40 will cut a 0.25 in. arc on the workpiece.

G21 METRIC UNITS

Format: N_ G21

The G21 command sets the system to accept all data in metric units, with the millimeter as the standard unit of measure.

Example: G21

In this example the MCU accepts any and all data as metric units. This controller requires all decimals to be indicated with a decimal point. Trailing or leading zeros are optional. This command can be placed on the same line as other system setting commands (for example, G90 and G40).

Sample Program G21EX21:

Workpiece Size:	Length 100 mm, Diameter 50 mm
Tool:	Tool #1, Neutral Tool
Tool Start Position:	X2",Z3"

```
%
:1013
N5 G90 G21 G40          (All data in millimeters)
N15 T0303
N17 M03
N20 G00 Z2 M08
N25 X45
N30 G01 Z-50 F1
N35 X40
N40 Z2
N45 X35
N50 Z-25
N55 X30
N60 Z-10
N65 G00 X100 M09
N70 Z100
N75 T0300 M05
N80 M02
```

G28 AUTOMATIC ZERO RETURN

Format: N_ G28

or N_ G28 X_ Y_ Z_

The G28 command is used for automatic tool changing. Basically it allows the existing tool to be positioned automatically to the predefined zero return position via an intermediate position.

All axes are positioned to the intermediate point at the rapid traverse rate, and then from the intermediate point to the zero return position (Fig. 6-6).

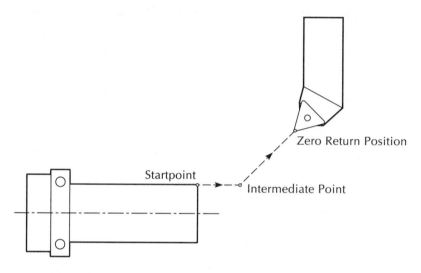

Figure 6-6 Shows cutter moving from the start point to the intermediate point and finally to the zero return position

Sample Program G28EX28:

Workpiece Size:	Length 4", Diameter 2.5"
Tool:	Tool #1, Right-hand Tool
Tool Start Position:	X2",Z3"
Zero Return Position:	X2",Z3"

```
%
:1028
N5 G20 G40
N10 T0101
N12 M03 M08
N15 G00 X2.25
N20 Z0.1
N25 G01 Z-2 F0.012
N30 G28 X4 Z0.5 M09    (Rapid move to zero return position)
N35 T0100 M05
N40 M02
```

G29 RETURN FROM ZERO RETURN POSITION

Format: N_ G29

   or   N_ G29 X_ Y_ Z_

The G29 command is used immediately after a G28 command to return the tool to a specified point via the intermediate point specified by the previous G28 command (Fig. 6-7).

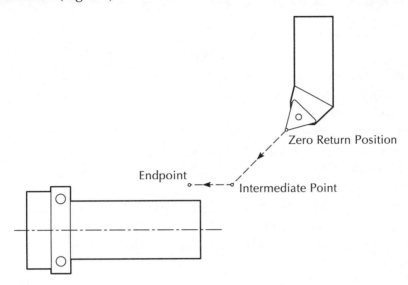

Zero Return Position

Endpoint   Intermediate Point

Figure 6-7 Shows cutter moving from the start point to the intermediate point and finally to the zero return position.

Sample Program G29EX29:

Workpiece Size:	Length 4", Diameter 2.5"
Tool:	Tool #1, Right-hand Tool
	Tool #2, Finishing Tool
Tool Start Position:	X2",Z3"
Zero Return Position:	X2",Z3"

```
%
:1029
N5 G20
N10 T0101
N12 M03 M08
N15 G00 X2.25
N20 Z0.1
N25 G01 Z-2 F0.012
N30 G28 X4 Z0.5 M09
N35 M05
N40 T02
```

```
N45  M03  M08
N50  G29  X2.25  Z0.1        (Return from zero return position)
N55  G01  Z-2
N60  G28  X4  Z0.5  M09
N65  T0100  M05
N70  M02
```

G40 TOOL NOSE RADIUS (TNR) COMPENSATION CANCEL

Format: `N_  G40`

The G40 command cancels any compensation that was applied to the tool
during a program and acts as a safeguard to cancel any cutter compensation
applied previously.

TNR compensation is used to compensate for the small radius on single-
point turning and boring tools. Normally, CNC programs are written so that
the tool tip follows the toolpath. However, some tools have a small radius on
the cutting edge that will make the point programmed not be actually on the
cutting surface. In this case, the tool must be offset either left or right. However,
tool nose radius compensation is modal, so the compensation must be canceled
once it is no longer required. The G40 command does this.

Sample Program G40EX40:

Workpiece Size:	Length 4", Diameter 2"
Tool:	Tool #1, Right-hand Facing Tool
Tool Start Position:	X2,Z3

```
%
:1040
N5  G20  G40              (Set TNR cancel at beginning)
N10  T0101
N15  M03  M08
N17  G41
N20  G00  Z-0.1
N25  X2.1
N30  G01  X1  F0.012
N35  G40  G00  Z3  M09    (TNR cancel with rapid to start)
N40  X4
N45  T0100  M05
N50  M02
```

G41 TOOL NOSE RADIUS COMPENSATION LEFT

Format: N_ G41

The G41 command applies tool nose radius compensation left to allow the programmer to program with turning and boring tools using actual coordinates, not allowing for the radius of the tool. The offset register value will compensate for the difference caused by the small radius on the tool. (See Fig. 6-8.)

TNR compensation is used to compensate for the small radius on single-point turning and boring tools.

Once compensation is instated, it remains in effect until cancelled by a G40 command. You must remember to cancel tool nose radius compensation when you return a tool to the toolchange position.

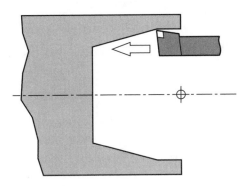

Figure 6-8

Sample Program G41EX41:

Workpiece Size:	Length 4", Diameter 2"
Tool:	Tool #8, Left-hand Facing Tool
	Tool #10, 1" Drill
	Tool #12, Center Drill
Tool Start Position:	X2,Z3

```
%
:1041
N5 G20 G40
N10 T1212 M08
N15 G98 M03 S2000
N20 G00 X0
N25 Z0.1
N30 G01 Z-0.2 F2
N35 G00 Z3
N40 X4 T1200
N45 T1010
N50 G00 X0
```

```
N55  Z0.1
N60  G74 Z-2 F0.5 D0 K0.25
N65  G00 Z3
N70  T1000 X4
N75  G99 T0808
N80  G41 G00 X0.8                    (TNR compensation left)
N85  Z0.2
N90  G01 Z-1.75 F0.012
N95  X0.9
N100 Z-0.25
N105 G03 X2 Z0 R0.5
N110 G40 G00 X4 Z3 M09
N115 T0800 M05
N120 M02
```

G42 TOOL NOSE RADIUS COMPENSATION RIGHT

Format: N_ G42 D_

The G42 command applies tool nose radius compensation right to allow the programmer to program with turning and boring tools using actual coordinates, not allowing for the radius of the tool. The offset register value will compensate for the difference caused by the small radius on the tool. (See Fig. 6-9.)

TNR compensation is used to compensate for the small radius on single-point turning and boring tools.

Once compensation is instated, it remains in effect until cancelled by a G40 command. You must remember to cancel tool nose radius compensation when you return a tool to the toolchange position.

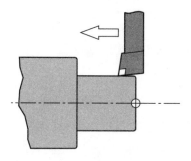

Figure 6-9

Sample Program G42EX42:

Workpiece Size:	Length 4", Diameter 2"
Tool:	Tool #1, Right-hand Facing Tool
	Tool #2, Right-hand Finishing Tool
Tool Start Position:	X2,Z3

```
%
:1042
N5 G20 G40
N10 T0101
N15 M03
N20 G00 Z0.1 M08
N25 X1.75
N30 G01 Z-2 F0.012
N35 G00 X2 Z0.1
N40 X1.5
N45 G01 Z-1.5
N50 G00 X1.75 Z0.1
N55 X1
N60 G01 Z0
N65 G03 X1.5 Z-0.25 I0 K-0.25
N70 G00 X4 Z3 T0100
N75 G00 T0202
N80 G42 G00 X0          (TNR compensation right)
N85 Z0.1
N90 G01 Z0
N95 X1
N100 G03 X1.5 Z-0.25 R0.25
N105 G01 Z-1.5
N110 X1.75
N115 Z-2
N120 X2.1
N125 G40 G00 X4 Z3 M09
N130 T0200 M05
N135 M02
```

G70 FINISHING CYCLE

Format: N_ G70

The G70 command calculates the finished part profile, then executes a finishing (or profile) pass on the finished workpiece.

It is specified by entering G70, followed by the letter address P (start block) and the letter address Q (end block). The main concept is that the programmer defines the finish contour of the part. This command is generally used to finish up after a G71 or G72 command.

When the G70 command is executed, it reads all program blocks, then formulates a profiling cycle. This finishing pass is then cut, following the finish contour of the part. The program then jumps to the line preceding the command.

This command is used to profile a part once all material-removing operations have been completed.

Example: G70 P20 Q45

In this example the MCU executes all commands between N20 and N45, resulting in, essentially, a profile pass (Fig. 6-10).

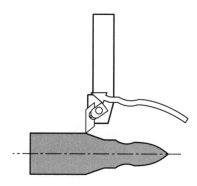

Figure 6-10 The tool follows the profile of the part specified by the G70 command. All data between the start and end blocks are considered.

Sample Program G70EX70:

Workpiece Size:	Length 4", Diameter 2"
Tool:	Tool #1, Right-hand Facing Tool
	Tool #2, Right-hand Finishing Tool
Tool Start Position:	X2,Z3

```
%
:1070
N5 G90 G20
N10 T0101
N15 M03
N20 G00 X2 Z0.1 M08
N35 G71 P40 Q55 U0.05 W0.05 D625 F0.012
N40 G01 X0 Z0
N45 G03 X0.5 Z-0.25 I0 K-0.25
N50 G01 X1.75 Z-1.0
N55 X2.1
N60 T0100 G00 X4 Z3
N65 T0202
N70 G00 X2 Z0.1
N75 G70 P40 Q55 F0.006          (Finish cycle from N40 to N55)
N80 G00 X4 Z3 M09
N85 T0200 M05
N90 M30
```

G71 TURNING CYCLE

Format: N_ G71_ P_ Q_ U_ W_ D_ F_

P   Start block of segment

Q   End block of segment

U   Amount of stock to be left for finishing in X

W   Amount of stock to be left for finishing in Z

D   Depth of cut for each pass in thousands of an inch or millimeter

F   Feedrate for finish pass

The G71 command automatically turns down a workpiece to a specified diameter at a specified depth of cut. It reads a program segment and determines the number of passes, the depth of cut for each pass, and the number of repeat passes for the cycle.

The G71 command can cut four types of patterns. Each must be programmed as a separate group of blocks. Cutting is done by parallel moves of the tool in the Z-axis direction and the U and W signs are as shown in Fig. 6-11.

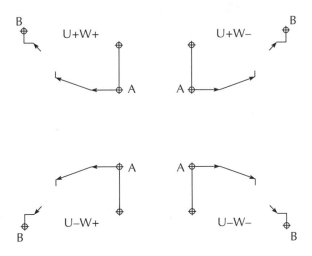

Figure 6-11 Positive and negative U and W signs

Example: G71 P40 Q100 U.025 W.025 D625 F0.012

In this example, the MCU reads the data between N40 and N100 and removes material according to this profile. The cycle has a depth of cut of 1/16 in. for each pass at 0.012 ipr. (See Fig. 6-12.)

In the following sample program use the SIMULATE EDIT option.

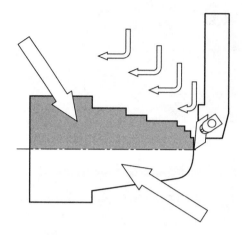

Figure 6-12 The G71 command turns down the part to the diameter specified in the program segment. The upper half of the part shows the G71 command and how it "steps" down to size. The lower half of the profile shows how the G70 command cleans up with a finishing pass.

Sample Program G71EX71:

Workpiece Size:	Length 4", Diameter 2"
Tool:	Tool #1, Right-hand Facing Tool
	Tool #2, Right-hand Finishing Tool
Tool Start Position:	X2,Z3

```
%
:1071
N5 G90 G20
N10 T0101
N15 M03
N20 G00 X2 Z0.1 M08
N35 G71 P40 Q55 U0.05 W0.05 D625 F0.012  (Rough turning)
N40 G01 X0 Z0
N45 G03 X1 Z-0.5 I0 K-0.5
N50 G01 Z-1.0
N55 X2.1 Z-1.5
N60 T0100 G00 X4 Z3
N65 T0202
N70 G00 X2 Z0.1
N75 G70 P40 Q55 F0.006
N80 G00 X4 Z3 M09
N85 T0200 M05
N90 M30
```

G72 ROUGH FACING CYCLE

Format: N_ G72 P_ Q_ U_ W_ D_ F_

P   Start block

Q   End block

U   Amount of stock to be left for finishing in X

W   Amount of stock to be left for finishing in Z

D   Depth of cut for finish pass in thousands of an inch or millimeter

F   Feedrate (this is optional)

The G72 command automatically faces off a part to a predefined depth of cut, with preset offsets and feedrates.

Example: G72 P25 Q45 U0.05 W0.05 D500 F0.012

In this example, the MCU reads the commands in N25 through N45, then executes a facing operation, in abidance with the profile defined. (See Fig. 6-13.)

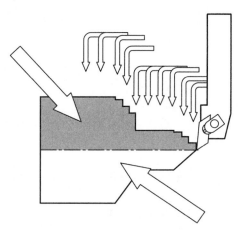

Figure 6-13 The G72 command roughs out the profile as specified in the program segment. Then the G70 command cleans it up with a finish pass.

The G72 command must either be inserted into the program after the program segment is completed or be written in the File Editor. If the command is written in simulate EDIT mode, the program will look for the start and end blocks, which do not yet exist, thereby creating errors.

Sample Program G72EX72:

Workpiece Size: Length 4", Diameter 1"

Tool: Tool #1, Right-hand Facing Tool

                                    Tool #2, Right-hand Finishing Tool

Tool Start Position: X2,Z3

```
%
:1072
N5 G90 G20
N10 T0101
N15 M03
N20 G00 X1 Z0.1 M08
N25 G72 P30 Q50 U0.05 W0.05 D500 F0.012   (Rough facing)
N30 G01 X0 Z0.1
N35 X0.25
N40 Z-0.125
N45 X0.5 Z-0.25
N50 G02 X1 Z-0.5 I0.25 K0
N55 G00 X4 Z3 T0100
N60 T0202
N65 G00 X1 Z0.1
N70 G70 P30 Q50 F0.006
N75 G00 X4
N80 Z3 M09
N85 T0200 M05
N90 M30
```

G74 PECK DRILLING CYCLE

Format: N_ G74 X0 Z_K_ F_

The G74 command executes a peck drilling cycle with automatic retracts and incremental depths of cut.

    This command is specified by G74 and several letter addresses as follows:

X0   X is always 0

Z   Total depth

K   Peck depth

F   Feed rate

Example: G74 X0 Z-1.0 K0.125 F0.015

In this example, a hole is peck drilled to a total depth of 1 in. using 0.125 in. for the depth of each peck. (See Fig. 6-14.)

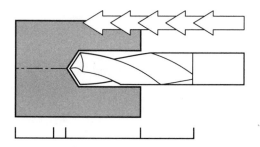

Figure 6-14 The G74 command relies on the command variables to execute properly. Z is the desired total depth, and K is how far the tool drills on each peck before retracting.

Sample Program G74EX74:

Workpiece Size:	Length 4", Diameter 1"
Tool:	Tool #12, Center Drill
	Tool #10, 1/2" Drill
Tool Start Position:	X2,Z3

```
%
:1074
N5 G20 G98
N10 T1212 M08
N15 M03 S2000
N20 G00 X0
N25 Z0.1
N30 G01 Z-0.2 F2
N35 G00 Z3
N40 X3 T1200
N45 T1010
N50 G00 X0
N55 Z0.1
N60 G74 X0 Z-1.5 K0.125 F0.5   (Drilling cycle)
N65 G00 Z3
N70 X4 M09
N75 T1000 M05
N80 M30
```

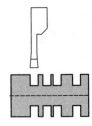

G75 GROOVING CYCLE

Format: `N_ G75 X_ Z_ F_ D_ I_ K_`

X   Diameter of groove

Z   Z position of groove

F   Incremental retract

D   Depth/X offset

K   Z movement

I   X movement

The G75 command is used to machine grooves. (See Fig. 6-15.)

Example: `G75 X0.25 Z-0.75 F0.125 I0.125 K0.125`

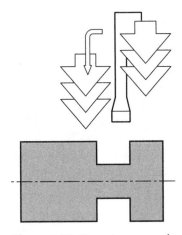

Figure 6-15 Grooving example

This command defaults to the last specified feedrate. The F address is the retract distance, so the feedrate cannot be set within the grooving cycle.

Sample Program G75EX75:

Workpiece Size:	Length 4", Diameter 1"
Tool:	Tool #5, Grooving Tool
Tool Start Position:	X2,Z3

```
%
:1075
N5 G90 G20
N10 T0505 F0.015
N15 M03
```

```
N20 G00 Z-0.5 M08
N25 X1.2
N30 G75 X0.5 Z-0.75 F0.125 D0 I0.125 K0.125   (Grooving
                                               cycle)
N35 G00 X4
N40 Z3 M09
N45 T0500 M05
N50 M30
```

G76 THREADING CYCLE

Format: N_ G76 X_ Z_ D_ K_ A_ F_

The G76 command performs all threading operations in a cycle, with automatic depth change and toolpath calculation.

It is specified by the G76 command and several letter addresses as follows:

X   Minor diameter of thread

Z   Position at end of thread

D   Depth of first pass (the control uses the first depth of cut to determine the number of passes)

K   Depth of thread

F   Pitch of thread (thread pitch = 1/thread/in.)

A   Tool angle (if the tool angle is given, the tool will continue to cut on the leading edge of the tool; if no tool angle is given the tool will cut on both sides)

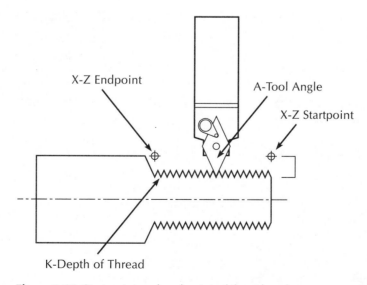

Figure 6-18 Start point and end point of thread cycle

Example: `G76 X0.5 Z-1.0 D625 K0.25 A55 F0.1`

In this example, the tool cuts a thread starting at its present location and ending at the specified XZ end point. The D value specifies each cut depth, and the K defines the overall depth. The A defines tool angle, and the F defines the pitch.

Sample Program G76EX76:

Workpiece Size:	Length 4", Diameter 1"
Tool:	Tool #6, Neutral Tool
Tool Start Position:	X2,Z3

```
%
:1076
N5 G90 G20
N10 T0606 M08
N15 M03
N20 G00 X1
N25 Z0.1
N25 G76 X0.96 Z-2 D625 K0.125 A55 F0.1  (Threading cycle)
N30 G00 X4
N35 Z3 M09
N35 T0600 M05
N40 M30
```

G90 ABSOLUTE POSITIONING

Format: `N_ G90`

The G90 command sets the system to accept all coordinates as absolute data and can be switched only with the G91 command.

Example: <u>G90</u>

In this example, any coordinate data entered after this command are absolute coordinates.

Sample Program G90EX90:

| *Workpiece Size:* | Length 4", Diameter 2" |
| *Tool:* | Tool #1, Right-hand Tool |

```
%
:1090
N5 G90      (Input all data in absolute mode)
```

```
N10  G20
N15  T0101
N20  M03
N25  G00 X1.75 M08
N30  Z0.1
N35  G01 Z-2 F0.015
N40  G00 X2 Z0.1
N45  X1.5
N50  G01 Z-1.75
N55  G00 X1.75 Z0.1
N60  X1.25
N65  G01 Z-1.5
N70  G00 X1.5 Z0.1
N75  X1
N80  G01 Z-1.25
N85  X2 Z-2.25
N90  G00 X4 Z3 M09
N95  T0100 M09
N100 M02
```

G91 INCREMENTAL POSITIONING

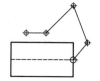

Format: N_ G91

The G91 command sets the system to accept all coordinates as incremental data and can be switched with the G90 command within a program.

Example: G91

In this example, any coordinates entered after this command are incremental coordinates.

Sample Program G91EX91:

Workpiece Size:	Length 4", Diameter 2"
Tool:	Tool #1, Right-hand Tool

```
%
:1091
N5  G90 G20
N10 T0101
N15 M03
N25 G00 X1.75
N30 Z0.1
N35 G91 G01 Z-1.85 F0.015    (Data input in Incremental)
```

```
N40 G00 X0.25 Z1.85
N45 X-0.5
N50 G01 Z-1.6
N55 G00 X0.25 Z1.6
N60 X-0.5
N65 G01 Z-1.35
N70 G00 X0.25 Z1.35
N75 X-0.5
N80 G01 Z-1.1
N85 X1 Z-1
N90 G90 G00 X4 Z3 M09
N95 T0100 M05
N100 M02
```

G98 LINEAR FEEDRATE PER TIME

Format: N_ G98

The G98 command sets the linear feedrate to units per time (minutes). The type of units (inch or millimeter) depends on which type of unit is active.

It causes all feedmoves (G01, G02, and G03, as well as the canned cycles) to accept units per minute as the defining rate. It sets only the feedrate to units per minute; it does not set the feedrate.

Sample Program G98EX98:

Workpiece Size:	Length 4", Diameter 2"
Tool:	Tool #10, 1" Drill
	Tool #12, Center Drill
Tool Start Position:	X2,Z3

```
%
:1041
N5 G20 G40 G99
N10 T1212 M08
N15 G98 M03 S2000          (Set feed in inches per minute)
N20 G00 X0
N25 Z0.1
N30 G01 Z-0.2 F2
N35 G00 Z3
N40 X4 T1200
N45 T1010
N50 G00 X0
N55 Z0.1
```

```
N60 G74 Z-1 F0.5 D0 K0.25
N65 G99 G00 Z3                    (Set feed in inches per revolution)
N70 T1000 X4
N75 M05
N80 M02
```

G99 FEEDRATE PER REVOLUTION

Format: N_ G99

The G99 command sets the feedrate to units per revolution. The type of unit
(inch or millimeter) depends on which type of units is active.

It causes all feedmoves (G01, G02, and G03, as well as the canned cycles)
to accept units per revolution as the defining rate. It is the default setting on
most CNC turning centers.

Sample Program G99EX99:

Workpiece Size:	Length 4", Diameter 2"
Tool:	Tool #8, Left-hand Facing Tool
	Tool #10, 1" Drill
	Tool #12, Center Drill
Tool Start Position:	X2,Z3

```
%
:1041
N5 G20 G40 G99                   (Set to inches per revolution)
N10 T1212 M08
N15 G98 M03 S2000                (Set to inches per minute)
N20 G00 X0
N25 Z0.1
N30 G01 Z-0.2 F2
N35 G00 Z3
N40 X4 T1200
N45 T1010
N50 G00 X0
N55 Z0.1
N60 G74 Z-1 F0.5 D0 K0.25
N65 G99 G00 Z3                   (Reset to inches per revolution)
N70 T1000 X4
N75 T0101
N80 G00 X0.75
N85 Z0.1
N90 G01 Z0 F0.015
```

```
N95 X1.5
N100 G03 X2 Z-0.25 I0 K-0.25
N105 G01 X1.75 Z-1.5
N110 X2 Z-3
N115 G00 X4 Z3 M09
N120 T0100 M05
N125 M02
```

M-CODES

M-codes are miscellaneous functions, which include actions necessary for machining but not those that are actual tool movements (for example, auxiliary functions). These include spindle on and off, tool changes, coolant on and off, program stops, and other similar related functions. The following codes are described in more detail in the following pages:

M00	Program Stop
M01	Optional Program Stop
M02	Program End
M03	Spindle On Clockwise
M04	Spindle On Counterclockwise
M05	Spindle Stop
M07	Coolant 1 On
M08	Coolant 2 On
M09	Coolant Off
M30	End of Program, Reset to Start

Note: Two or more M-codes cannot be included on the same line.

M00 PROGRAM STOP

Format: N_ M00

The M00 command is a temporary program stop function. All functions are temporarily suspended and remain so until reactivated by user input.

When the MCU encounters an M00 command, it shuts down all machine controls (spindle, coolant, all axes, and auxiliaries). The MCU then waits for user input to continue the program. The screen prompt "ENTER to

CONTINUE" is displayed on screen. The MCU will reinstate all functions only after Enter is pressed.

The MCU retains all program blocks and coordinate data until after the machine control is returned to its normal state. (The computer remembers all points and tool position information so that there is no chance of "losing the zero.")

Example: `N250 M00`

In this example, the program cycles through until the M00 command is encountered. The machine and all operations then halt at `N250` and await user input to continue the program.

Sample Program M00EX0:

Workpiece Size:	Length 4", Diameter 2"
Tool:	Tool #1, Right-hand Tool
Tool Start Position:	X2,Z3

```
%
:1000
N5 T0101
N10 M03
N15 G00 X2.1 M08
N20 Z-0.1
N25 G01 X0 F0.015
N30 G00 X4 Z0
N35 M00                    (Program stop—MCU waits)
N40 X2.1 Z-0.3
N45 G01 X1.4 Z-0.2
N50 X1
N55 Z0.1
N60 G00 Z3
N65 X4 M09
N70 T0100 M05
N75 M02
```

M01 OPTIONAL PROGRAM STOP

Format: `N_ M01`

The M01 command is an optional program stop that stops the program only if the M01 switch is set to ON.

In the OPTIONS menu, is an option entitled "O.Stop." Its default position is OFF(-). To turn it on, highlight it with the cursor, then press Enter. The switch will be set to ON(+).

With the M01 switch on, the MCU halts all machine functions temporarily. The monitor displays the screen prompt "ENTER to CONTINUE." After the user presses Enter, the lathe will carry on as before, without any loss of position.

Example: N25 M01

In this example, the machine and all operations halt temporarily at N25, provided the switch is on.

The following sample program is identical to that for the M00 command except M00 is replaced with M01. If the M01 switch is not turned on, the program will ignore the command.

Sample Program M01EX1:

Workpiece Size:	Length 4", Diameter 2"
Tool:	Tool #1, Right-hand Tool
Tool Start Position:	X2,Z3
Optional Stop:	On

```
%
:1000
N5 T0101
N10 M03
N15 G00 X2.1 M08
N20 Z-0.1
N25 G01 X0 F0.015
N30 G00 X4 Z0
N35 M01                    (Optional program stop)
N40 X2.1 Z-0.3
N45 G01 X1.4 Z-0.2
N50 X1
N55 Z0.1
N60 G00 Z3
N65 X4 M09
N70 T0100 M05
N75 M02
N80
```

M02 PROGRAM END

Format: N_ M02

The M02 command indicates the end of the main program cycle operation. Upon encountering this command, the MCU switches off all machine operations (spindle, coolant, all axes, and any auxiliaries) and terminates the program.

The M02 command is always by itself on the last line of the program.

Sample Program M02EX2:

Workpiece Size:	Length 4", Diameter 2"
Tool:	Tool #1, Right-hand Tool
	Tool #2, Right-hand Finishing Tool
Tool Start Position:	X2,Z3

```
%
:1070
N5 G90 G20
N10 T0101
N15 M03
N20 G00 X2 Z0.1 M08
N35 G71 P40 Q60 U0.05 W0.05 D625 F0.012
N40 G01 X0 Z0
N45 G03 X0.5 Z-0.25 I0 K-0.25
N50 G01 X1.5 Z-0.75
N55 Z-1.25
N60 X2.1
N65 T0100 G00 X4 Z3
N70 T0202
N75 G00 X2 Z0.1
N80 G70 P40 Q60 F0.006
N85 G00 X2.125 Z-1.5
N90 G01 X2 F0.012
N95 G02 Z-3 R2
N100 G00 X4 Z3 M09
N90 T0200 M05
N95 M02                    (Program end)
```

M03 SPINDLE ON CLOCKWISE

Format: N_ M03 S_

The M03 command switches the spindle on so that it rotates clockwise.

The spindle will rotate clockwise at the specified speed (rpm) until instructed by the MCU to stop. You can set up the rpm by entering an S code followed by the desired value (for example, S2000). Otherwise the MCU will determine the rpm based on the desired feedrate per revolution.

Example: `M03 S2000`

In this example, the spindle is turned on at an initial rate of 2000 rpm.

Sample Program M03EX3:

Workpiece Size: Length 100 mm, Diameter 50 mm
Tool: Tool #1, Neutral Tool
Tool Start Position: X2",Z3"

```
%
:1021
N5 G90 G21 G40
N15 T0303
N17 M03                    (Spindle on clockwise)
N20 G00 Z2 M08
N25 X45
N30 G01 Z-60 F1
N35 X40
N40 Z-10
N45 X35
N50 Z-25
N55 X30
N60 Z-10
N65 G00 X100 M09
N70 Z100
N75 T0300 M05              (Spindle off)
N80 M02
```

M04 SPINDLE ON COUNTERCLOCKWISE

Format: `N_ M04 S_`

The M04 command switches the spindle on so that is rotates counterclockwise. It is specified by the M04 command, the letter address S, and then the required rpm.

The spindle will rotate counterclockwise at the specified speed (rpm) until instructed by the MCU to stop.

You can change the spindle speed at any point during the program by redefining the S value.

Example: `M04 S2000`

In this example, the spindle is turned on at an initial rate of 2000 rpm.

Sample Program M04EX4:

Workpiece Size:	Length 4", Diameter 2"
Tool:	Tool #1, Right-hand Finishing Tool
Tool Start Position:	X2,Z3

```
%
:1002
N5 G20 G40
N10 T0202
N15 M04                        (Spindle on counterclockwise)
N20 G00 X1.7
N22 Z0.1 M08
N25 G01 Z-0.5 F0.012
N30 G00 X2
N35 Z0.1
N40 X1.4
N45 G01 Z-0.25
N50 G00 X1.5 Z0.1
N55 X1
N60 G01 Z-0.1
N65 G00 X1.1 Z0.1
N70 X0
N75 G01 Z0
N80 G03 X2 Z-1 I0 K-1
N85 G00 X4 Z3 M09
N90 T0200 M05                  (Spindle off)
N95 M02
```

M05 SPINDLE STOP

Format: N_ M05

The M05 command stops the spindle rotation.

Although the commands (M00, M01, M02, and M30) switch the spindle off temporarily, only the M05 command switches the spindle off directly.

Example: N350 M05

In this example, the machine spindle stops at N350.

Sample Program M05EX5:

Workpiece Size:	Length 4", Diameter 2"
Tool:	Tool #1, Right-hand Tool
Tool Start Position:	X2,Z3

```
%
:1001
N5 G20 G40
N10 T0101
N15 M03
N20 G00 X2.375 M08
N22 Z0.1
N25 G01 Z-2.0 F0.015
N30 G00 X2.5
N35 Z0.1
N40 X2.25
N45 G01 Z-2
N50 G00 X2.375
N55 Z0.1
N60 X2.125
N65 G01 Z-2
N70 G00 X2.25
N75 Z0.1
N80 X1.875
N85 G01 Z0
N90 X2.125 Z-0.125
N95 G00 X4 M09
N100 Z3
N105 T0100 M05          (Turn spindle off)
N110 M30
```

M07 COOLANT 1 ON

Format: N_ M07

The M07 command switches on the first coolant flow.

Coolant is required when you are turning materials such as mild steel. It provides lubrication, cools the tool, and carries away some of the chips. When you are machining lighter materials such as aluminium or wax, coolant is not always required.

Example: N475 M07

In this example, the coolant flow from the number one hose is turned on when the MCU encounters the M007 command.

The status of this command can be verified by inspecting the status window for the coolant on prompt. M07 is turned off by the M09 command after turning is completed.

Sample Program M07EX7:

Workpiece Size: Length 4", Diameter 2"
Tool: Tool #3, Neutral Tool
Tool Start Position: X2,Z3

```
%
:1021
N5 G90 G20 G40
N15 T0303
N17 M03
N20 G00 X2.1 M07        (Coolant Hose #1 on)
N25 Z-1.25
N30 G01 X1.75 F0.015
N35 Z-2.75
N40 X1.5
N45 Z-1.25
N50 G02 Z0 R1 F0.006
N55 G00 X4 Z3 M09        (Coolant off)
N60 T0300 M05
N65 M02
```

M08 COOLANT 2 ON

Format: N_ M08

The M08 command switches on the second coolant flow.

Example: N75 M08

In this example, the coolant flow from the number two hose is turned on when the MCU encounters this command.

Sample Program M08EX8:

Workpiece Size: Length 4", Diameter 2"
Tool: Tool #1, Neutral Tool
Tool Start Position: X2,Z3

```
%
:1008
N5 G90 G20 G40
N15 T0303
N17 M03
N20 G00 X2.1 M08        (Coolant Hose #2 on)
```

```
N25 Z-1.25
N30 G01 X1.75 F0.015
N35 Z-2.75
N40 Z-2.5
N45 X1.5
N50 Z-1.5
N55 G00 X2.1
N60 Z-1
N65 G01 X1.75
N70 Z-0.25
N75 G00 X4
N80 Z3 M09               (Coolant off)
N85 T0300 M05
N90 M02
```

M09 COOLANT OFF

Format: N_ M09

The M09 command switches off the coolant flow.

The coolant is switched off automatically when a tool change, a program end, or program stop is encountered. The operator is responsible for switching the coolant off when required. Refer to the status window to verify if coolant is on or off.

Example: N10 M09

In this example, all coolants (from both hose number one and hose number two) is turned off when the MCU encounters the M09 command.

Sample Program M09EX9:

Workpiece Size:	Length 4", Diameter 2"
Tool:	Tool #1, Neutral Tool
Tool Start Position:	X2,Z3

```
%
:1009
N5 G90 G20 G40
N15 T0303
N17 M03
N20 G00 X2.1 M08         (Coolant on)
N25 Z-2.75
N30 G01 X1.75 F0.015
N35 Z-0.25
```

```
N40  X1.5
N45  Z-1.5
N50  X1.25
N55  X1.5 Z-0.25
N60  G00 X4
N65  Z3 M09                    (Coolant hose off)
N70  T0300 M05
N75  M02
```

M30 END OF PROGRAM, RESET TO START

Format: `N_ M30`

The M30 command stops program execution and awaits user input before continuing the program. It then rewinds the program memory to the beginning. On older CNC or NC machines that use paper tape, this command will rewind the tape to the beginning of the program.

The screen prompt "ENTER to CONTINUE" is displayed on screen (as a safety measure to prevent accidental program end).

Example: `N50 M30`

In this example, program execution is stopped at `N50`.

Sample Program M30EX30:

Workpiece Size:	Length 4", Diameter 2"
Tool:	Tool #1, Right-hand Tool
Tool Start Position:	X2,Z3

```
  %
:1002
N5  G20 G40
N10  T0101
N15  M03
N20  G00 Z0.05 X1.75 M08
N25  G01 Z-2.5 F0.015
N30  X2 Z-2.75
N35  G00 X2.1 Z0.05
N40  X1.25
N45  G01 Z0
N50  G03 X1.75 Z-0.25 I0 K-0.25
N55  G00 X4 Z3 M09
N60  T0100 M05
N65  M30
```

LETTER ADDRESSES

Letter addresses are variables used in G- and M-codes. Most G-codes contain a variable, defined by the programmer, for each specific function. Each letter used in CNC programming is called an address or word. The words used for programming are as follows:

F	Assigns a feedrate
G	Preparatory function,
I	X-axis location of ARC center
K	Z-axis location of ARC center
M	Miscellaneous function
N	Block number (specifies the start of a block)
P	Start Block Dwell time
Q	Block End
D	Depth
R	Radius
S	Sets the spindle speed
T	Specifies the tool to be used
A	Tool Angle
U	X stock
W	Z stock
X	X-axis Coordinate
Z	Z-axis Coordinate

Word addresses are described in more detail next.

Letter	Address	Description
F	Feedrate	Specifies a feedrate in feed (inches or millimeters) per minute or feed per revolution.
		In threading, designates the thread pitch. Note that some controllers use F to designate the thread lead.
G	Preparatory function	Specifies a preparatory function. Allows for various modes (for example, rapid and feed) to be set during a program.

Letter	Address	Description
I	X value for G02/G03	Specifies the X distance and direction from a start point to a center point in the X-axis (see G02 and G03).
K	Z value for G02/G03	Specifies the Z distance and direction from a start point to a center point in the Z-axis (see G02 and G03).
		Also can specify the final depth of a thread during threading operations.
M	Miscellaneous code	Controls coolant on/off, spindle rotation, and so on.
N	Block number	Specifies a block, or sequence, number. Used for program line identification. Allows the programmer to organize each line and is helpful while you are editing. In CNCEZ, increments by five to allow extra lines to be inserted if needed during editing.
P	Start block	Used within multiple repetitive cycles to specify the block number of the first block of the finish pass definition.
	Dwell time	Can also specify the length of time in seconds in a dwell command (see G04).
Q	Block end	Used within multiple repetitive cycles to specify the block number of the last block of the finish pass definition.
D	Depth	Specifies the depth of cut of the first pass in threading.
R	Radius	For circular interpolation, replaces the I and K to provide an easier way to designate the radius of a circular movement.
S	Spindle speed	Specifies the spindle speed in revolutions per minute or surface units (feet or meters) per minute.
T	Tool number	Specifies the turret library position and the offset register number to which to be indexed. (For example, to index to station #3 and call offset #3, program T0303.

Letter	Address	Description
A	Tool angle	Used in a threading cycle to specify the tool angle.
U	X stock	Used in multiple repetitive cycles (see G70 and G71) to specify the amount of stock to be left on the face for finishing.
W	Z stock	Used in multiple repetitive cycles (see G70 and G71) to specify the amount of stock to be left on the face for finishing.
X	X-axis	Designates a coordinate along the X-axis.
Z	Z-axis	Designates a coordinate along the Z-axis.

STEP-BY-STEP TURNING EXAMPLES

Work through each of the following examples step by step. In the first example, each step is described in more detail than it is in the remaining examples, so be sure to work through it.

If you have any difficulties with the programs or simply want to test and see them without entering them in first, they can be found in the **\CNCEZ\DEMOTURN** directory.

EXAMPLE #1: I-TURN1.TRN

This program introduces you to the basic G- and M-codes. When executed, it turns the workpiece down from an original diameter of 1.0 in. The completed part is shown in Fig. 6-17.

Workpiece Size:	1" Diameter by 2" Length
Tool:	Tool #1, Right-hand Turning Tool
Tool Start Position:	X2,Z3

```
%
:1001
N5 G20 G40
N10 T0101 M03
N15 G00 X1 Z0.25 M08
N20 G01 Z-0.75 F0.015
N25 G00 X1.1
N30 Z0.05
```

```
N35 X0.9375
N40 G01 Z-0.75 F0.012
N45 G00 X1
N50 Z0.05
N55 X0.8745
N60 G01 Z-0.75
N65 G00 X0.5
N70 Z0.05
N75 X0.8125
N80 G01 Z-0.375
N85 G00 X1
N90 Z0.05
N95 X0.75
N100 G01 Z-0.375
N105 G00 X2 M09
N110 Z2
N115 T0100 M05
N120 M30
```

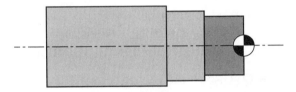

Figure 6-17 The completed part

STEP 1: Execute the batch file CNCEZ.BAT, which is in the root directory.

```
C:\CNCEZ [Enter]
```

After the batch file is run, the opening menu appears on the screen (Fig. 6-18).

```
CNC PROGRAMMING MADE EASY

  1 ...    CNC Milling Simulator
  2 ...    CNC Turning Simulator
  3 ...    Exit
```

Figure 6-18 Opening menu for CNC Programming Made Easy

STEP 2: Choose the turning option either by using the cursor keys to high-light the required option and then pressing Enter or by typing the appropriate menu number option and pressing Enter.

The main system screen appears (Fig. 6-19).

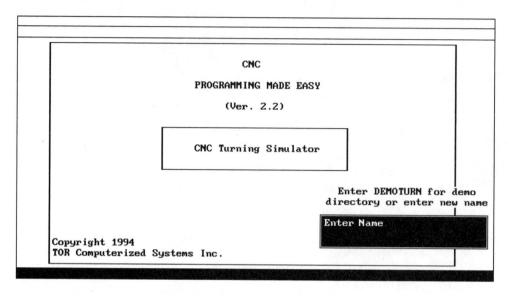

Figure 6-19 Main system screen for CNC Turning Simulator

STEP 3: You are prompted to enter DEMOTURN (for the default directory) or the name of a new directory. In this chapter, you will create a new directory to store all your files. Call this directory **PROJECTS**.

Enter DEMOTURN for demo directory or enter new name: **PROJECTS [Enter]**

At the "Create New Directory?" prompt, select **YES**.

The CNC graphical user interface is displayed (Fig. 6-20).

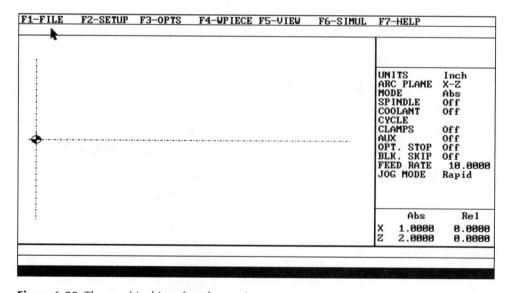

Figure 6-20 The graphical interface for turning

STEP 4:   Create a new file called **I-TURN1.**

Move the pointer to the Menu Bar and select **F1-FILE**.
Select **NEW** (Fig. 6-21).
Enter the file name: **I-TURN1 [Enter]** (Fig. 6-22).

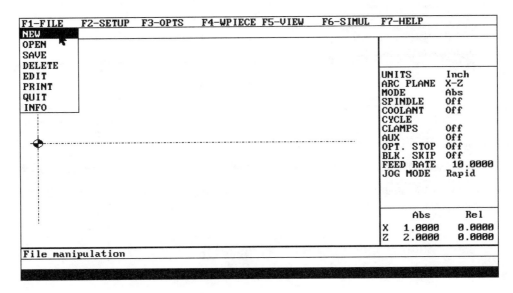

Figure 6-21 Selecting NEW from the F1-FILE menu

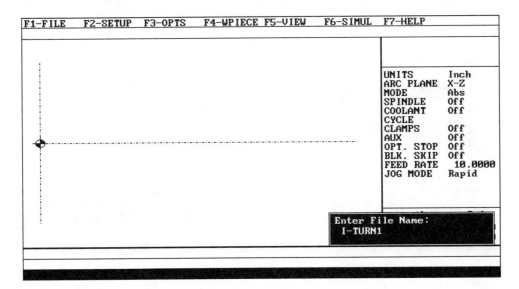

Figure 6-22 Prompt to enter file name

STEP 5:   Set up the workpiece (stock material) for this program.

From the Menu Bar, select **F4-WPIECE**.
Select **WORKPIECE** (Fig. 6-23).

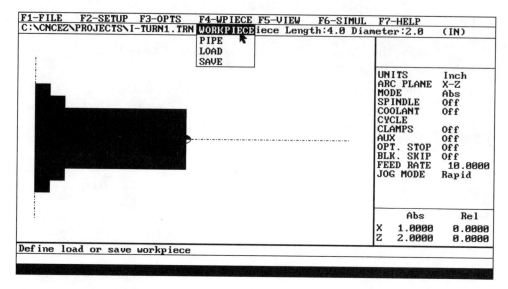

Figure 6-23 Selecting WORKPIECE from F4-WPIECE menu

Enter Length (in): **2 [Enter]** (Fig. 6-24).
Enter Diameter (in): **1 [Enter]** (Fig. 6-25).

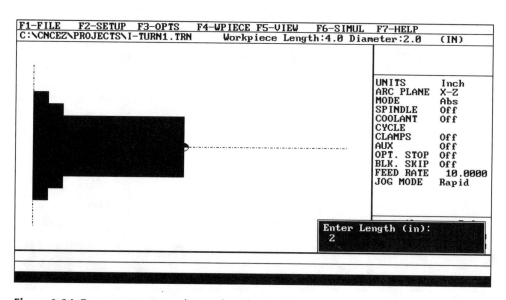

Figure 6-24 Prompt to enter workpiece length

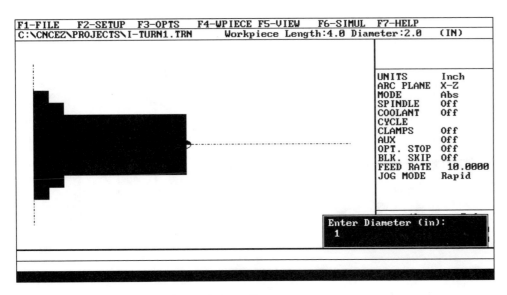

Figure 6-25 Prompt to enter the workpiece diameter

STEP 6:   This CNC program will use the default tool library that is shipped with the software. The program uses Tool #1 which is defaulted in the turret to be a right-hand tool. Look at the tool library at Tool #1.

From the Menu Bar, select **F2-SETUP**.
Select **TOOLS**, (Fig. 6-26).
Move the pointer over **Tool #1** to see the results (Figs. 6-27 and 6-28).

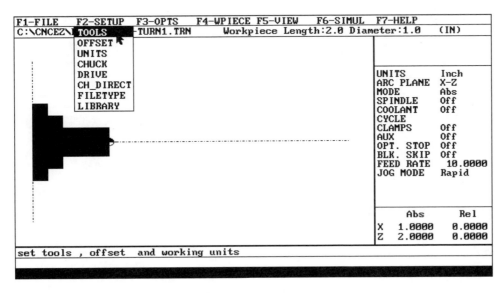

Figure 6-26 Selecting TOOLS from the F2-SETUP menu

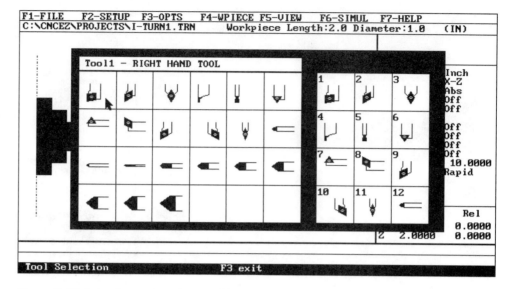

Figure 6-27 Selecting Tool #1 from tool library

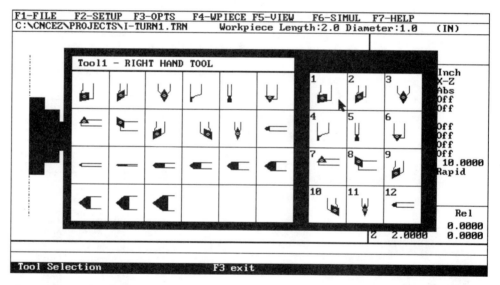

Figure 6-28 Selecting Tool Carousel #1

Click on Tool Carousel #1 to make this the right-hand tool.
Press **F3** to exit the tool library.

STEP 7: Begin entering the program and simulate the cutter path. Use the SIMULATE/EDIT option.

From the Menu Bar, select **F6-SIMUL**.
Select **EDIT** (Fig. 6-29).

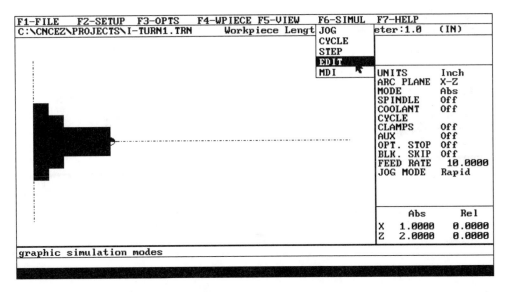

Figure 6-29 Selecting EDIT from the F6-SIMUL menu

STEP 8: Program setup phase. You must enter all the setup parameters before you can enter all the actual cutting moves (Figs. 6-30, 6-31, and 6-32).

>% [Enter]	Program start flag
>:1001 [Enter]	Program number 1001, (Fig. 6-30)

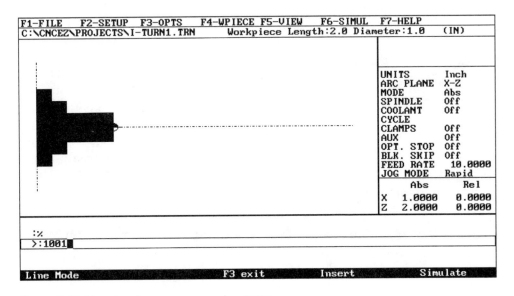

Figure 6-30 Entering the program number 1001

>:N5 G20 G40 [Enter]	Inch input and TNR cancel
>:N10 T0101 M03 [Enter]	Tool #1, spindle on clockwise (Fig. 6-31)

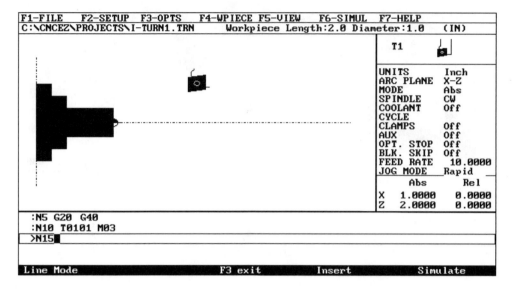

Figure 6-31 Result from entering T0101 M03

STEP 9: Material removal phase. Begin cutting the workpiece using G00 and G01.

>**N15 G00 X1 Z0.25 M08 [Enter]** Rapiding to X1,Z0.25 (Fig. 6-32)

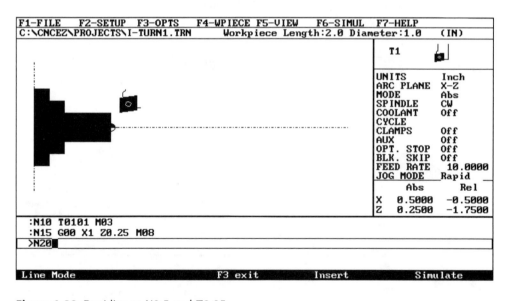

Figure 6-32 Rapiding to X0.5 and Z0.25

>**N20 G01 Z-0.75 F0.015 [Enter]** G01 feed move to Z–0.75 (Fig. 6-33)

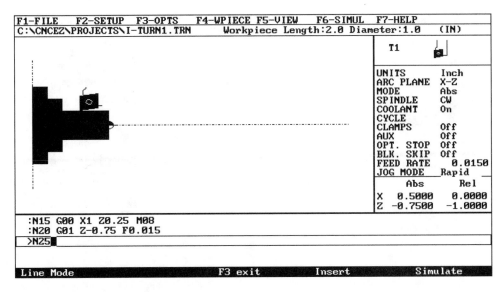

Figure 6-33 Performing a G01 to Z–0.75

>N25 G00 X1.1 [Enter]	G00 up to X1.1
>N30 Z0.05 [Enter]	G00 to Z0.05
>N35 X0.9375 [Enter]	G00 down to X0.9375
>N40 G01 Z-0.75 F0.012 [Enter]	G01 feed move to Z–0.75 at 0.012 ipr (Fig. 6-34)

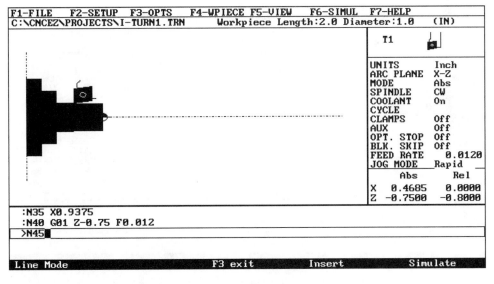

Figure 6-34 Performing another G01 to Z–0.75 on N40

>N45 G00 X1 [Enter]	G00 up to X1
>N50 Z0.05 [Enter]	G00 right to Z0.05
>N55 X0.8745 [Enter]	G00 down to X0.8745
>N60 G01 Z-0.75 [Enter]	G01 feed move to Z–0.75 at 0.012 ipr (Fig. 6-35)

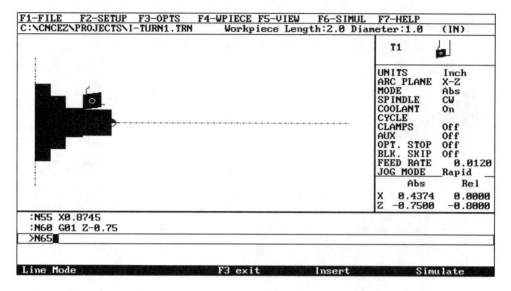

Figure 6-35 Performing another G01 to Z–0.75 on N60

>N65 G00 X1 [Enter]	G00 up to X1
>N70 Z0.05 [Enter]	G00 right to Z0.05
>N75 X0.8125 [Enter]	G00 down to X0.8125
>N80 G01 Z-0.375 [Enter]	G01 feed move to Z–0.375 at 0.012 ipr (Fig. 6-36)

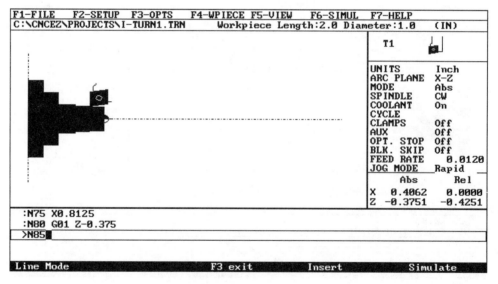

Figure 6-36 Performing a G01 to Z–0.375 on N80

>N85 G00 X1 [Enter]	G00 rapid to X1
>N90 Z0.05 [Enter]	G00 rapid to Z0.05
>N95 X0.75 [Enter]	G00 rapid to X0.75
>N100 G01 Z-0.375 [Enter]	G01 feed move to Z–0.375
>N105 G00 X2 M09 [Enter]	G00 rapid to X1 and coolant off
>N110 Z2 [Enter]	G00 rapid to Z2 position

STEP 10: Program shutdown phase. Turn off the spindle and program end (Fig. 6-37).

>N115 T0100 M05 [Enter]	M05 spindle off
>N120 M30 [Enter]	End of program (Fig. 6-37)
>N65 Press F3	Exit from **Simulate/Edit** mode

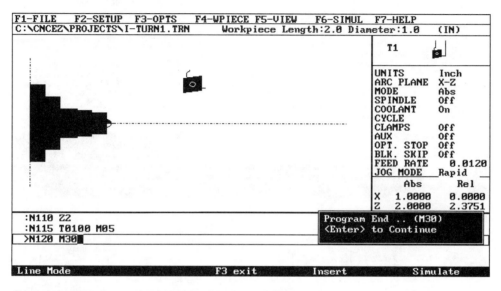

Figure 6-37   End of program prompt

STEP 11: The program is complete. Rerun it using the SIMULATE/CYCLE option.

From the Menu Bar, select **F6-SIML**.
Select **CYCLE**, (Fig. 6-38).

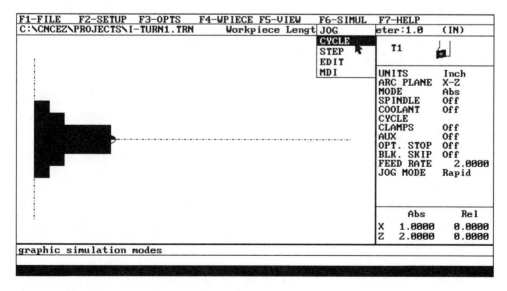

Figure 6-38 Selecting CYCLE from the F6-SIMUL menu

STEP 12: End of program (Fig. 6-39)

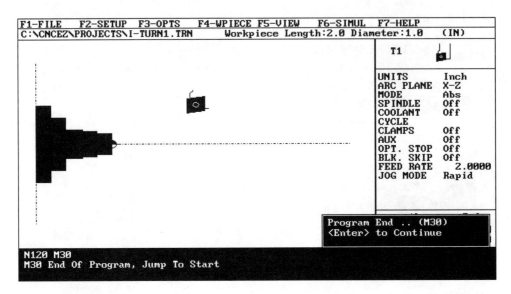

```
F1-FILE    F2-SETUP  F3-OPTS   F4-WPIECE F5-VIEW   F6-SIMUL  F7-HELP
C:\CNCEZ\PROJECTS\I-TURN1.TRN       Workpiece Length:2.0 Diameter:1.0   (IN)

                                        T1

                                        UNITS       Inch
                                        ARC PLANE   X-Z
                                        MODE        Abs
                                        SPINDLE     Off
                                        COOLANT     Off
                                        CYCLE
                                        CLAMPS      Off
                                        AUX         Off
                                        OPT. STOP   Off
                                        BLK. SKIP   Off
                                        FEED RATE      2.0000
                                        JOG MODE    Rapid

                                     Program End .. (M30)
                                     <Enter> to Continue

N120 M30
M30 End Of Program, Jump To Start
```

Figure 6-39 End of program

EXAMPLE #2: I-TURN2.TRN

This program introduces you to the basic circular interpolation routines. The completed part is shown in Fig. 6-40.

Workpiece Size:	2" Diameter by 4" Length
Tool:	Tool #1, Right-hand Turning Tool
Tool Start Position:	X2,Z3

```
%
:1002
N5 G20 G40
N10 T0101
N15 M03
N20 G00 X1.8 Z0.05
N25 M08
N30 G01 Z-2.5 F0.015
N35 G00 X2
N40 Z0.05
N45 X1.6
N50 G01 Z-2
N55 G00 X1.8
N60 Z0.05
N65 X1.4
N70 G01 Z-1.5
N75 X2 Z-3
```

```
N80  G00 Z0.05
N85  X1.2
N90  G01 Z-0.5
N95  G00 X1.4
N100 Z0.05
N105 X1
N110 G01 Z-0.5
N115 G03 X1.4 Z-0.7 I0 K-0.2
N120 G00 Z-0.1
N125 X1
N135 G02 X0.8 Z0 I-0.1 K0
N140 G00 X2 Z2
N145 M09
N150 T0100 M05
N155 M30
```

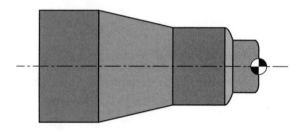

Figure 6-40 The completed part

STEP 1: Create a new file called **I-TURN2**.

Move the pointer to the Menu Bar and select **F1-FILE**.
Select **NEW**.
Enter the file name: **I-TURN2 [Enter]**.

STEP 2: Set up the workpiece (stock material) for this program.

From the Menu Bar, select **F4-WPIECE**.
Select **WORKPIECE**.
Enter Length (in): **4 [Enter]**
Enter Diameter (in): **2 [Enter]**

STEP 3: Begin entering the program and simulate the cutter path. Use the SIMULATE/EDIT option.

From the Menu Bar, select **F6-SIMUL**.
Select **EDIT**.

STEP 4: Program setup phase. You must enter all the setup parameters before you can enter all the actual cutting moves.

>% [Enter]	Program start flag
>:1002 [Enter]	Program number 1002
>:N05 G20 G40 [Enter]	Inch programming and TNR cancel
>:N10 T0101 [Enter]	Tool change to Tool #1
>N15 M03 [Enter]	(Fig. 6-41)

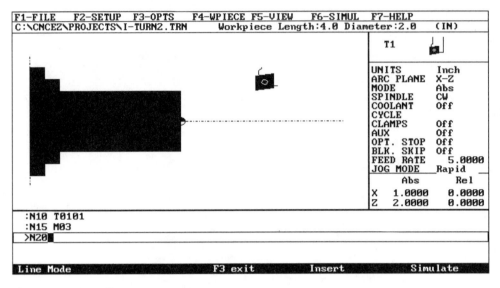

Figure 6-41 Spindle on

STEP 5: Material removal phase. Begin cutting the workpiece.

>N20 G00 X1.8 Z0.05 [Enter]	Rapiding to X1.8,Z0.05
>N25 M08 [Enter]	Coolant on (Fig. 6-42)

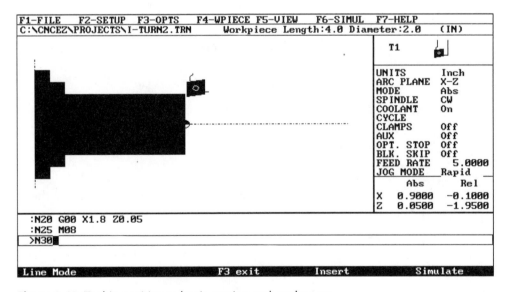

Figure 6-42 Tool in position to begin cutting and coolant on

>N30 G01 Z-2.5 F0.015 [Enter]   G01 feed move to Z–2.5 at 0.015
                                 ipr (Fig. 6-43)

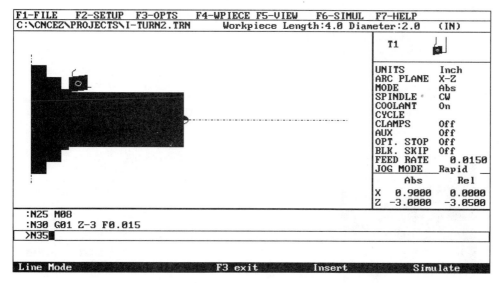

Figure 6-43 The first cut

>N35 G00 X2 [Enter]	G00 rapid to X2
>N40 Z0.05 [Enter]	G00 rapid to Z0.05
>N45 X1.6 [Enter]	G00 rapid to X1.6
>N50 G01 Z-2 [Enter]	G01 feed move to Z–1
>N55 G00 X1.8 [Enter]	G00 rapid to X1.8
>N60 Z0.05 [Enter]	G00 rapid to Z0.05
>N65 X1.4 [Enter]	G00 rapid to X1.4
>N70 G01 Z-1.5 [Enter]	G01 feed move to Z–1.5
>N75 X2 Z-3 [Enter]	G01 diagonal feed move to X2,Z–3 (Fig. 6-44)

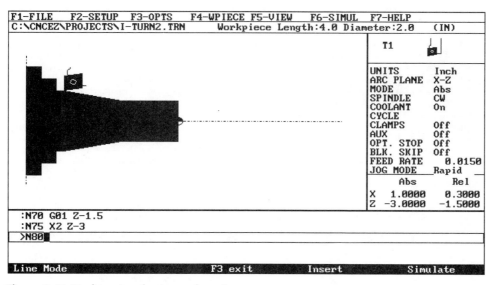

Figure 6-44 Tool turning the tapered portion

>N80 G00 Z0.05 [Enter]   G00 rapid to Z0.05
>N85 X1.2 [Enter]   G00 rapid to X1.2
>N90 G01 Z-0.5 [Enter]   G01 feed move to Z–0.5
>N95 G00 X1.4 [Enter]   G00 rapid to X1.4
>N100 Z0.05 [Enter]   G00 rapid to Z0.05
>N105 X1 [Enter]   G00 rapid to X1
>N110 G01 Z-0.5 [Enter]   G01 feed move to Z–0.5 (Fig. 6-45)

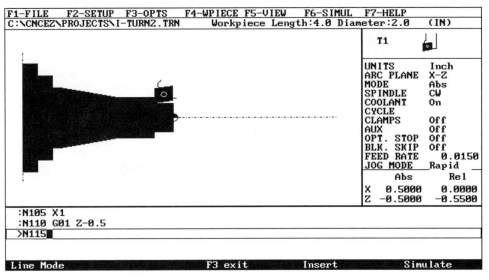

Figure 6-45 Result of G01 feed move

>N115 G03 X1.4 Z-0.7 I0 K-0.2 [Enter]   G03 circular interpolation counterclockwise (Fig. 6-46)

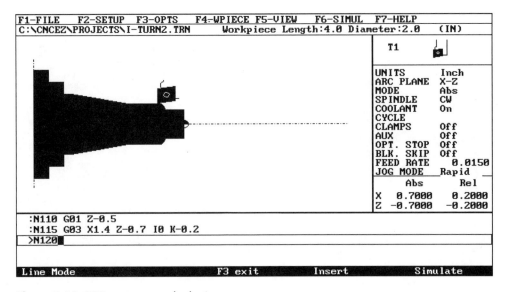

Figure 6-46 G03 arc counterclockwise

>N120 G00 Z-0.1 [Enter]   Rapid move to Z0.1
>N125 X1.1 [Enter]   Rapid move to X1
>N130 G01 X1 [Enter]   Feed move to X1
>N135 G02 X0.8 Z0 I-0.1 K0 [Enter]   G02 arc clockwise (Fig. 6-47)

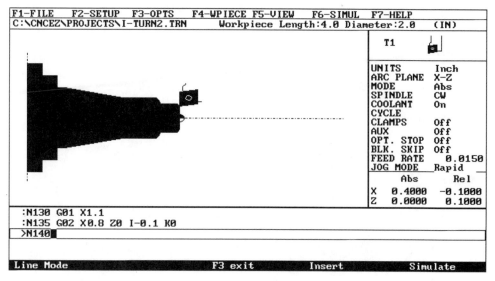

Figure 6-47 Result of G02 arc move

>N140 G00 X2 Z2 [Enter]   Rapid to X2,Z2
>N145 M09 [Enter]   Coolant off
>N150 T0100 M05 [Enter]   Spindle off
>N155 M30 [Enter]   End of program (Fig. 6-48))

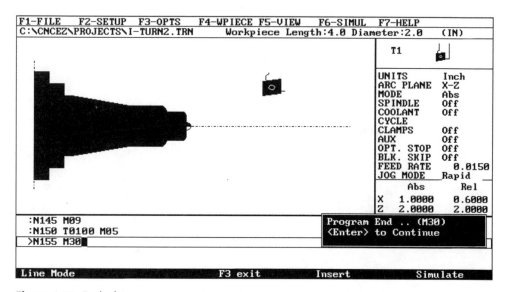

Figure 6-50 End of program prompt

EXAMPLE #3: I-TURN3.TRN

This program introduces you to the G71 Turning Cycle and G70 Finishing Cycle commands. The completed part is shown in Fig. 6-49.

Workpiece Size: 4" Diameter by 2" Length
Tool: Tool #1, Right-hand Turning Tool
Tool Start Position: X2,Z3

```
%
:1003
N5 G90 G20 G40
N10 T0101
N15 M03
N20 G00 X2.1 Z0.05
N25 G71 P30 Q50 U0.025 W0.005 D625 F0.012
N30 G01 X1 Z0
N35 G03 X1.5 Z-0.25 I0 K-0.25
N40 G01 X1.75 Z-2
N45 G03 X2 Z-2.125 I0 K-0.125
N50 G01 X2.2
N55 G70 P30 Q50 F0.006
N60 G00 X2 Z2
N65 T0100 M05
N70 M30
```

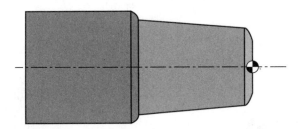

Figure 6-49 The completed part

STEP 1:   Create a new file called **I-TURN3**.

Move the pointer to the Menu Bar, and select **F1-FILE**.
Select **NEW**.
Enter the file name: **I-TURN3 [Enter]**.

STEP 2:   Set up the workpiece (stock material) for this program.

From the Menu Bar, select **F4-WPIECE**.
Select **WORKPIECE**.

Enter Length (in): **4 [Enter]**
Enter Diameter (in): **2 [Enter]**

STEP 3: Begin entering the program and simulate the cutter path. Use the SIMULATE/EDIT option.

From the Menu Bar, select **F6-SIMUL**.
Select **EDIT**.

STEP 4: Program setup phase. You must enter all the setup parameters before you can enter all the actual cutting moves.

>% [Enter]	Program start flag
>:1003 [Enter]	Program number 1003
>:N05 G90 G20 G40 [Enter]	Absolute and inch programming
>:N10 T0101 [Enter]	Tool change to Tool #1
>N15 M03 [Enter]	Spindle on clockwise

STEP 5: Material removal phase.

>N20 G00 X2.1 Z0.05 [Enter]   (Fig. 6-50)

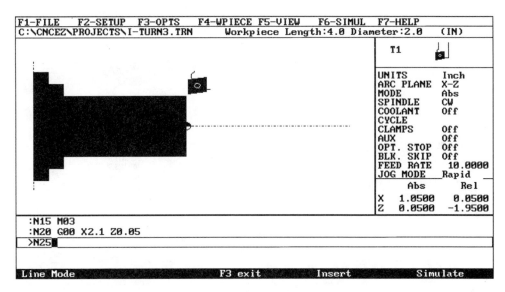

Figure 6-50 Tool at cycle ready position

Before entering the G71 and G70 commands, you must first create the profile. The profile will begin on N30 and will end on N50. (This is just a simulation, so don't worry about the depth of cut right now. This will be taken care of by the G71 command.)

>N25 G00 X1 Z0 [Enter]	A temporary line that will later be replaced by the G71 command
>N30 G01 X1 Z0 [Enter]	Feed move to X1 and Z0

>N35 G03 X1.5 Z-0.25 I0 K-0.25 [Enter]   Arc Feed move
>N40 G01 X1.75 Z-2 [Enter]   Fig. 6-51

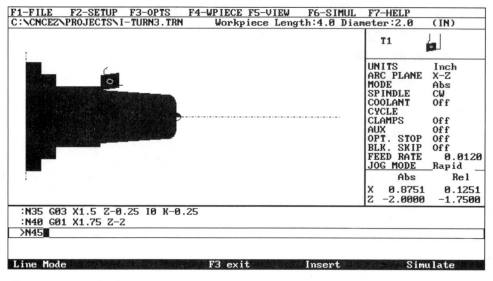

Figure 6-51 Result after N40

>N45 G03 X2 Z-2.125 I0 K-0.125 [Enter]   Arc feed move
>N50 G01 X2.2 [Enter]   Fig. 6-52

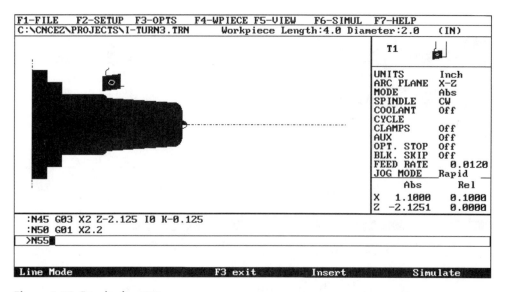

Figure 6-52 Result after N50

>N55 G00 X1 Z0 [Enter]   A temporary line that will be replaced
    by the G70 command
>N60 G00 X2 Z2 [Enter]   Rapid move to X2 and Z2
>N65 T0100 M05 [Enter]   Spindle off
>N70 M30 [Enter]   Fig. 6-53

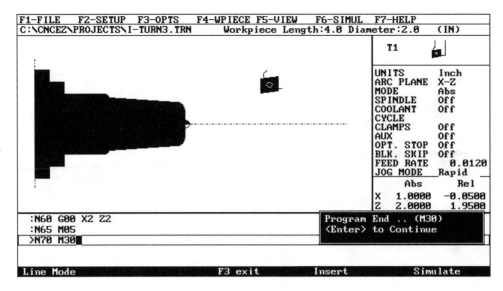

Figure 6-53 The completed profile

STEP 6:   Use the F1-FILE/EDIT option to insert the G71 and G70 commands. (Due to how the F6-SIMUL/EDIT option works, it is much easier and faster to go to the F1-FILE/EDIT option to insert the commands.)

To exit the current mode, press **F3**.
From the Menu Bar, select **F1-FILE**.
From the F1-FILE menu, select **EDIT** (Fig. 6-54).

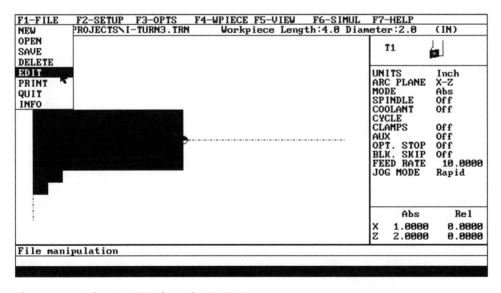

Figure 6-54 Selecting EDIT from the F1-FILE menu

As shown in Figs. 6-55 and 6-56, the editor can be displayed in two ways. The partial view is the way the editor first looks on screen. By pressing F1, you see the full screen.

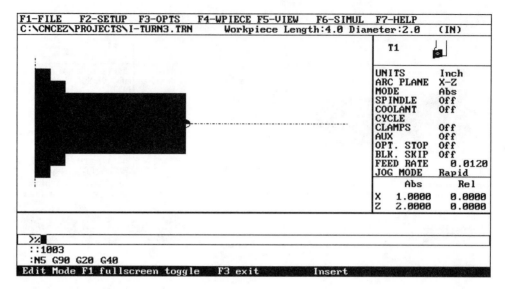

```
F1-FILE   F2-SETUP  F3-OPTS   F4-WPIECE F5-VIEW   F6-SIMUL  F7-HELP
C:\CNCEZ\PROJECTS\I-TURN3.TRN       Workpiece Length:4.0 Diameter:2.0    (IN)

                                            T1          ⟨⟩

                                     UNITS       Inch
                                     ARC PLANE   X-Z
                                     MODE        Abs
                                     SPINDLE     Off
                                     COOLANT     Off
                                     CYCLE
                                     CLAMPS      Off
                                     AUX         Off
                                     OPT. STOP   Off
                                     BLK. SKIP   Off
                                     FEED RATE     0.0120
                                     JOG MODE    Rapid
                                           Abs        Rel
                                     X   1.0000     0.0000
                                     Z   2.0000     0.0000


 >%
 ::1003
 :N5 G90 G20 G40
Edit Mode F1 fullscreen toggle    F3 exit          Insert
```

Figure 6-55 Partial editor

To select the full-screen editor, press F1, (Fig. 6-56).

Here you must replace <u>N25</u> and <u>N55</u> with the following, also shown in Fig. 6-56:

>**N25 G71 P30 Q50 U0.025 W0.005 D625 F0.012**   Turning cycle
>**N55 G70 P30 Q50 F0.006**   Finishing cycle

```
F1-FILE    F2-SETUP   F3-OPTS    F4-WPIECE F5-VIEW   F6-SIMUL  F7-HELP
C:\CNCEZ\PROJECTS\I-TURN3.TRN       Workpiece Length:4.0 Diameter:2.0    (IN)


 :%
 ::1003
 :N5 G90 G20 G40
 :N10 T0101
 :N15 M03
 :N20 G00 X2.1 Z0.05
 :N25 G71 P30 Q50 U0.025 W0.005 D625 F0.012
>N30 G01 X1 Z0
 :N35 G03 X1.5 Z-0.25 I0 K-0.25
 :N40 G01 X1.75 Z-2
 :N45 G03 X2 Z-2.125 I0 K-0.125
 :N50 G01 X2.2
 :N55 G70 P30 Q50 F0.01
 :N60 G00 X2 Z2
 :N65 T0100 M05
 :N70 M30
 :N75

Edit Mode F1 fullscreen toggle    F3 exit          Insert
```

Figure 6-56 The full-screen editor

STEP 7:   Go to F6-SIMUL and run the complete program using the CYCLE option.

To exit from the editor mode, press **F3**.

From the Menu Bar, select **F6-SIMUL**.
From the F6-SIMUL menu, select **CYCLE**.

You will now see the program simulated and see how the G71 and G70 command take care of many lines of programming (Fig. 6-57).

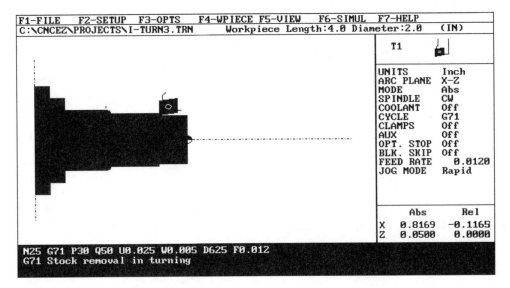

Figure 6-57 G71 command being executed

STEP 8: End of program (Fig. 6-58)

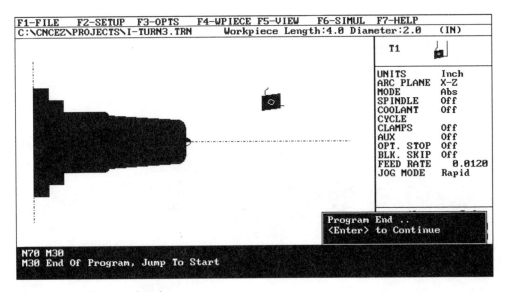

Figure 6-58 The completed part

EXAMPLE #4: I-TURN4.TRN

This example demonstrates the G72 Facing Cycle and the G74 Drilling Cycle commands. The completed part is shown in Fig. 6-59.

Workpiece Size:	2" Diameter by 3" Length
Tool:	Tool #2, Right-hand Turning Tool
	Tool #3, 3/8" Drill
Tool Start Position:	X2,Z3

```
%
:1004
N5 G90 G20 G40
N10 T0202
N15 M03
N20 M08
N25 G00 X2 Z0.05
N30 G72 P35 Q50 U0.05 W0.005 D500 F0.012
N35 G01 X1 Z0.05
N40 Z-1
N45 X2 Z-1.5
N50 X2.2
N55 G70 P35 Q50 F0.006
N60 T0200 G00 X4 Z3
N65 T0303
N70 G00 X0 Z0.1
N75 G74 Z-1 F0.05 D0 K0.125
N80 G00 X4 Z3 M09
N85 T0300 M05
N90 M30
```

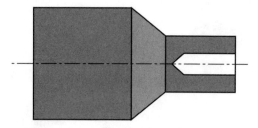

Figure 6-59 The completed part

STEP 1: Create a new file called **I-TURN4**.

Move the pointer to the Menu Bar and select **F1-FILE**.
Select **NEW**.
Enter the file name: **I-TURN4 [Enter]**.

STEP 2: Set up the workpiece (stock material) for this program.

From the Menu Bar, select **F4-WPIECE**.
Select **WORKPIECE**.
Enter Length (in): **3 [Enter]**
Enter Diameter (in): **2 [Enter]**

STEP 3: Begin entering the program and simulate the cutter path. Use the SIMULATE/EDIT option.

From the Menu Bar, select **F6-SIMUL**.
Select **EDIT**.

STEP 4: Program setup phase. You must enter all the setup parameters before you can enter all the actual cutting moves.

>% [Enter]	Program start flag
>:1004 [Enter]	Program number 1004
>:N05 G90 G20 G40 [Enter]	Absolute and inch programming
>:N10 T0202 [Enter]	Tool change to Tool #2
>N15 M03 [Enter]	Spindle on clockwise
>N20 M08 [Enter]	Coolant pump 1 on

STEP 5: Material removal phase.

>N25 G00 X2 Z0.05 [Enter]   Fig. 6-60

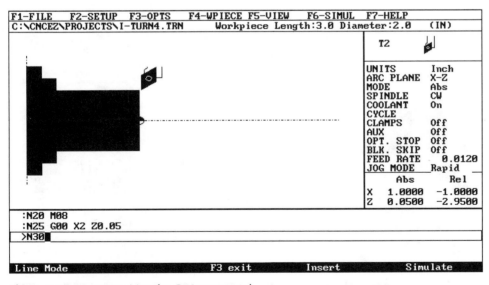

Figure 6-60 Home position for G72 command

>N30 G00 X1 Z0.05 [Enter]   To be replaced later with G72
>N35 G01 X1 Z0.05 [Enter]   Beginning of profile
>N40 Z-1 [Enter]   Feed in to Z–1
>N45 X2 Z-1.5 [Enter]   Diagonal feed to X2 and Z–1.5
>N50 X2.2 [Enter]   End of profile (Fig. 6-61)

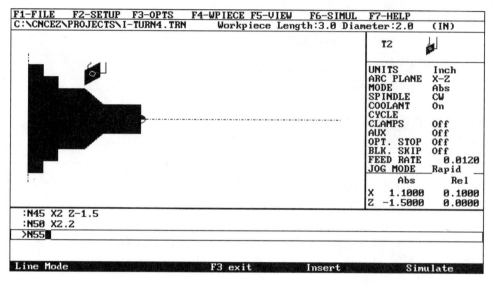

Figure 6-61 Shows profile

>N55 G00 Z0.05 [Enter]   To be replaced by G70
>N60 T0200 G00 X4 Z2 [Enter] Fig. 6-62

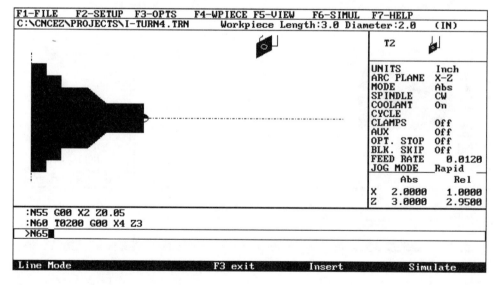

Figure 6-62 In tool change position

STEP 6: Use the F1-FILE/EDIT option to insert the G72 and G70 commands.

To exit the current mode, press **F3**.
From the Menu Bar, select **F1-FILE**.
From the F1-FILE menu, select **EDIT**.
To select the full-screen editor, press **F1**.

Here you must replace N30 and N55 with the following, also shown in Fig. 6-63.

>**N30 G72 P35 Q50 U0.05 W0.005 D500 F0.012**   Facing cycle
>**N55 G70 P35 Q50 F0.006**   Finishing cycle

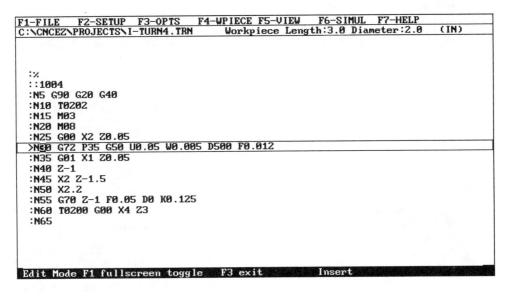

Figure 6-63 Replacing N30 and N55 with G72 and G70

STEP 7: Go to F6-SIMUL/EDIT to complete the program.

To exit from the editor mode, press **F3**.
From the Menu Bar, select **F6-SIMUL**.
From the F6-SIMUL menu, select **EDIT**.

You will now see the program simulated and see how the G72 and G70 commands take care of many lines of programming (Figs. 6-64 and 6-65).

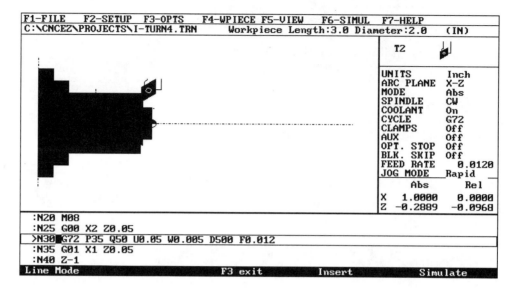

Figure 6-64 The program running the G72 command

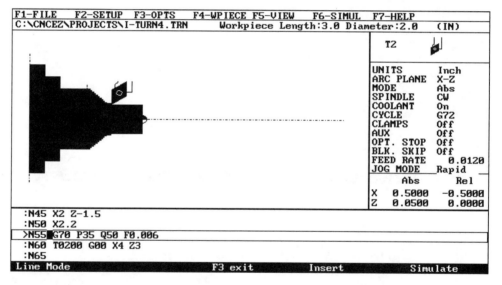

Figure 6-65 The program executing the G70 command

STEP 8: Enter the drill cycle command.

>N65 T0303 [Enter]	Fig. 6-66
>N70 G00 X0 Z0.1 [Enter]	Rapid move to X0 and Z0.1
>N75 G74 Z-1 F0.05 D0 K0.125 [Enter]	Fig. 6-67

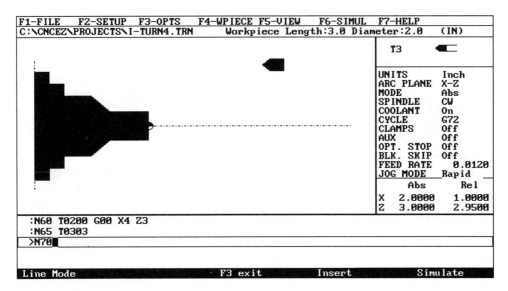

Figure 6-66 Calling for a tool change to a 3/8in. drill

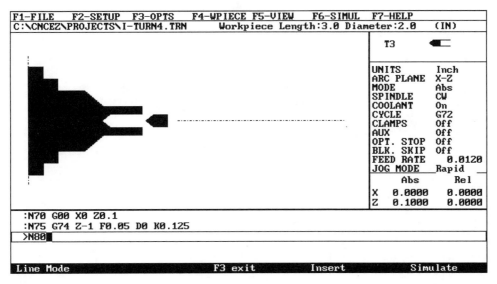

Figure 6-67 After the G74 command

STEP 9: Program shutdown phase

>**N80 G00 X4 Z3 M09 [Enter]**   Rapid move to X4,Z3 and cool-
ant off

>**N85 T0300 M05 [Enter]**   Spindle off

>**N90 M30 [Enter]**   Fig. 6-68

STEP 10: End of program

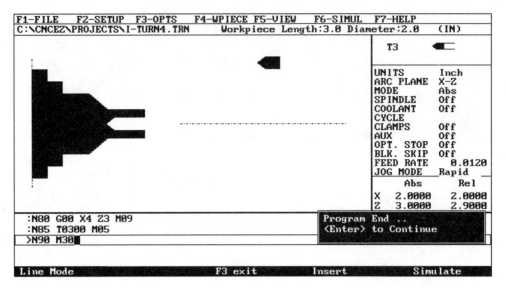

Figure 6-68 Program end

EXAMPLE #5: I-TURN5.TRN

Workpiece Size: 2" Diameter by 4" Length

Tool: Tool #1, Right-hand Turning Tool

                         Tool #2, Right-hand Finishing Tool

                         Tool #3, Grooving Tool

                         Tool #5, Neutral Tool

Tool Start Position: X2,Z3

```
%
:1005
N5 G90 G20 G40
N10 T0101
N15 M03
N20 G00 X2.05 Z0.05 M07
N25 G71 P30 Q40 U0.05 W0.05 D500 F0.012
N30 G01 X1.5 Z0.05
N35 Z-3
N40 X2.05
N45 T0100 G00 X4 Z3
N50 T0202
N55 G00 X2.05 Z0.05
N60 G70 P30 Q40 F0.006
N65 T0200 G00 X4 Z3
```

```
N70  T0505
N75  G00 X2.25 Z-3
N80  G75 X1.25 Z-0.25 F0.25 D0 I0.125 K0.125
N85  T0500 G00 X4 Z3
N90  T0303
N95  G00 X1.5 Z0.05
N100 G01 Z0 F0.012
N105 G76 X1.5 Z-2.75 D625 K0.125 A55 F0.1
N110 G00 X4 Z3 M09
N115 T0300 M05
N120 M02
```

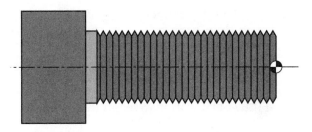

Figure 6-69 The completed part

STEP 1:   Create a new file called **I-TURN5**.

Move the pointer to the Menu Bar and select **F1-FILE**.
Select **NEW**.
Enter the file name: **I-TURN5 [Enter]**.

STEP 2:   Set up the workpiece (stock material) for this program.

From the Menu Bar, select **F4-WPIECE**.
Select **WORKPIECE**.
Enter Length (in): **4 [Enter]**
Enter Diameter (in): **2 [Enter]**

STEP 3:   Begin entering the program and simulate the cutter path. Use the SIMULATE/EDIT option.

From the Menu Bar, select **F6-SIMUL**.
Select **EDIT**.

STEP 4:   Program setup phase. You must enter all the setup parameters before you can enter all the actual cutting moves.

>% [Enter]	Program start flag
>:1005 [Enter]	Program number 1005
>:N05 G90 G20 G40 [Enter]	Absolute and inch programming
>:N10 T0101 [Enter]	Tool change to Tool #1
>N15 M03 [Enter]	Spindle on clockwise

STEP 5: Material removal phase

>N20 G00 X2.05 Z0.05 M07 [Enter]	Rapid move to X2.05,Z0.05
>N25 G00 X2.05 Z0.05 [Enter]	To be replaced with G71
>N30 G01 X1.5 Z0.05 [Enter]	Feed move to X1.5 and Z0.05
>N35 Z-3 [Enter]	Feed move to Z–3
>N40 X2.05 [Enter]	Feed move to X2.05
>N45 T0100 G00 X4 Z3 [Enter]	Rapid to X4,Z3 and Tool #1 cancel
>N50 T0202 [Enter]	Tool change to Tool #2
>N55 G00 X2.05 Z0.05 [Enter]	Rapid to X2.05,Z0.05

STEP 6: Use the F1-FILE/EDIT option to insert the G71 and G70 commands.

To exit the current mode, press **F3**.
From the Menu Bar, select **F1-FILE**.
From the F1-FILE menu, select **EDIT**.
To select the full-screen editor, press **F1**.

Here you must replace N25 and N60 with the following:

>N25 G71 P30 Q40 U0.05 W0.05 D500 F0.012 [Enter]	Turning cycle
>N60 G70 P30 Q40 F0.006	Finishing cycle

STEP 7: Go to F6-SIMUL/EDIT to complete the program.

To exit from the editor mode, press **F3**.
From the Menu Bar, select **F6-SIMUL**.
From the F6-SIMUL menu, select **EDIT**.

You will now see the program simulated and see how the G71 and G70 commands takes care of many lines of programming (Fig. 6-70).

STEP 8: Enter the G75 command (Fig. 6-71).

>N65 T0200 G00 X4 Z3 [Enter]	Rapid to tool change position
>N70 T0505 [Enter]	Tool change to Tool #5
>N75 G00 X2.25 Z-3	Rapid to X2.25,Z–3
>N80 G75 X1.5 Z-0.25 F0.25 D0 I0.125 K0.125 [Enter]	Grooving cycle

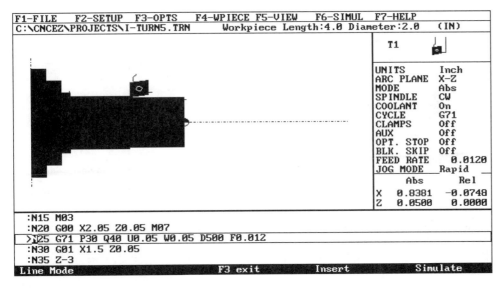

```
F1-FILE   F2-SETUP   F3-OPTS   F4-WPIECE F5-VIEW   F6-SIMUL   F7-HELP
C:\CNCEZ\PROJECTS\I-TURN5.TRN      Workpiece Length:4.0 Diameter:2.0   (IN)
```

T1	
UNITS	Inch
ARC PLANE	X-Z
MODE	Abs
SPINDLE	CW
COOLANT	On
CYCLE	G71
CLAMPS	Off
AUX	Off
OPT. STOP	Off
BLK. SKIP	Off
FEED RATE	0.0120
JOG MODE	Rapid

	Abs	Rel
X	0.8381	-0.0748
Z	0.0500	0.0000

```
:N15 M03
:N20 G00 X2.05 Z0.05 M07
>N25 G71 P30 Q40 U0.05 W0.05 D500 F0.012
:N30 G01 X1.5 Z0.05
:N35 Z-3
```

```
Line Mode                F3 exit          Insert          Simulate
```

Figure 6-70 Executing the G71 command

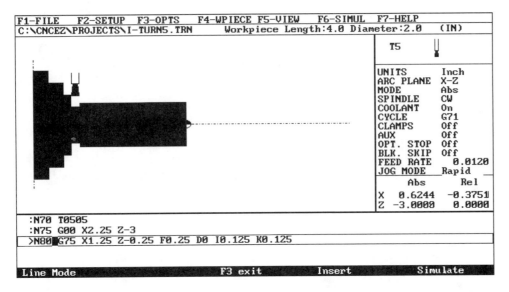

```
F1-FILE   F2-SETUP   F3-OPTS   F4-WPIECE F5-VIEW   F6-SIMUL   F7-HELP
C:\CNCEZ\PROJECTS\I-TURN5.TRN      Workpiece Length:4.0 Diameter:2.0   (IN)
```

T5	
UNITS	Inch
ARC PLANE	X-Z
MODE	Abs
SPINDLE	CW
COOLANT	On
CYCLE	G71
CLAMPS	Off
AUX	Off
OPT. STOP	Off
BLK. SKIP	Off
FEED RATE	0.0120
JOG MODE	Rapid

	Abs	Rel
X	0.6244	-0.3751
Z	-3.0000	0.0000

```
:N70 T0505
:N75 G00 X2.25 Z-3
>N80 G75 X1.25 Z-0.25 F0.25 D0 I0.125 K0.125
```

```
Line Mode                F3 exit          Insert          Simulate
```

Figure 6-71 Grooving cycle

STEP 9: Enter the G76 command (Fig. 6-72).

> **>N85 T0500 G00 X4 Z3 [Enter]**   Rapid to X4,Z3 and Tool #5 cancel
>
> **>N90 T0303 [Enter]**   Tool change to Tool #3
>
> **>N95 G00 X1.5 Z0.05 [Enter]**   Rapid move to X1.5,Z0.05
>
> **>N100 G01 Z0 F0.012 [Enter]**   Feed move to Z0
>
> **>N105 G76 X1.5 Z-2.75 D625 K0.125 A55 F0.1 [Enter]**   Threading cycle (Fig. 6-72)
>
> **>N110 G00 X4 Z3 M09 [Enter]**   Rapid to X4,Z3 and coolant off

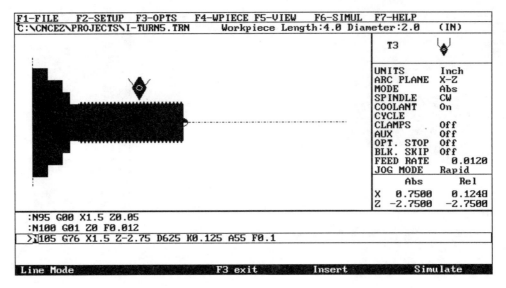

Figure 6-72 Threading cycle in progress

STEP 10: Program shutdown phase

>**N115 T0300 M05 [Enter]**   Spindle off and cancel tool
>**N120 M02 [Enter]**   End of program

STEP 11: End of program

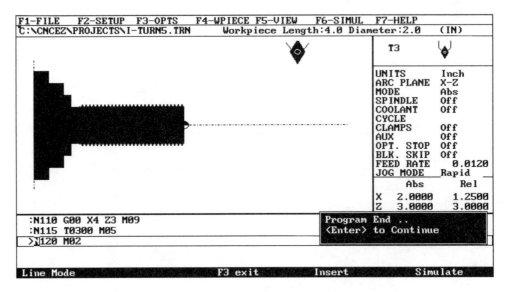

Figure 6-73 End of program prompt

LAB EXERCISE

1. What does the preparatory function G00 command do? _____

_____

_____

_____

2. How is tool nose radius compensation called? _____

_____

_____

_____

3. Give an example of a linear feed move. _____

_____

_____

_____

4. What does the address U stand for when a G71 command is programmed?

_____

_____

_____

5. What does a G76 command specify? _____

_____

_____

_____

6. Which G-code and additional letter address are used to call up a dwell
   cycle? _____

_____

_____

_____

7. Write an example start line for a G74 peck drilling cycle. _____

_____

_____

_____

8. Which M-code is used to specify spindle on clockwise? _____

_____

_____

_____

Chapter 7

Introduction to CAD/CAM

CHAPTER OBJECTIVES

After studying this chapter, the student should have knowledge of the following:

Basics of computer-aided design

Basics of computer-aided manufacturing

Introduction to AutoCAD

Introduction to Mastercam

THE BASIC CAD/CAM SYSTEM

Originally CAD/CAM systems comprised mostly expensive mainframe computers and microcomputers. Because of advancements in computer technology, the personal computer (PC) is now quickly becoming the computer of choice for users. CAD/CAM software can be general in design so that it can be used in all disciplines, or it can be specialized with a specific design goal in mind. A good example of a specialized system is one used primarily for a task such as circuit board design. An excellent choice for an all-round CAD software is AutoCAD by Autodesk, Inc. AutoCAD is an open architecture CAD software, which means it can be run with virtually thousands of third-party add-on packages for a users' specific application.

A typical PC-based CAD system can consist of the following:

- An IBM or compatible personal computer

  The minimum system requirements for AutoCADR12 as recommended by Autodesk, Inc. are as follows:

  – IBM 386- or 486-class machine or true compatible or PS/2 modules 60, 70 or 80

  – An 80387 or 80487 math coprocessor

  – A minimum of 8MB of RAM

  – A minimum of 11MB of free hard disk space (full installation requires at least 23MB)

  – DOS 5.0 or later

  – An AutoCAD-supported video display monitor. The minimum is generally an IBM VGA standard that supports 640X480 pixels. Many types of video cards are available, including numerous CAD accelerator cards from various manufacturers.

- An input device

  Some input devices that can be used include a Microsoft or compatible mouse and/or a digitizing tablet such as a Summagraphics Summasketch 3 or a Kurta XGT Tablet.

- An output device

  Some output devices supported by AutoCAD include various printers and plotters such as the Hewlett Packard Draftpro and the Calcomp Drawingmaster.

COMPUTER-AIDED DESIGN

CAD (computer-aided design), at its most basic, is a geometric modeling system used to produce two-dimensional or three-dimensional engineering drawings of parts. Although the term is sometimes used to describe computer-aided drafting, CAD is the use of a computer to aid in the total design process.

Design is a process that involves identifying a need, generating possible solutions to meet that need, evaluating each solution to determine its merits (engineering analysis), identifying the solution to be developed based on merit, and then developing a detailed model so that it can be built.

The computer can aid in most steps in the design process. The extent to which it can depends on the cost and availability of computer hardware and software. Over the last decade, the cost has dropped considerably to the point where a CAD system is very affordable even by the smallest of companies. This is still the trend, so more functions are being added to the existing power of CAD. Functions like finite element analysis (FEA), finite element modeling (FEM), parametric design, and three-dimensional modeling. Currently, the primary use of CAD is in the production of three-dimensional geometric models from which engineering drawings and CNC part programs are produced almost automatically.

The engineering or shop drawing, once considered the culmination of all design efforts, is now mostly considered just a reference document to assist in manufacturing quality control. Even this function will someday probably disappear as corporations go paperless. A drawing is developed in the computer-aided design process, without the need to fabricate a prototype, so all the testing and analysis can be performed and a part program can be generated. Once the part is fabricated, it can then go through a computer-assisted, quality-control check. All this can be performed without your ever having to pick-up a shop drawing.

The major goals of CAD for manufacturing are

- to increase productivity and

- to create a database for manufacturing.

CAD helps the designer or draftsperson to visualize a design on the computer screen. The designer can make a change and get almost immediate feedback on the results. Current CAD software also allows for analysis and testing of components before manufacture and the presentation of the finished product.

A good CAD system has the following characteristics:

1. Easy to learn

   It should be a step-by-step process and should be done in a logical manner. It should be menu-driven and highly graphical with as much data as possible displayed on screen. It also should have an online tutorial so the student can get started quickly, online context sensitive help accessible from any point in the program, and online documentation.

2. Easy to work with

It should be adaptable to your particular application and should not require a specialist to operate it.

3. Have macro commands

A macro is a single key or command sequence that causes the execution of a string of commands.

4. Have its own embedded programming language

The CAD software should have its own customization language.

5. Be expandable

It should be able to grow with you. You should also be able to easily change peripheral devices such as display monitors or plotters.

6. Have an open database

It should do more than just create drawings. It should be able to generate bills of material and hold prices and other database information.

7. Be compatible with other CAD/CAM and analysis programs

It should be able to easily exchange geometric models with other programs using standard model interchange file formats such as IGES, DXF, and STL. IGES is the current standard for three-dimensional geometric model exchange involving parametric surfaces (for example, NURBS). DXF (Autodesk) is the de facto standard for PC geometric model exchange. STL (stereolithography) is the de facto standard for rapid prototyping system models (three-dimensional polygon models only). Most analysis programs (for example, finite element, boundary element, computational fluids, kinematics, and so on) accept one or more of these file formats to import a geometric model for analysis.

AUTOCAD

AutoCAD is used by more than 600,000 customers in 85 countries, making it the world's largest-selling PC-based CAD package. Using AutoCAD, you can create a three-dimensional model of a design, then automatically create two-dimensional working drawings from that model. For presentation purposes, these three-dimensional models can be used again to create true three-dimensional renderings for both visualization and presentation purposes. AutoCAD is used in all fields ranging from mechanical engineering, architecture, landscape design, and civil engineering to cartography and interior design.

AutoCAD uses an intuitive graphical interface that allows you to execute commands via pull-down menus, icon menus, dialog boxes, the command line, or a digitizer template. Using a mouse or digitizer, you can select tools from the easy-to-use menus to quickly create geometric shapes of any complexity. These shapes can then be edited and changed quickly with commands such as mirror, trim, copy, stretch, fillet, chamfer, erase, rotate, move, and scale. Zoom and pan commands let you view the entire drawing on the screen or zoom in to an area no matter how small. AutoCAD also provides full-dimension control according to ISO, DIN, ANSI, and other standards. With AutoCAD's text tools, you can annotate your drawing just as easily. After you complete your drawing, AutoCAD's plotting tools let you plot your drawings exactly as they appear on screen. You can use up to 255 combinations of line types, colors, widths, and pen speeds for the same plotter.

AutoCAD also uses an open architecture, which means you can customize AutoCAD to suit your specific requirements. There are over 1000 off-the-shelf, third-party packages that customize AutoCAD you can add on to in order to meet specific needs. These programs integrate with AutoCAD to create specialized systems for architectural design, mechanical drafting, structural engineering, mapping, mining, landscape design, fashion design, circuit board design, and dozens of other applications.

AutoCAD's ability to adapt to and work with specific programs helps make AutoCAD even more useful. AutoCAD drawings can also be transferred to other CAD or CAM packages such as Mastercam and Smartcam via an IGES or DXF file format.

The major benefits of a CAD package like AutoCAD are as follows:

- Automates repetitive tasks

- Reduces duplicate efforts

- Allows you to communicate with others via electronic means

- Makes drawing revisions easier to perform

- Enables you to customize your environment and tailor AutoCAD to meet your needs

- Lets you create extremely accurate and high-quality drawings

- Provides impressive presentations

- Supports a wide selection of hardware

COMPUTER-AIDED MANUFACTURING

CAM (computer-aided manufacturing) utilizes computers in the control and operations of a manufacturing process.

There are two main applications for computer-aided manufacturing:

1. Those whereby the computer directly controls a manufacturing operation

2. Those whereby the computer is used to support the manufacturing process, for example, inventory control, and CNC part programming

In the past, CAM, as it applies to NC part programming, also was called computer-assisted programming. Generally, the CAM process involves either defining the part geometry or calling it up from an existing file and then describing the cutter tool path including feeds, speeds, direction, coolant, and clamping. Next, the program is run through a process called post-processing in which a CNC file is generated.

Therefore there are three distinct steps in the CAM process, as follows:

1. Input or define the part geometry

   Most CAM systems enable the programmer to describe the part geometry. They also allow the importing of data from other software packages such as CAD. Today's CAD systems actually evolved from early computer-assisted programming and computer graphics programming systems.

2. Describe the cutter toolpath

   Describing the toolpath involves selecting the tools to be used for the particular job, specifying the feeds and speeds, and activating the clamps and coolant. There are many CAM systems on the market today and each works slightly differently. The systems that are more difficult to use use the part geometry described as the centerline cutter toolpath. The part program is modified by erasing certain geometry or by changing the tool information to create offsets and pockets. The packages that are better and easier to use employ the part geometry as a reference, and the programmer describes the tool path with it.

3. Generate the final CNC program

   The final CNC program is generated when the post-processor is run. In many older CAM systems, the post-processor was a separate software package. Today's have integrated post-processor systems. Many companies make their living developing post-processors for other companies. A post-processor, whether integrated or separate, is customized for a particular machine tool. As discussed in Chapter 1, there are so many variations of machine tool controllers, that you have a different post-processor for each.

MASTERCAM

CAM software such as Mastercam helps provide the CNC programmer with a valuable productivity tool for both the generation of CNC part programs and process planning. It helps reduce the time it takes to generate accurate machine-ready NC programs. CAD drawings from software such as AutoCAD are easily translated into programs that can be downloaded to a CNC machine directly from the computer. Mastercam CAD/CAM solutions are provided for two-dimensional, two and one-half-dimensional, and three-dimensional machining, including two- through five-axis milling, lathes, two- and four-axis wire EDM, sheet-metal punching and unfolding, plasma cutting, and lasers. All Mastercam products have a double-precision three-dimensional database, powerful, integrated CAD system, and an easy-to-use intuitive user interface that helps users learn CAM quickly and easily. Thousands of companies, technical schools, colleges, and universities have chosen Mastercam for its power and ease of use.

Standard CAD features in Mastercam include standard geometry and surface creation. The easy-to-use CAD system allows for the creation of the following entities in two-dimensional or three-dimensional: points, lines, arcs, fillets, splines, ellipses, rectangles, chamfers, and letters, as well as surfaces such as Loft, Coons, Ruled, Revolved, Swept, Draft, and Trimmed. Also included are IGES, DXF, CADL, and ASCII bi-directional data converters. Other features include

- Dimensioning in any plane or view

- Cross-hatching

- Multiple viewports

- Dynamic rotation, panning, and zooming

- Plotting capabilities

CAM features in Mastercam include the following:

- Graphical toolpath editing with full toolpath simulation

- Built-in tool libraries and materials files

- Canned cycle support

- Links to third-party applications

- Surface machining

- Drilling

- Pocketing

- Cycle time estimation

The following example shows the typical steps for creating geometry in Mastercam and producing the final CNC code. For this example, the Mastercam milling module is used.

EXAMPLE OF CREATING GEOMETRY IN MASTERCAM

After you enter the Mastercam milling module, the main drawing screen appears (Fig. 7-1).

The Mastercam screen consists of a graphics drawing area (center of screen), a menu area (left edge of screen), and a command area (bottom of screen).

```
Main Menu:                                          Mastercam
Analyze      |
Create       |
File         |
Modify       |
Xform        |
Delete       |
Screen       |
Toolpaths    |
NC Utils     |
Exit         |
BACKUP       |
MAIN MENU    |
-PM-         |
Z      0.0000|
Color:    10 |
Level:     1 |
Mask:    OFF |
Tplane: OFF  |
Cplane:    T |
Gview:     T |
```

Figure 7-1 Mastercam main drawing screen

When you move the mouse or pointing device, a cross-hair or cursor moves around the graphics drawing area. By moving the cursor to the menu area on the screen's left edge, you can select a menu option. You select an option by moving the cursor so that it highlights the option and then picking it with the pick button of your pointing device. You can also choose a menu option from the keyboard by typing in the capitalized letter shown for a particular menu option. For example, to choose File, press F on your keyboard.

Using Mastercam and the part drawing in Fig. 7-2, generate the CNC part program that you can finally test on CNCEZ. (This is the same part drawing used in Exercise 7 in Chapter 8.)

STEP 1: Create a rectangle to show the stock material. First, create the rough stock. Remember that in order to start from a known position, the PRZ will be the lower left-hand corner and top of the workpiece.

From the MAIN menu, select **Create**.
Select **Rectangle**.
Select **1 Point**.
Select **Values**.

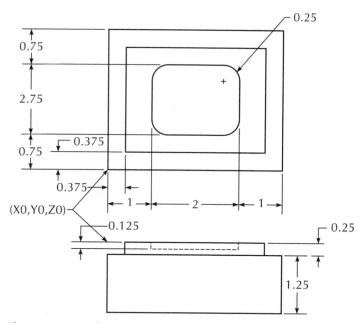

Figure 7-2 Part drawing showing 1/8in. pocket and 1/4in. milled profile

Mastercam prompts you on the command line (bottom of screen) for the lower left-hand corner of the rectangle.

Enter the following: **X0Y0 [Enter]**.
When prompted for the width, enter **4 [Enter]**.
When prompted for the height, enter **3 [Enter]**.

You have now created a rectangle that will represent the stock of the workpiece to be machined.

To see all of the rectangle on the screen, use the Fit command: Press and hold Alt and press F1. The drawing will redraw automatically on the screen and fit itself to the entire screen area. The Fit command has just fit all objects on the screen; it has not changed the dimensions of the object.

You can use the function keys to access Mastercam macros that execute some of the more frequently used commands, as follows:

F1 = ZOOM	ALT+F1 = FIT TO SCREEN
F2 = UNZOOM	
F3 = REPAINT	
F4 = ANALYZE	ALT+F4 = CURSOR POSITION
F5 = DELETE	ALT+F5 = DELETE WINDOW
F6 = FILE	
F7 = MODIFY	
F8 = XFORM	
F9 = DISPLAY INFO	ALT+F9 = VIEW
F10 = HELP	

Another important key is Escape (Esc). Pressing it, you interrupt an operation and back up one menu at a time.

STEP 2: Create a rectangle, which will be the basic shape of a lip around the outside of the part.

To return Mastercam to the MAIN menu options, select **MAIN MENU** from the menu area.

You can return to the MAIN menu at any time by choosing MAIN MENU. To back up one menu at a time, choose the BACK UP option.

From the main menu, select **Create**.
Select **Rectangle**.
Select **1 Point**.
Select **Values**.

Mastercam prompts you on the command line for the lower left-hand corner of the rectangle.

Enter the following: **X.375Y.375 [Enter]**
When prompted for the width, enter **3.25 [Enter]**.
When prompted for the height, enter **2.25 [Enter]**.

You have created a rectangle that will represent a raised ridge around the outside of the part. (Fig. 7-3).

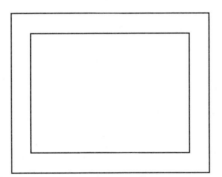

Figure 7-3 Part with raised ridge

Next, transform the rectangle that forms the lip to its final depth of cut value. In this example, the depth is –0.25 inch.

Return to the MAIN menu.
Select **Xform**.
Select **Delete**.
Select **Translate**.
Select **Window**.

Place a window around the inner rectangle.
Select **Done**.
Select **Rectangle**.
Enter the following: **Z–0.25 [Enter]**.
Press F3 to redraw the screen.

The lip is now a different color to show it has been translated to Z–0.25.

STEP 3: Create a rectangle that will be the basic shape of an internal pocket.

From the MAIN menu, select Create.
Select **Rectangle**.
Select **1 Point**.
Select **Values**.

Mastercam prompts you on the command line for the lower left-hand corner of the rectangle.

Enter the following: **X1Y0.75 [Enter]**.
Enter the Width: **2 [Enter]**.
Enter the Height: **1.5 [Enter]**.

You have created a rectangle that will represent the internal pocket (Fig. 7-4).

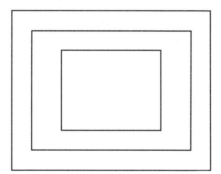

Figure 7-4 Part with rectangle

STEP 4: Fillet the four corners of the internal pocket.

From the MAIN menu, select Modify.
Select **Fillet**.
Select **Radius**.
Enter the radius of the fillet: **0.25 [Enter]**.

In Mastercam, the fillet radius must be larger than the radius of the cutter to be used.

You can now fillet the line of the first intersection as shown in Fig. 7-5. After completing the first fillet, continue with the remaining intersections in the same manner.

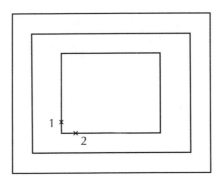

Figure 7-5 Filleted intersection

Next, transform the pocket to its final depth of cut. In this example, the depth is –0.125 inch.

Return to the MAIN menu and select **Xform**.
Select **Delete**.
Select **Translate**.
Select **Window**.
Create a window around the pocket.
Select **Done**.
Select **Rectangle**.
Enter the following: **Z–0.125 [Enter]**.
Press F3 to redraw the screen.

STEP 5: Save the part geometry.

The geometry is now set at the proper depths for machining. You should save the geometry before creating the toolpaths, which is step 6.

Return to the MAIN menu, then select **FILE**.
Select **Save**.
Enter CAMEXER1 [Enter].

STEP 6: Next, create the toolpath. For machining this part, use the following plan:

1. Rough cut around and finish profile the lip.
2. Cut out and finish the internal pocket.

You will use both the contour and the pocket toolpath commands. The contour toolpath is used for when a cutter is to follow the center of a line or follow tangent to that line (cutter compensation to the left or right of the line). The pocket toolpath is used when a cavity with or without internal pockets is to be cut out.

From the MAIN menu, select **Toolpaths**.
Select **Contour**.

Mastercam prompts you for an NCI file name. In Mastercam, the toolpath file is referred to as an NCI file. The NCI file will be converted to CNC code for a particular machine tool using the post-processor.

Enter **CAMEXER1 [Enter]**.

Use the chain command to select the rectangle that forms the lip on the part.

Select **Chain**.
Select the lower left-hand corner of the rectangle (Fig. 7-6).

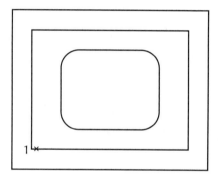

Figure 7-6 Selecting the lower left-hand corner

To complete the chain, select **Close**.

The rectangle closes and its color changes to show that the chain is complete.

To end the chained profile, select **End Here**.
Select **Done**.

Next, set the machining parameters for this toolpath section.

Select **Params**.
Use the parameter setting without any modification.

The parameter screens have many different options; not all of the parameters have to be changed to complete this toolpath. Definitions for each parameter are in the Mastercam documentation.

The contour toolpath has two parameter screens. The first is specific to contouring; the second is generally the same for all toolpaths.

To move between the parameter screen options, move the pointing device up and down. To choose an option, press the left pick button. To set an option, press Enter.

Entry/exit line direction = **tangent**
Entry/exit line length = **0.0000**
Entry/exit arc : Radius = **0.0000** Angle = **90.000**
Number of roughing cuts = **2**
Roughing cut spacing = **0.1**
Number of finish passes = **1**
Finish pass spacing = **0.05**

When this parameter screen is set, select **Next screen**.

Make the necessary changes so that the second parameter screen matches the following parameters:

Cutter compensation in control = **off**
Roll cutter around sharp corners
Cutter compensation in computer = **right center**
Tool library: **TOOLS.mtl** Material: **NONE**
Tool ref. = **0.25END** Tool n. = **2** Dia. ofst. = **0** Len. ofst. = **0**
Cutter diameter = **0.2500**
Amount of stock to leave = **0.0000**
Feedrate = **8.0000** Plunge rate = **4.0000** Spindle speed = **2500**
Coolant = **off**
Rapid depth = **0.1250** Contour depth = **-0.2500**
Starting sequence number = **1** Increment = **1** Program n. = **1234**
No rotary axis
Linear array: Nx, Ny = **1 1** Dx, Dy = **0.0000 0.0000**
Depth cuts: Rough: **2 cuts at 0.1250** Finish: **0 cuts at 0.0000**
Home position = **X0.0000 Y0.0000 Z1.0000**
Misc. real [1] = **0.0** Wk Coordinate System (G53 = 1..G59 = 7) = **1**
Tool Plane: **OFF** Tool Origin: **OFF**
Display: **Tool(static, endpoints, run, delay = 0.0)** Toolpath
Select this line when through setting parameters

Select the last line with the mouse. The rectangle should now have three light-blue cutter paths around the outside. If the cutter paths are to the inside, your chain direction has gone clockwise instead of counterclockwise. Return to the MAIN menu without saving the toolpath and try again.

To accept the toolpath segment, select **Yes**.

The machining will now be continued by moving onto the pocket.

From the TOOLPATHS Menu, select **Pocket**.

Use the chain command to select the rectangle that forms the pocket.

Select **Chain**.
Select the lower left-hand corner of the pocket (Fig. 7-7).

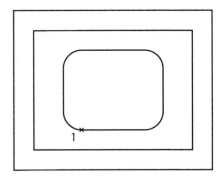

Figure 7-7 Selecting the lower left-
hand corner of the pocket

To close in order to end the chain, select **Close**.

The rectangle closes and its color changes to show that the chain is complete.

To end the chained profile, select **End Here**.
Select **Done**.

Next, set the machining parameters for this toolpath section.
Use the parameter setting without any modification.
The parameter screens have many different options; not all of them have to be changed to complete this toolpath. Definitions for each parameter are in the Mastercam documentation.
The pocket toolpath has two parameter screens. The first is specific to pocket; the second is generally the same for all toolpaths.
To move between the parameter screen options, move the mouse up and down. To choose an option, press the left mouse button. To set an option, press Enter.

ROUGHING
Cutting method = **Zig zag**
Roughing angle = **0.000**
Roughing cut spacing = **0.100**
Pocket depth = **–0.125** (This is the total depth of the pocket.)

FINISHING
Number of finish passes = **1**
Finishing pass spacing = **0.001**
Entry/exit line direction = **tangent**
Entry/exit line length = **0.0000**
Entry/exit arc : Radius = **0.0000 Angle = 90.000**
Machining sequence = **region**
Machine finish passes at: **final depth**
Use additional finish parameters? **No**

After setting this parameter screen, select **Next screen**.
Make the necessary changes so that the second parameter screen matches the following parameters:

Roll cutter around sharp corners
Tool library: **TOOLS.mtl** Material: **NONE**
Tool ref. = **0.25END** Tool n. = **2** Dia. ofst. =**0** Len. ofst. = **0**
Cutter diameter = **0.2500**
Amount of stock to leave = **0.0000**
Feedrate = **8.0000** Plunge rate = **4.0000** Spindle speed = **2500**
Coolant = **off**
Rapid depth = **0.1250**
Starting sequence number = **1** Increment = **1** Program n. = **1234**
No rotary axis
Linear array: Nx, Ny = **1 1** Dx, Dy = **0.0000 0.0000**
Depth cuts: Rough: **1 cut at 0.0000** Finish: **0 cut at 0.0000**
Home position = **X0.0000 Y0.0000 Z1.0000**
Misc. real [1] = **0** Wk Coordinate System **(G53=1..G59=7)=1**
Tool Plane: **OFF** Tool Origin: **OFF**
Display: **Tool(static, endpoints, run, delay = 0.00) Toolpath**
Select this line when through setting parameter

Select the last line with the mouse.
The inside of the pocket should now have a white line following inside of the pocket's shape.

Select **All** (Watch the toolpath move in the pocket.).
Select **Done**.
To accept the toolpath, select **Yes**.
To end the toolpath generation, select **End program**.
To run the post-processor, select **Yes**.
To continue, press **[Enter]**.

This completes the toolpath moves, runs the post-processor, and generates the finished CNC program, as follows:

```
%
:1234
N001 G90 G80 G40
N002 M06 T02
N003 S2500 M03
N004 Z.125
N005 X.375 Y.100
N006 G01 Z-.125 F4.0
N007 X3.625 F8.0
N008 G03 X3.900 Y.375 J0.275
N009 G01 Y2.625
N010 G03 X3.625 Y2.900 I-0.275
N011 G01 X.375
N012 G03 X.100 Y2.625 J-0.275
N013 G01 Y.375
N014 G03 X.375 Y.100 I0.275
N015 G01 Y.200 F4.0
N016 X3.625 F8.0
N017 G03 X3.800 Y.375 J0.175
N018 G01 Y2.625
N019 G03 X3.625 Y2.800 I-0.175
N020 G01 X.375
N021 G03 X.200 Y2.625 J-0.175
N022 G01 Y.375
N023 G03 X.375 Y.200 I0.175
N024 G01 Y.250 F4.0
N025 X3.625 F8.0
N026 G03 X3.750 Y.375 J0.125
N027 G01 Y2.625
N028 G03 X3.625 Y2.750 I-0.125
N029 G01 X.375
N030 G03 X.250 Y2.625 J-0.125
N031 G01 Y.375
N032 G03 X.375 Y.250 I0.125
N033 G00 Z.125
N034 Y.100
N035 G01 Z-.250 F4.0
N036 X3.625 F8.0
N037 G03 X3.900 Y.375 J0.275
N038 G01 Y2.625
N039 G03 X3.625 Y2.900 I-0.275
```

```
N040 G01 X.375
N041 G03 X.100 Y2.625 J-0.275
N042 G01 Y.375
N043 G03 X.375 Y.100 I0.275
N044 G01 Y.200 F4.0
N045 X3.625 F8.0
N046 G03 X3.800 Y.375 J0.175
N047 G01 Y2.625
N048 G03 X3.625 Y2.800 I-0.175
N049 G01 X.375
N050 G03 X.200 Y2.625 J-0.175
N051 G01 Y.375
N052 G03 X.375 Y.200 I0.175
N053 G01 Y.250 F4.0
N054 X3.625 F8.0
N055 G03 X3.750 Y.375 J0.125
N056 G01 Y2.625
N057 G03 X3.625 Y2.750 I-0.125
N058 G01 X.375
N059 G03 X.250 Y2.625 J-0.125
N060 G01 Y.375
N061 G03 X.375 Y.250 I0.125
N062 G00 Z.125
N063 X1.245 Y.876
N064 G01 Z-.125 F4.0
N065 X2.755 F8.0
N066 G03 X2.871 Y.972 I-0.005 J0.124
N067 G01 X1.129
N068 G02 X1.126 Y1.000 I0.121 J0.028
N069 G01 Y1.068
N070 X2.874
N071 Y1.164
N072 X1.126
N073 Y1.260
N074 X2.874
N075 Y1.356
N076 X1.126
N077 Y1.452
N078 X2.874
N079 Y1.548
N080 X1.126
N081 Y1.644
N082 X2.874
N083 Y1.740
```

```
N084 X1.126
N085 Y1.836
N086 X2.874
N087 Y1.932
N088 X1.126
N089 Y2.000
N090 G02 X1.129 Y2.028 I0.124
N091 G01 X2.871
N092 G03 X2.755 Y2.124 I-0.121 J-0.028
N093 G01 X1.245
N094 G02 X1.250 I0.005 J-0.124
N095 G01 X2.750
N096 G02 X2.874 Y2.000 J-0.124
N097 G01 Y1.000
N098 X2.875
N099 Y2.000
N100 G03 X2.750 Y2.125 I-0.125
N101 G01 X1.250
N102 G03 X1.125 Y2.000 J-0.125
N103 G01 Y1.000
N104 G03 X1.250 Y.875 I0.125
N105 G01 X2.750
N106 G03 X2.875 Y1.000 J0.125
N107 G00 Z.125
N108 G00 X0 Y0 Z1
N109 M05
N110 M30
```

THE CAD/CAM SYSTEM

CAD and CAM together create a direct link between product design and manufacturing. As discussed in this chapter, the CAD system is used to develop a geometric model of the part. This model then is used by the CAM system to generate part programs for CNC machine tools. The computer is the common element in both procedures. Both the CAD and CAM functions may be performed either by the same system or by separate systems located in different rooms or even different countries. The network between engineering, design, and manufacturing computers becomes the critical information highway that ties the CAD and CAM functions together.

If the connection between CAD and CAM is extended to its logical limits within a company, we then have the concept of the computer-integrated enterprise (CIE). In the CIE, all aspects of the enterprise are computer-aided, from management and sales to product design and manufacturing. A manager can access product geometric models, engineering analysis, and manufacturing quality control data. A design engineer can access market surveys, manufacturing process plans, and product life cycle data. A part programmer can access part geometric models, tool inventories, and current machine performance data. The critical technology that enables a CIE to work is the computer network, which includes workstations or PCs available to all who need them, a network connecting all the workstations or PCs, and file servers to route data to where it is needed. In a networked environment, file and data standards are crucial to facilitate data exchange between different workstations or PCs and growth to newer technologies as they become available.

OVERALL BENEFITS OF CAD/CAM

Increased productivity is generally the justification for using a CAD/CAM system. Productivity increases with faster turn around, better quality and more accuracy.

CAD/CAM systems allow for rapid development and editing of designs and documentation. When a three-dimensional geometric model is produced in the design process, it then becomes a common element for engineering analysis, machining process planning (including CNC part programming), documentation (including engineering drawings), quality control, and so on. The tight coupling of CAD and CAM considerably shortens the time it takes to bring a new product to market.

More specifically, CAD/CAM will produce benefits in the following areas:

- **Design** An efficient CAD system enables a designer to look at complex geometries and examine many different design alternatives. It also facilitates tedious operations such as maintaining standard part libraries, computing inertial (mass) properties, interfacing with analysis programs, and exchanging data with other software packages.

- **Drafting** Computer-aided drafting greatly facilitates the production, editing, storage, and plotting of complex engineering drawings. Edited drawings need only be replotted, not redrawn. Standard part libraries can be utilized. If the CAD system uses a three-dimensional geometric model as its primary data, then the production of engineering drawings is a simple matter of selecting the desired views, watching the computer generate the bulk of the drawing, selecting the desired dimensions, and annotating the appropriate features. Changes to the geometric model are automatically reflected in the engineering drawings.

- **Manufacturing** CAM provides the facility to generate CNC part programs directly from a three-dimensional geometric model or a two-dimensional engineering drawing. In addition, the CAM system tracks the machine capabilities, tool lists, materials properties, recommended feeds and speeds, and so on. The CAM system can also track many stored part programs and download them to a CNC machine tool as needed. Part programs can be verified offline using virtual machine tool simulations. Facilitating communication between the computer and the CNC machine greatly speeds up machining process planning.

- **Management Control** Project management methods range from autocratic (one person makes all the decisions) to the democratic (design teams are formed for each product and each team member has a say in all aspects of the product's design, production, and distribution). Whatever the management method used, the enhanced communication and data availability provided by a CAD/CAM system enables those who make decisions to have access to a wide range of data, from geometric models to part programs. Access to more information can lead to more-informed decisions. This is the essence of the CIE, whereby the computer network is used to collect, correlate, store, and distribute all the data used by a company, whether they be financial, marketing, engineering, manufacturing, quality control, product liability, or what ever.

- **Concurrent Engineering** Efficient CAD/CAM operations can facilitate concurrent engineering, which essentially is the running of many of the CAD and CAM functions in parallel. Concurrent engineering is designed to reduce product development time and thereby enhance competitiveness in a world economy. It relies heavily on communication, both personal and over computer networks, between all principal players in product development.

- **Product Quality** CAD/CAM helps improve overall product quality by providing for data storage and distribution, facilitating communication, decreasing product design time, increasing design process flexibility, facilitating change anywhere along the product design path, and allowing improved verification of part geometry and CNC part programs.

Following are the results of these benefits:

- The design more closely meets the product requirements, so the design goal can be closely met.

- Design/analysis time is reduced, hence shortening the time to bring the product to market.

- Production levels increase.

- Increased profit equals increased revenues, which result from a higher-quality product minus decreased cost of production.

LAB EXERCISE

1. What is CAD? _____

_____

_____

_____

_____

2. What are the major goals of CAD?

a) _____

_____

_____

_____

b) _____

_____

_____

_____

3. What is CAM? _____

_____

_____

_____

4. What are the two main applications for CAM?

a) _____

_____

_____

_____

b) _____

_____

_____

_____

5. Does CAD/CAM establish a direct link between product design and manufacture? Explain. _____

_____

_____

_____

_____

Chapter 8

Workbook Exercises

This chapter is intended to reinforce the concepts covered in Chapters 1–7 in order to help you reaffirm the basic concepts of CNC. The exercises get progressively more difficult. They are also combined with a series of exercise questions to help you understand the theoretical concepts. If you have problems with the exercises, you should go back through the chapters and review the material again.

WORKBOOK EXERCISE 1

Answer the following questions:

1. What are the two axes of motion on a basic CNC lathe? _____

_____

_____

_____

_____

2. What G-code sets the PRZ for milling? _____

_____

_____

_____

_____

3. What are miscellaneous functions? _____

_____

_____

_____

_____

4. What are the three primary axes of motion on a basic CNC mill? _____

_____

_____

_____

_____

5. What coordinate system are you working in when you are programming
   from a fixed PRZ? _____

_____

_____

_____

6. What is a preparatory function? _____

_____

_____

_____

7. Are most G-codes considered to be modal commands? _____

_____

_____

_____

8. What does performing a dwell mean? _____

_____

_____

_____

_____

9. How do a G01 and a G02 command differ? _____

_____

_____

_____

_____

10. In CNC milling, what is the purpose of cutter diameter compensation?

_____

_____

_____

_____

11. What does the I specify when a circular interpolations is programmed?

_____

_____

_____

_____

12. Which G-code is used to cancel any cutter compensation? _____

_____

_____

_____

_____

13. Give the letter address that corresponds to the following:

Feedrate: _____

Spindle speed: _____

Block number: _____

Miscellaneous function: _____

Preparatory function: _____

X-axis location: _____

Tool number: _____

WORKBOOK EXERCISE 2

Calculate the diametrical coordinates for the following turned part:

Coordinate Sheet

#	X	Z
1		
2		
3		
4		
5		
6		
7		
8		
9		
10		
11		
12		
13		
14		

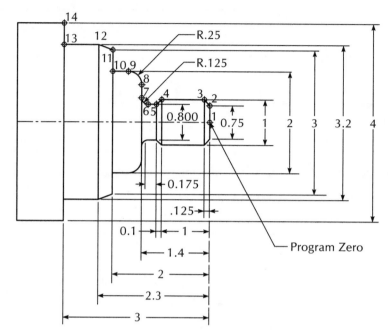

Figure 8-1 Turned part for Exercise 2

WORKBOOK EXERCISE 3

Calculate the coordinates for the following milling part:

Coordinate Sheet

#	X	Y	Z
1			
2			
3			
4			
5			
6			
7			
8			
9			
10			

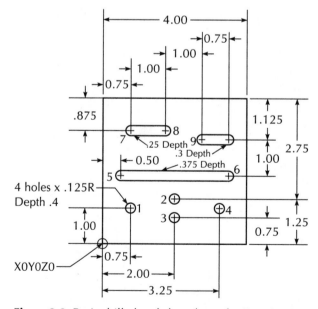

Figure 8-2 Basic drilled and slotted part for Exercise 3

WORKBOOK EXERCISE 4

Calculate the coordinates and complete the program for the finishing pass of the following lathe part:

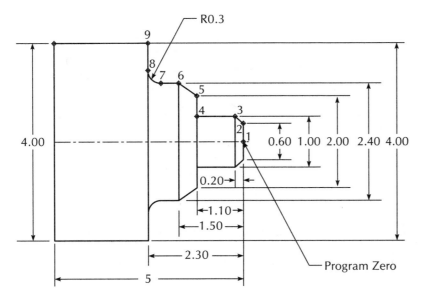

Coordinate Sheet

#	X	Z
1		
2		
3		
4		
5		
6		
7		
8		
9		

Figure 8-3 Turned part for Exercise 4

Workpiece Size:	4" Diameter by 5" Length
Tool:	Tool #1, Right-hand Turning Tool
Tool Start Position:	X4,Z3

%	Program start flag
:1004	Program number
N5 G__ G__ G__	Absolute, inches, comp. off
N10 T_____	Tool change to Tool #1
N15 M0__	Spindle on clockwise
N20 G0__ X0 Z0.1 M0__	Rapid to X0,Z0.1, Coolant 1 on
N25 G0__ Z__ F0.012	Feed to point #1 at 0.012 ipr
N30 X__	Feed to point #2
N35 X__ Z__	Feed to point #3
N40 Z__	Feed to point #4
N45 X__	Feed to point #5
N50 X__ Z__	Feed to point #6
N55 Z__	Feed to point #7
N60 G0__ X__ Z__ I0.3 K0	Circular feed to point #8
N65 G0__ X__	Feed to point #9
N70 G0__ Z3 M0__	Rapid to Z3, Coolant off
N75 T0100 M0__	Tool comp. off, Spindle off
N80 M0__	Program end

WORKBOOK EXERCISE 5

Calculate the coordinates and complete the program for the following milling part.

Coordinate Sheet

#	X	Y	Z
1			
2			
3			
4			
5			
6			
7			

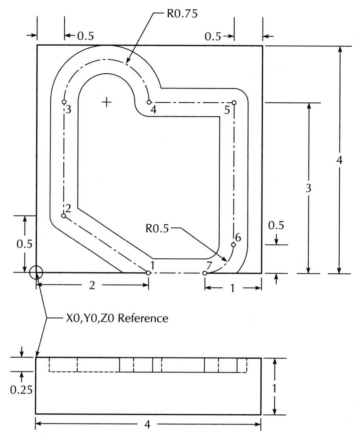

Figure 8-4 Slotted part for Exercise 5

Workpiece Size:	X4,Y4,Z1
Tool:	Tool #4, 1/2" Slot Drill
Tool Start Position:	X0,Y0,Z1

%	Program start flag
:1005	Program number
N5 G__ G__ G40 G80	Absolute, inches, comp. and cycle off
N10 M____ T____	Tool change to Tool #4
N15 M0__ S_____	Spindle on clockwise at 2000 rpm
N20 G0__ X2 Y-0.375 M0__	Rapid to X2,Y-0.375, Coolant 2 On
N25 Z-0.25	Rapid down to Z-0.25
N30 G01 Y__ F15	Feed move to point #1 at 15 ipm
N35 X__ Y__	Feed move to point #2

```
N40  Y__                     Feed move to point #3
N45  G02 X__ I0.75           Circular feed move to point #4
N50  G01 X__                 Feed move to point #5
N55  Y__                     Feed move to point #6
N60  G02 X__ Y__ I-0.5       Circular feed move to point #7
N65  G01 X__                 Feed move to point #1
N70  G00 Z1                  Rapid to Z1
N75  X0 M0__                 Rapid to X0, Coolant off
N80  M0__                    Spindle off
N85  M3__                    Program end
```

WORKBOOK EXERCISE 6

Calculate the coordinates and complete the program for the following turning part. You must choose your tools from the tool library and properly calculate the speeds, feeds, and depth of cuts required. Remember to use a Coordinate Sheet and to plan your sequence of operations.

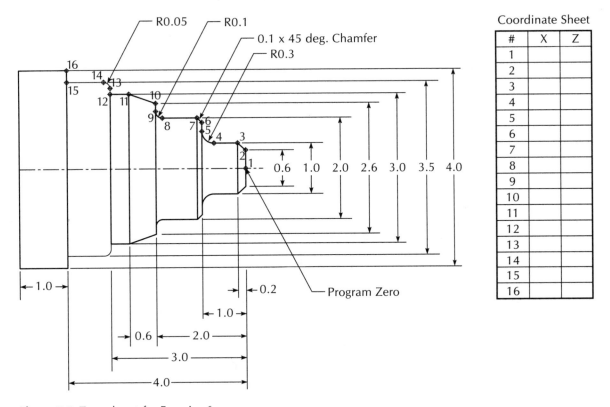

Figure 8-5 Turned part for Exercise 6

Workpiece Size: _____

Tool: _____

_____

_____

Tool Start Position: X2,Z3

CNC PROGRAMMING SHEET		PART NAME:		PROG BY:		
		MACHINE:		DATE:		PAGE:
		SET UP INFORMATION:				

N SEQ	G Code	X Pos'n	Y Pos'n	Z Pos'n	I J K Pos'n	F Feed	R Radius or Retract	S Speed	T Tool	M Misc

N SEQ	G Code	X Pos'n	Y Pos'n	Z Pos'n	I J K Pos'n		F Feed	R Radius or Retract	S Speed	T Tool	M Misc

WORKBOOK EXERCISE 7

Calculate the coordinates and create the program for the following milling part. Assume a 3/4 in. slot drill for the entire operation. You must calculate the feeds and speeds based on the material you will be cutting. Remember to use a Coordinate Sheet and to plan your sequence of operations.

Coordinate Sheet

#	X	Y	Z
1			
2			
3			
4			
5			
6			
7			
8			

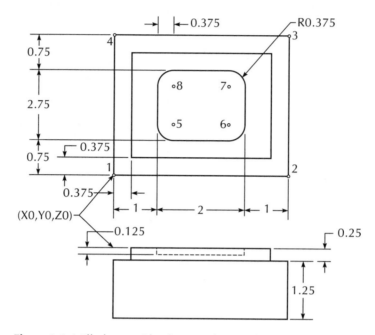

Figure 8-6 Milled part with 1/8in. pockect and 1/4in. milled profile

Workpiece Size: _____

Tool: _____

_____

_____

Tool Start Position: X0,Y0,Z1

CNC PROGRAMMING SHEET		PART NAME:		PROG BY:		
		MACHINE:		DATE:		PAGE:
		SET UP INFORMATION:				

N SEQ	G Code	X Pos'n	Y Pos'n	Z Pos'n	I J K Pos'n		F Feed	R Radius or Retract	S Speed	T Tool	M Misc

N SEQ	G Code	X Pos'n	Y Pos'n	Z Pos'n	I J K Pos'n		F Feed	R Radius or Retract	S Speed	T Tool	M Misc

Appendix A

Answers to LAB Exercises

Chapter 1

LAB EXERCISE

1. *What is CNC?*

   Computer numerical control. The process of manufacturing machined parts as controlled and allocated by a computerized controller.

2. *How did CNC come to be developed?*

   As a direct result of the war effort in World War II to ensure that both product quality and order quantity requirements were met.

3. *What is DNC?*

   Direct numerical control. The process by which a computer directly controls a numerical control machine tool.

4. *List the steps in the CNC process.*

   1. Develop the part drawing.
   2. Decide which machine will produce the part.
   3. Choose the tooling required.
   4. Decide on the machining sequence.
   5. Do math calculations for the program coordinates.
   6. Calculate the speeds and feed required for the tooling and part material.
   7. Write the NC program.
   8. Prepare setup sheets and tool lists.
   9. Send the program to machine.
   10. Verify the program.
   11. Run the program if no changes are required.

5. *Name some objectives of CNC.*

   1. Increased production
   2. Improved quality
   3. Improved accuracy
   4. Stabilizing manufacturing costs
   5. Providing the ability to do more complex jobs

6. *What are some characteristics of CNC-produced parts?*

   1. Be similar in terms of raw material.

   2. Be of various sizes and shapes.

   3. Be a small to medium batch size.

   4. Have parts whose sequences of steps for completing them are similar.

7. *Describe in your own words the CNC process.*

   NC programming is much the same as conventional machining. The machinist still has sole responsibility for the operation of the machine, although this control is no longer via manual turning of the axis handwheels, but rather via the controller and efficient NC planning and programming.

Chapter 2: In-Text Exercises

MILLING EXERCISE

Exercise 1: Absolute Positioning

A. X–1.25,Y2	B. X–4,Y2	C. X–4,Y0.5
D. X–4.5,Y–2.5	E. X–2.5,Y–4.5	F. X3,Y–3.5
G. X4,Y–2	H. X4,Y2	

Exercise 2: Incremental Positioning

A. X–1.25,Y2	B. X–2.75,Y0	C. X0,Y–1.5
D. X–0.5,Y–3	E. X2,Y–2	F. X5.5,Y1
G. X1,Y1.5	H. X0,Y4	

TURNING EXERCISE

Exercise 1: Using Incremental Coordinates, find the diametrical X and Z points on the profile.

A. X4,Z2	B. X0,Z–6	C. X–4,Z1
D. X0,Z–6	E. X2,Z–2	

Exercise 2: Using Absolute Coordinates, find the X and Z points on the profile.

A. X4,Z2	B. X4,Z–4	C. X2,Z–3
D. X2,Z–9	E. X3,Z–10	

Chapter 2: Lab Exercise

1. *What is the standard coordinate system called?*

   Cartesian coordinate system

2. *What are the three axes used on the CNC mill?*

   X, Y, and Z

3. *What are the two axes used on the CNC lathe?*

   X and Z

4. *What are the two types of coordinate systems? Explain the difference between them?*

   The absolute and the incremental coordinate systems. The absolute system has a fixed origin point, the incremental system does not (uses the last position as a reference).

5. *Does the X-axis run on a CNC milling machine vertically or horizontally?*

   Horizontally

6. *What are the three planes in the Cartesian coordinate system?*

   X Y, X Z, Y Z

7. *What is the PRZ?*

   Program Reference Zero

8. *Where do you find the PRZ on the following?*

   Milling workpiece: The lower left-hand corner and top surface of the part

   Turning workpiece: The furthest Z-axis edge and center of the workpiece

Chapter 3: Lab Exercise

1. *What do the following letter addresses stand for?*

   X: X-axis coordinate

   Y: Y-axis coordinate

   Z: Z-axis coordinate

   F: F assigns the feedrate

2. *What are the basic definitions of the following letter addresses?*

   G: Preparatory function

   M: Miscellaneous function

3. *What is a preparatory function?*

   Functions for control of the machine that involve actual tool moves

4. *What are two reasons for using cutting fluids?*

   1. Reduce heat
   2. Reduce tool wear

5. *What are the factors that affect how a cutting tool performs ?*
   1. Tool material
   2. Shape of the tool point
   3. Form of the tool

6. *Describe the PRZ for milling.*
   The lower left-hand corner and top of the work surface

Chapter 5: Lab Exercise

1. *What does the preparatory function G01 do?*
   Linear interpolation command

2. *How are tool length offsets called?*
   Using a G43 or G44

3. *Give an example of a rapid positioning in move.*
   G00 X1

4. *What does the address F stand for when a G01 command is programmed?*
   Linear feedrate

5. What plane does a G18 specify?
   XZ plane

6. *Which G-code and additional letter address are used to call up cutter compensation left?*
   G41 D_

7. *Write an example start line for a G81 drilling cycle.*
   N10 G81 Z−.25 R.125 F5

8. *Which M-code is used to specify program end, reset to start?*
   M30

Chapter 6: Lab Exercise

1. *What does the preparatory function G00 do?*
   Positioning in rapid

2. *How is tool nose radius compensation called?*
   G41 or G42

3. *Give an example of a linear feed move.*

   G01 Z3

4. *What does the address U stand for when a G71 command is programmed?*

   Amount of stock to be left for finishing in X

5. *What does a G76 specify?*

   Threading

6. *Which G-code and additional letter address are used to call up a dwell cycle?*

   G04 P_

7. *Write an example start line for a G74 peck drilling cycle.*

   N45 G74 Z–1 F.5 D.125 K.125

8. *Which M-code is used to specify spindle on clockwise?*

   M03

Chapter 7: Lab Exercise

1. *What is CAD?*

   Computer-aided design

2. *What are the major goals of CAD?*

   a) To increase productivity

   b) To create a database for manufacturing

3. *What is CAM?*

   Computer-aided manufacturing

4. *What are the two main applications for CAM?*

   a) Computer directly controlling a manufacturing operation

   b) Computer used to support the manufacturing process

5. *Does CAD/CAM establish a direct link between product design and manufacture? Explain.*

   Yes, the CAM system is used to develop the database for manufacturing and the CAM system helps in the manufacturing process.

Chapter 8: Workbook Exercises

Workbook Exercise 1

1. *What are the two axes of motion on a basic CNC lathe?*

   X and Z

2. *What G-code sets the PRZ for milling?*

   G92

3. *What are miscellaneous functions?*

   Actions necessary for machining but not for tool movement

4. *What are the three axes of motion on a basic CNC mill?*

   X, Y, and Z

5. *What coordinate system are you working in when you are programming from a fixed PRZ?*

   Absolute

6. *What is a preparatory function?*

   Functions for control of the machine that involve actual tool moves

7. *Are most G-codes considered to be modal commands?*

   Yes, most are

8. *What does performing a dwell mean?*

   A delay in the program's execution

9. *How do a G01 and a G02 command differ?*

   G01 is linear; the G02 is an arc.

10. *In CNC milling, what is the purpose of cutter diameter compensation?*

    To offset the tool center path left or right

11. *What does the I specify when a circular interpolation is programmed?*

    Distance from start point of an arc to center point in X

12. *Which G-code is used to cancel any cutter compensation?*

    G40

13. *Give the letter address that corresponds to the following:*

Feedrate:	F
Spindle speed:	S

Block number:	N
Miscellaneous function:	M
Preparatory function:	G
X-axis location:	X
Tool number:	T

Workbook Exercise 2

The coordinates for the turned part:

1. X0,Z0
2. X0.75,Z0
3. X1,Z–0.125
4. X1,Z–1
5. X0.8,Z–1.1
6. X0.8,Z–1.275
7. X1.05,Z–1.4
8. X1.5,Z–1.4
9. X2,Z–1.65
10. X2,Z–2
11. X3,Z–2
12. X3.2,Z–2.3
13. X3.2,Z–3
14. X4,Z–3

Workbook Exercise 3

The coordinates for the milled part:

1. X0.75,Y1,Z–0.4
2. X2,Y1.25,Z–0.4
3. X2,Y0.75,Z–0.4
4. X3.25,Y1,Z–0.4
5. X5,Y1.875,Z–0.25
6. X3.5,Y1.875,Z–0.25
7. X0.75,Y3.125,Z–0.25
8. X1.75,Y3.125,Z–0.25
9. X2.75,Y2.875,Z–0.3
10. X3.5,Y2.875,Z–0.3

Workbook Exercise 4

The coordinates:

1. X0,Z0
2. X0.6,Z0
3. X1,Z–0.2
4. X1,Z–1.1
5. X2,Z–1.1
6. X2.4,Z–1.5
7. X2.4,Z–2
8. X3,Z–2.3
9. X4,Z–2.3

The completed program:

Workpiece Size:	4" Diameter by 5" Length
Tool:	Tool #1, Right-hand Turning Tool
Tool Start Position:	X4,Z3

%	Program start flag
:1004	Program number
N5 G90 G20 G40	Absolute, inches, comp. off
N10 T0101	Tool change to Tool #1
N15 M03	Spindle on clockwise
N20 G00 X0 Z0.1 M07	Rapid to X0,Z0.1, coolant 1 on
N25 G00 Z0 F0.012	Feed to point #1 at 0.012 ipr
N30 X0.6	Feed to point #2
N35 X1 Z–0.2	Feed to point #3
N40 Z–1.1	Feed to point #4
N45 X2	Feed to point #5
N50 X2.4 Z–1.5	Feed to point #6
N55 Z–2	Feed to point #7
N60 G02 X3 Z–2.3 I0.3 K0	Circular feed to point #8
N65 G01 X4	Feed to point #9
N70 G00 Z3 M09	Rapid to Z3, coolant off
N75 T0100 M05	Tool comp. off, spindle off
N80 M02	Program end

Workbook Exercise 5

The coordinates:

1. X2,Y0,Z–0.25
2. X0.5,Y1,Z–0.25
3. X0.5,Y3,Z–0.25
4. X2,Y3,Z–0.25

5. X3.5,Y3,Z–0.25

6. X3.5,Y0.5,Z–0.25

7. X3,Y0,Z–0.25

The completed program:

Workpiece Size:	X4,Y4,Z1
Tool:	Tool #4, 1/2" Slot Drill
Tool Start Position:	X0,Y0,Z1

%	Program start flag
:1005	Program number
N5 G90 G20 G40 G80	Absolute, inches, comp. and cycle off
N10 M06 T04	Tool change to Tool #4
N15 M03 S2000	Spindle on clockwise at 2000 rpm
N20 G00 X2 Y–0.375 M08	Rapid to X2,Y–0.375, coolant 2 On
N25 Z–0.25	Rapid down to Z–0.25
N30 G01 Y0 F15	Feed move to point #1
N35 X0.5 Y1	Feed move to point #2
N40 Y3	Feed move to point #3
N45 G02 X2 I0.75	Circular feed move to point #4
N50 G01 X3.5	Feed move to point #5
N55 Y0.5	Feed move to point #6
N60 G02 X3 Y0 I–0.5	Circular feed move to point #7
N65 G01 X2	Feed move to point #1
N70 G00 Z1	Rapid to Z1
N75 X0 M09	Rapid to X0, Coolant off
N80 M05	Spindle off
N85 M30	Program end

Workbook Exercise 6

The coordinates:

1. X0,Z0

2. X0.6,Z0

3. X1,Z–0.2

4. X1,Z–0.7

5. X1.6,Z–1

6. X1.8,Z–1

7. X2,Z–1.1

8. X2,Z–1.9

9. X2.2,Z–2

10. X2.6,Z–2

11. X3,Z–2.6

12. X3,Z–3

13. X3.4,Z–3
14. X3.5,Z–3.05
15. X3.5,Z–4
16. X4,Z–4

The completed part program:

Workpiece Size:	4" Diameter by 5" Length
Tool:	Tool #1, Right-hand Turning Tool
	Tool #2, Right-hand Finishing Tool
Tool Start Position:	X4,Z3

%	Program start flag
:1006	Program number
N5 G90 G20 G40	Absolute, inches, cutter comp. off
N10 T0101	Tool change to Tool #1
N15 M03	Spindle on clockwise
N20 G00 Z0.1 M07	Rapid to Z0.1, coolant #1 On
N25 G71 P30 Q105 U0.05 W0.05	
D625 F0.012	Turning cycle
N30 G01 X0 Z0	Feed move to point #1
N35 X0.6	Feed move to point #2
N40 X1 Z–0.2	Feed move to point #3
N45 Z–0.7	Feed move to point #4
N50 G02 X1.6 Z–1 I0.3 K0	Circular feed move to point #5
N55 G01 X1.8	Feed move to point #6
N60 X2 Z–1.1	Feed move to point #7
N65 Z–1.9	Feed move to point #8
N70 G02 X2.2 Z–2 I0.1 K0	Feed move to point #9
N75 G01 X2.6	Feed move to point #10
N80 X3 Z–2.6	Feed move to point #11
N85 Z–3	Feed move to point #12
N90 X3.4	Feed move to point #13
N95 G03 X3.5 Z–3.05 I0 K–0.05	Circular feed move to point #14
N100 G01 Z–4	Feed move to point #15
N105 X4	Feed move to point #16
N110 G00 Z3 T0100	Rapid move to Z3
N115 T0202	Tool change to Tool #2
N120 G00 Z0.1	Rapid move to Z0.1
N125 G70 P30 Q105 F0.006	Finish pass on profile at 0.006 ipr
N130 G00 Z3 M09	Rapid to Z3 and coolant pump off
N135 T0200 M05	Tool cancel and spindle off
N140 M02	Program end

Workbook Exercise 7

The coordinates:

1. X0,Y0,Z–0.25
2. X4,Y0,Z–0.25
3. X4,Y3,Z–0.25
4. X0,Y3,Z–0.25
5. X1.375,Y1.125,Z–0.125
6. X2.625,Y1.125,Z–0.125
7. X2.625,Y1.875,Z–0.125
8. X1.375,Y1.875,Z–0.125

The completed part program:

Workpiece Size:	X4,Y3,Z1.5
Tool:	Tool #6, 3/4" Slot Drill
Tool Start Position:	X0,Y0,Z1

%	Program start flag
:1007	Program number
N5 G90 G20 G40 G80	Setup defaults
N10 M06 T6	Tool change to Tool #6
N15 M03 S1500	Spindle on clockwise at 1500 rpm
N20 G00 X–0.5 M08	Rapid move to X–0.5, Coolant on
N25 Z–0.25	Rapid move down to Z–0.25
N30 G01 X4 F15	Feed move to point #2 at 15 ipm
N35 Y3	Feed move to point #3
N40 X0	Feed move to point #4
N45 Y0	Feed move to point #1
N50 G00 Z0.25	Rapid move up to Z0.25
N55 X1.375 Y1.125	Rapid move over to X1.375,Y1.125
N60 G01 Z–0.125 F5	Feed move down to point #5
N65 X2.625	Feed move to point #6
N70 Y1.875	Feed move to point #7
N75 X1.375	Feed move to point #8
N80 Y1.125	Feed move to point #5
N85 G00 Z1	Rapid move up to Z1
N90 X0 Y0 M09	Rapid move to X0,Y0 and coolant off
N95 M05	Spindle off
N100 M02	Program end

Appendix B

Cutting Speeds and Feeds

Formulas

SPINDLE RPM

$$RPM = \frac{4CS}{D}$$

CS   Material cutting speed in surface feet per minute/meters per minute (sfm/mpm).

D   Diameter of the part (turning) or diameter of the cutter (milling).

FEEDRATES (Inch)

Lathe

Feed (in./min) = rpm × r

r   Feedrate in inches per revolution (ipr),
(usually .001 – .020 ipr)

Mill

Feed = rpm × T × N

T   Chip load per tooth

N   Number of teeth on cutter

FEEDRATES (metric)

Lathe

Feed (mm/min) = rpm × r

r   Feedrate in mm per revolution.

Mill

Feed = rpm × T × N

T   Chip load per tooth

N   Number of teeth on cutter

MILLING MATERIAL TABLE (INCH VERSION)

(All cutting speeds in surface feet per minute, chip load per tooth)

Material	Cutting Speed	Chip load
Aluminum and magnesium—HSS cutter	250	0.005
Brass and bronze, soft—HSS cutter	220	0.005
Copper—HSS cutter	150	0.005
Cast iron, soft—HSS cutter	75	0.005
Cast iron, hard—HSS cutter	50	0.003
Steel—HSS cutter	25	0.004
Stainless steel, hard—HSS cutter	35	0.003
Stainless steel, free machining—HSS cutter	70	0.003
Titanium—HSS cutter	35	0.003
Ferritic low alloys—HSS cutter	40	0.002
Austenitic alloys—HSS cutter	20	0.001
Nickel base alloys—HSS cutter	5	0.001
Cobalt base alloys—HSS cutter	5	0.001

MILLING MATERIAL TABLE (METRIC VERSION)

(All cutting speeds in surface meters per minute; chip load expressed in mm/flute)

Material	Cutting speed	Chip load
Aluminum and magnesium—HSS cutter	180	0.12
Brass and bronze, soft—HSS cutter	70	0.12
Brass and bronze, hard—HSS cutter	45	0.08
Copper—HSS cutter	45	0.12
Cast iron, soft—HSS cutter	23	0.12
Cast iron, hard—HSS cutter	14	0.07
Steel—HSS cutter	8	0.10
Stainless steel, hard—HSS cutter	11	0.08
Stainless steel, free machining—HSS cutter	21	0.08
Titanium—HSS cutter	11	0.08
Ferritic low alloys—HSS cutter	12	0.05
Austenitic alloys—HSS cutter	6	0.03
Nickel base alloys—HSS cutter	2	0.03
Cobalt base alloys—HSS cutter	2	0.03

LATHE MATERIAL FILE (INCH VERSION)

Column one is the spindle speed in in./min
Column two is the feedrate in in./rev
Column three is the feedrate for roughing only in in./rev
Column four is the amount of each depth of cut in inches
Column five is the cutting operation

Aluminum

Speed	FR in./rev	FR in./min	Depth of cut	Operation
300	0.007			Drilling
800	0.01	0.005	0.15	Roughing
1000	0.003	0.011		Finishing
600	0.003	0.011		Grooving

Steel

Speed	FR in./rev	FR in./min	Depth of cut	Operation
120	0.005			Drilling
600	0.01	0.005	0.125	Roughing
800	0.003	0.01		Finishing
500	0.003	0.01		Grooving

Cast Iron

Speed	FR in./rev	FR in./min	Depth of cut	Operation
120	0.003			Drilling
550	0.01	0.005	0.125	Roughing
410	0.003	0.011		Finishing
300	0.003	0.011		Grooving

LATHE MATERIAL FILE (METRIC VERSION)
Column one is the spindle speed in m/min
Column two is the feedrate in mm/rev
Column three is the feedrate for roughing only in mm/rev
Column four is the amount of each depth of cut in mm
Column five is the cutting operation

Aluminum

Speed	FR mm/rev	FR mm/min	Depth of cut	Operation
91	0.18			Drilling
244	0.25	0.12	3	Roughing
305	0.08	0.28		Finishing
183	0.08	0.28		Grooving

Steel

Speed	FR mm/rev	FR mm/min	Depth of cut	Operation
37	0.13			Drilling
183	0.25	0.12	3	Roughing
244	0.08	0.25		Finishing
152	0.08	0.25		Grooving

Cast Iron

Speed	FR mm/rev	FR mm/min	Depth of cut	Operation
37	0.08			Drilling
168	0.25	0.12	3	Roughing
125	0.08	0.28		Finishing
91	0.08	0.28		Grooving

Appendix C

Blank Programming Sheets

	PART NAME:		PROG BY:		
PROGRAMMING SHEET	MACHINE:		DATE:		PAGE:
	SET UP INFORMATION:				

N SEQ	G Code	X Pos'n	Y Pos'n	Z Pos'n	I J K Pos'n	F Feed	R Radius or Retract	S Speed	T Tool	M Misc

PROGRAMMING SHEET	PART NAME:		PROG BY:		
	MACHINE:		DATE:		PAGE:
	SET UP INFORMATION:				

N SEQ	G Code	X Pos'n	Y Pos'n	Z Pos'n	I J K Pos'n	F Feed	R Radius or Retract	S Speed	T Tool	M Misc

PROGRAMMING SHEET	PART NAME:		PROG BY:		
	MACHINE:		DATE:		PAGE:
	SET UP INFORMATION:				

N SEQ	G Code	X Pos'n	Y Pos'n	Z Pos'n	I J K Pos'n	F Feed	R Radius or Retract	S Speed	T Tool	M Misc

PROGRAMMING SHEET		PART NAME:		PROG BY:		
		MACHINE:		DATE:		PAGE:
		SET UP INFORMATION:				

N SEQ	G Code	X Pos'n	Y Pos'n	Z Pos'n	I J K Pos'n	F Feed	R Radius or Retract	S Speed	T Tool	M Misc

PROGRAMMING SHEET	PART NAME:		PROG BY:	
	MACHINE:		DATE:	PAGE:
	SET UP INFORMATION:			

N SEQ	G Code	X Pos'n	Y Pos'n	Z Pos'n	I J K Pos'n		F Feed	R Radius or Retract	S Speed	T Tool	M Misc

PROGRAMMING SHEET		PART NAME:		PROG BY:		
		MACHINE:		DATE:	PAGE:	
		SET UP INFORMATION:				

N SEQ	G Code	X Pos'n	Y Pos'n	Z Pos'n	I J K Pos'n		F Feed	R Radius or Retract	S Speed	T Tool	M Misc

PROGRAMMING SHEET	PART NAME:		PROG BY:	
	MACHINE:		DATE:	PAGE:
	SET UP INFORMATION:			

N SEQ	G Code	X Pos'n	Y Pos'n	Z Pos'n	I J K Pos'n		F Feed	R Radius or Retract	S Speed	T Tool	M Misc

PROGRAMMING SHEET	PART NAME:		PROG BY:	
	MACHINE:		DATE:	PAGE:
	SET UP INFORMATION:			

N SEQ	G Code	X Pos'n	Y Pos'n	Z Pos'n	I J K Pos'n	F Feed	R Radius or Retract	S Speed	T Tool	M Misc

PROGRAMMING SHEET		PART NAME:		PROG BY:		
		MACHINE:		DATE:		PAGE:
		SET UP INFORMATION:				

N SEQ	G Code	X Pos'n	Y Pos'n	Z Pos'n	I J K Pos'n		F Feed	R Radius or Retract	S Speed	T Tool	M Misc

PROGRAMMING SHEET	PART NAME:					PROG BY:				
	MACHINE:					DATE:			PAGE:	
	SET UP INFORMATION:									
N SEQ	G Code	X Pos'n	Y Pos'n	Z Pos'n	I J K Pos'n	F Feed	R Radius or Retract	S Speed	T Tool	M Misc

Technical Support

Getting Technical Support

If you have a problem or question about the software or a program you are writing, help is available by sending a fax or your file to the following:

TOR Computerized Systems, Inc.
CNCEZ Technical Support
160 Applewood Crescent, #14
Concord, Ontario L4K 4H2
Canada
Fax: (905) 660-1382
Tel: (904) 660-3262
e-mail: frankn@torcomp.com

You can also visit our Internet web site at www.torcomp.com

When requesting assistance, make sure you provide us with as much information as possible, including the following:

1. **Address Information**
   Name
   Company
   Date
   Address
   Telephone number
   Fax number

2. **Hardware and Software Information**
   Product name
   Computer brand and model
   Operating system(s) and version
   Network software and version
   Amount of hard disk space
   Amount of memory (RAM)
   Type of graphics card(s)
   Whether you use a digitizer or mouse
   Printer: Serial   Parallel
   Print-out of CONFIG.SYS file
   Print-out of AUTOEXEC.BAT file

3. **CNC Program**
   If the program is too long, you can mail it on disk.

4. Problem Description
The sequence of steps
Program block numbers
Error message displayed

Basic Troubleshooting

Troubleshooting your system starts with a few basic steps you can follow to help
solve your problem.

Step 1: Try to recreate what you were doing before the problem occurred. For
example, did you load new software or hardware or have you tried a new
command or sequence of commands.

Step 2: Strip down your system files to the basics. Make a backup of your
CONFIG.SYS and AUTOEXEC.BAT files and then strip them down removing
any extra TSRs, screen savers, or other utilities. Once the problem is solved,
restore each file to its previous status one line at a time.

Sample CONFIG.SYS file:

```
Files=30
Buffers=20
Device=C:\dos\himem.sys
Dos=high
```

Sample AUTOEXEC.BAT file:

```
Prompt $p$g
Path=C:\;C:\DOS
Set temp=C:\DOS
```

Step 3: Read through this book carefully on the use of the software or specific
commands. If an error message is displayed, look at the following section
under error messages.

Error Messages

Error-N @ Address

The DOS SET TEMP command must be used in the AUTOEXEC.BAT file to
create an environment variable that can be used by CNCEZ, for example,

SET TEMP = C:\TEMP

where TEMP is a valid directory on the (root drive) of your computer's hard
disk.

Many programs use this variable when storing temporary files. Refer to your DOS users' manual for more information on the SET TEMP command.

Error-T @ Address

Your CNC program is an invalid file and is not recognized by CNCEZ. To correct this problem, check your program with a DOS ASCII editor and remove any erroneous characters.

Error In - exefile, error in raw-in-more

This error may occur on some 80286 computers. To correct this problem, remark out or remove the DOS\SETVER or any diskcache programs that are loaded in the CONFIG.SYS or AUTOEXEC.BAT files.

Error D @ Address

This occurs when a file is opened from a specific directory but before the simulation is run, the directory is changed. The file you are currently using is not located in the directory specified in the status line.

Special CNC Codes

If your CNC machine controller uses special codes or is conversational and you want to simulate it, send us complete details so that we can devise a possible solution.

Glossary

Absolute System - A measuring system in which all points are given with respect to a common datum point. The alternative is the incremental system.

Accuracy - Measured by the difference between the actual position of the machine slide and the position demanded.

Address - A letter that represents the meaning of the element of information immediately following it.

ANSI - Abbreviation for American National Standards Institute. It sets drafting standards.

Arc Clockwise - An arc generated by the tool motion in two axes in which the toolpath with respect to the workpiece is a clockwise when viewing the plane of motion the from positive direction of the perpendicular axis.

Arc Counterclockwise - An arc generated by the tool motion of two axes, in which path of the tool with respect to the workpiece is counterclockwise, when viewing the plane of motion from the positive direction of the perpendicular axis.

Array - A rectangular or circular pattern.

ASCII - Abbreviation for American Standard Code for Information Interchange. A standard set of 128 binary numbers representing keyboard information such as letters, numerals, and punctuation.

Assembly - A drawing including more than one related part that is joined or assembled with others.

Asynchronous Port - An electrical connection port on a computer for one type of communication. Also called a serial or RS-232 Communication (COM) port.

Attribute - Textual information associated with CAD geometry. Attributes can be assigned to drawing objects and extracted from the drawing database. Applications include creating bills of material.

Axis - A principal direction along which the movements of the tool or workpiece occur. There are usually three primary linear axes, mutually at right angles, designated as X, Y, and Z.

Bezier Curve - A polynomial curve passing near but not necessarily through a set of given points. Represents an equation of an order one less than the number of points being considered.

Binary - The numerical base, base 2, by which computers operate. The electrical circuitry of a computer is designed to recognize only two states, high and low, which easily translate to logical and arithmetic values of 1 and 0. For example, the binary number 11101 represents the decimal number 29.

Bit - A binary digit (1 or 0). For example, the binary number 10110111 is eight bits long.

Bitmap - The digital representation of an image in which bits are referenced (mapped) to pixels. In color graphics, a different value is used for each red, green, and blue component of a pixel.

Bspline Curve - A blended piecewise polynomial curve passing near a given set of control points. The blending functions provide more local control as opposed to curves like Bezier.

Buffer - An intermediate storage device (hardware or software) between data handling units.

Byte - A string of eight bits representing 256 different binary values. A kilobyte (kbyte or KB) is 1024 bytes.

Block - A group of words that defines one complete set of instructions.

Block Delete - Permits selected blocks of code to be ignored by the control system.

CAD - Abbreviation for computer-aided design, which uses graphics-oriented computer software for designing and drafting applications.

CAE - Abbreviation for computer-aided engineering, which uses graphics-oriented computer software for engineering and drafting applications involving mathematical analysis.

CAM - Abbreviation for computer-aided manufacturing, which is the use of computers to assist in phases of manufacturing.

Cancel - A command that nullifies any canned cycles or sequence commands.

Cartesian Coordinates - A means whereby the position of a point can be defined with reference to a set of axes at right angles to each other.

Chamfer - A beveled edge or corner between two intersecting lines or surfaces.

CIE - Abbreviation for computer-integrated engineering or computer-integrated enterprise.

CIM - Abbreviation for computer-integrated manufacturing, which involves a common computer database from which information for various manufacturing processes are stored and retrieved. This information usually includes drawings, numerical control data, and bill of materials.

Circular Interpolation - Enables the programmer to move a tool up to 360 degrees in an arc using only one block of information. The circular path may be generated in any two planes.

CNC - Abbreviation for computer numerical control.

Code - A system describing the assembling of characters for representing information.

Command - A signal or group of signals that initiates one step in the execution of a program.

Computer Numerical Control - (CNC) A numerical control system utilizing a computer as a controller.

Control Key - A key on the keyboard used in conjunction with other keys to perform special functions.

Coons Patch - A bicubic surface patch interpolated between four adjoining general space curves.

CPU - Abbreviation for central processing unit. The CPU controls, sequences, and synchronizes the activities of all the computer components and performs the various arithmetic and logic operations on the data.

Cross-hairs - A cursor usually comprising two perpendicular lines on the display screen and used to select coordinate locations.

CRT - Abbreviation for cathode ray tube. Denotes the video display tube used with computers.

Cursor - A pointer on a display screen that can be moved around and used to place textual or graphical information.

Cutter Diameter Compensation - Provides a means of using a cutter of a different diameter than originally intended in a program. The programmer may use either an oversized or undersized cutter and still maintain the programmed geometry.

Cutter Offset - The distance from the part surface to the axial center of a cutter.

Cycle - A sequence of operations that is repeated regularly. The time it takes for one such sequence to occur.

Data - Information used as a basis for reasoning or calculation.

Database - Related information organized and stored so that it can be easily retrieved and, typically, used by multiple applications. A noncomputer example of a database is a telephone directory.

Default - A parameter or variable that remains in effect until changed. It is what a computer program assumes in the absence of specific user instructions.

Digitize - Act of entering graphical location points into a computer with a tablet, puck, or stylus.

Digitizing Tablet - A graphics input device that generates coordinate data. It is used in conjunction with a puck or a stylus.

Directory - A portion of the storage space on a disk drive that can contain files. It is analogous to a file drawer in a filing cabinet.

Diskette - See floppy disk.

Display Screen - A video display tube or CRT used to transmit graphical information.

DOS - Abbreviation for disk operating system. Software that controls the operation of disk drives, memory usage, and I/O in a computer.

Drawing File - A collection of graphical data stored as a set (file) in a computer.

DXF - Abbreviation for drawing interchange file. A file format used to produce an ASCII description of an AutoCAD drawing file.

Dwell - A delay in a program's execution. A dwell halts all axis movement for a specified time.

Edit - To modify or prepare.

End Point - The exact location on a line or curve where it terminates.

Enter - A keyboard key that when pressed signals the computer to execute a command or terminate a line of text. Also sometimes called Return.

FEA - Abbreviation for finite element analysis. Numerical technique of approximately determining field variables such as displacements and stresses in a domain. This is done by breaking down the domain into a finite number of "pieces," also called "elements," and solving for the unknowns in those elements.

Feed - The programmed or manually established rate for movement of the cutting tool into the workpiece.

Feedrate (Code Word) - A code containing the letter F followed by digits. It determines the machine slide rate of feed.

FEM - Abbreviation for finite element modeling. The process of breaking down a geometric model into a mesh, called the finite element mesh model, that is used for finite element analysis.

File - A collection of data accessible to a computer either on a disk drive or main memory that represents textual and/or graphical information.

Fillet - A curved surface of constant radius blending two otherwise intersecting surfaces. A two-dimensional representation of this surface above involving two lines or curves and an arc.

Floppy Disk - A circular plastic disk coated with magnetic material mounted in a square cardboard or plastic holder. Used by a computer to store information for later use. Can be inserted or removed from a floppy disk drive at will. Also called a diskette.

G-Code - A word addressed by the letter G and followed by a numerical code defining preparatory functions or cycle types in a numerical control system.

Generation, NC - Typically refers to the automatic generation of NC instructions from a CAD model of part geometry.

Grid - An area on the graphics display covered with regularly spaced dots and that is used as a drawing aid.

Hard Disk - A rigid metal disk covered with magnetic material. Mounted permanently in a hard disk drive, it spins at a high velocity, is capable of storing large amounts of data, and works faster than a floppy disk drive does.

Hardcopy - A paper printout of information stored in a computer.

Hatching - A regular pattern of line segments covering an area bounded by lines and/or curves.

Icon - A graphical symbol typically used to convey a message or represent a command on the display screen.

Incremental System - A control system whichby each coordinate or positioned dimension, both input and feedback, is taken from the last position rather than from a common datum point, as in the absolute system.

Input - External information entered into the control system.

Interface - A condition of spatial intersection between two parts in an assembly. Also, the region of intersection of the two parts.

IPM - Abbreviation for inches per minute.

IPR - Abbreviation for inches per revolution.

ISO - Abbreviation for International Standardization Organization. An organization charged with establishing and promoting international standards.

Isometric - A view or drawing of an object in which the projections of the X, Y, and Z axes are spaced 120 degrees apart and the projection of the Z-axis is vertical.

JOG - A control function that manually operates an axis of the machine.

LAN - Abbreviation for local area network. One of several systems used to link computers together in order to share data, programs, and peripherals.

Letter Address - The manner by which information is directed to the system. All information must be preceded by its proper letter address, for example, X, Y, Z, or M.

Linear Interpolation - The movement of the tool in a linear (straight) path.

Macro - A single command made up of a string of commands.

Mainframe Computer - Arguably, a larger and faster computer than a minicomputer.

Manual Data Input - A method that enables an operator to insert data into the control.

Manual Part Programming - Programming method whereby the machining instructions are prepared by the operator on a document called the part program manuscript.

MCU - Abbreviation for machine control unit. Consists of the electronics and hardware that reads and interprets the programmed instructions and converts it into the mechanical actions of the machine tool.

Memory - An essential component of a computer. The place in which programs and data are stored. Memory includes both ROM (read-only memory) and RAM (random-access memory).

Menu - A list of commands available for selection. Can be available on a digitizing tablet or on the display screen.

Microcomputer - A computer principally designed for use by a single person.

Microprocessor - An integrated circuit chip (or set of chips) that acts as the CPU of a computer, for example, the Motorola 68020 and the Intel 80386.

MPM - Abbreviation for millimeters per minute.

MPR - Abbreviation for millimeters per revolution.

Minicomputer - A computer that is generally configured for simultaneous use by a small number of people. It generally has more powerful resources and peripherals than does a microcomputer.

Mirror - To create the reverse image of selected graphical items.

Modal - Information that once input into the system remains in effect until it is changed.

Mode - A software setting or operational state.

Model - A two- or three-dimensional representation of an object.

Modem - Stands for modulator/demodulator. The device that allows a computer to send and receive data over telephone lines.

Mouse - A hand-operated, relative-motion device resembling a digitizer puck and used to position the cursor on a computer display screen.

Multiuser - The ability of an operating system to allow multiple users on different terminals to share computer resources such as the CPU, storage, and memory.

Multitasking - The ability of an operating system to manage concurrent tasks on a computer.

NC (Numerical Control) - The technique of controlling a machine or process by using numbers, letters, and symbols.

Numerical Control System (NC) - A system in which a program of instructions is read by a machine control unit and decoded to cause movement in a machine tool or to control a process.

Network - An electronic linking of computers for communication.

NURBS - Stands for Non-Uniform Rational B-splines. A widely used parametric model for three-dimensional curves and surfaces.

Offset - A displacement in the axial direction of the tool that is the difference between the actual tool length and the programmed tool length.

Operating System - Also, disk operating system. Software that manages computer resources and allows a user access and control.

Origin - The intersection point of the axes in a coordinate system. For example, the origin of a Cartesian coordinate system is where the X-, Y-, and Z-axes meet, at (0,0,0).

Orthogonal - Two geometric entities whose slopes or tangents are perpendicular at their intersection.

Orthographic Projection - Also called the parallel projection, the two-dimensional representation of a three-dimensional object but without perspective. In drafting, it is typically the front, top, and right-side views of an object.

Part Program - A specific and complete set of instructions for the manufacture of a part on an NC machine.

Part Programmer - A person who prepares the planned sequence of events for the operation of a numerically controlled machine tool.

Peripheral - An accessory device to a computer such as a plotter, printer, or tape drive.

Pixel - Stands for "picture element." Pixels are the tiny dots that make up what is displayed on a CRT. Also called "pels."

Plotter - A computer-controlled device that produces text and images on paper or acetate by electrostatic, thermal, or mechanical means (with a pen).

Point-To-Point Control System - A system in which the tool is moved to a pre-defined location. Only positioning is performed and there is no cutting performed during the positioning move. Also called a positioning system.

Preparatory Function - An NC command that changes the mode of operation of the control. (Generally noted at the beginning of a block by the letter G plus two digits.)

Program - A sequence of steps that is executed in order to perform a given function.

Prompt - A message from the computer software requesting a response from the user.

Puck - A hand-operated device with one or more buttons resembling a mouse, it operates in conjunction with a digitizing tablet. Also called a transducer.

Quadrant - Any of the four parts into which a plane is divided by rectangular coordinate axes in that plane.

RPM - Abbreviation for revolutions per minute.

RAM - Abbreviation for random-access memory. The main memory of a computer. Programs and data can be read from and written to RAM.

Rapid - Positioning of the cutter near the workpiece at a high rate of travel speed before the cut is started.

Register - An internal memory storage location for the recording of information.

Relative Coordinates - Coordinates specified by differences in distances and/or angles measured from a previous set of coordinates rather than from the origin point.

Reset - To return a register to zero or to a specified initial condition.

Right-hand Rule - A method of determining the positive directions of the X-,Y-, and Z-axes of a coordinate system and the positive direction of rotation about an axis.

ROM - Abbreviation for read-only memory. The permanent memory of a computer that contains the computer's most fundamental operating instructions.

Save - To store data on a disk or tape.

Screen - A video display tube or CRT that displays graphical information.

Serial Interface - An electrical connection that permits the linking of computers and peripherals over long distances. Also called the RS-232C interface.

Spindle Speed (Code Word) - A code containing the letter S followed by digits. This code determines the rpm or cutting speed of the cutting spindle of the machine.

Stylus - An input device that looks like a pen and is used like a digitizer puck.

Tool Function - A command identifying a tool and calling for its selection. The address is normally a T word.

Tool Length Compensation - A register that eliminates the need for preset tooling. Allows the programmer to program all tools as if they are of equal lengths.

Tool Offset - A correction for the tool position parallel to a controlled axis.

Turnkey - A computer system sold complete and ready to use for a specific application. You just "turn the key."

Unit - A user-defined distance, such as inches, meters, and miles.

View - A graphical representation of a two-dimensional drawing or a three-dimensional model from a specific location (viewpoint) in space.

Viewpoint - A location in three-dimensional model space from which a model is viewed.

Wireframe Model - A two- or three-dimensional representation of an object consisting of boundary lines or edges of an object.

Word - A command or combination of commands that stores information that the machine tool acts upon.

Word Address Format - The specific group of symbols in a block of information by one or more alphabetical characters which identify the meaning of the word.

X-Axis - Axis of motion that is always horizontal and parallel to the workholding surface.

Y-Axis - Axis of motion that is perpendicular to both the X- and Z-axes.

Z-Axis - Axis of motion that is always parallel to the principal spindle of the machine.

Index